Foundational Essays in James Joyce Studies

THE FLORIDA JAMES JOYCE SERIES

UNIVERSITY PRESS OF FLORIDA

Florida A&M University, Tallahassee
Florida Atlantic University, Boca Raton
Florida Gulf Coast University, Ft. Myers
Florida International University, Miami
Florida State University, Tallahassee
New College of Florida, Sarasota
University of Central Florida, Orlando
University of Florida, Gainesville
University of North Florida, Jacksonville
University of South Florida, Tampa
University of West Florida, Pensacola

FOUNDATIONAL ESSAYS IN JAMES JOYCE STUDIES

EDITED BY

MICHAEL PATRICK GILLESPIE

Foreword by Sebastian D. G. Knowles, series editor

University Press of Florida

Gainesville · Tallahassee · Tampa · Boca Raton

Pensacola · Orlando · Miami · Jacksonville · Ft. Myers · Sarasota

22 21 20 19 18 17   6 5 4 3 2 1

First cloth printing, 2011
First paperback printing, 2017

A record of cataloging-in-publication data is available from the Library
of Congress.
ISBN 978-0-8130-3529-1 (cloth)
ISBN 978-0-8130-5482-7 (pbk.)

The University Press of Florida is the scholarly publishing agency for the
State University System of Florida, comprising Florida A&M Univer-
sity, Florida Atlantic University, Florida Gulf Coast University, Florida
International University, Florida State University, New College of Florida,
University of Central Florida, University of Florida, University of North
Florida, University of South Florida, and University of West Florida.

University Press of Florida
15 Northwest 15th Street
Gainesville, FL 32611-2079
http://upress.ufl.edu

To A. Nicholas Fargnoli
a fine teacher, an excellent scholar,
and a superb friend

Contents

Foreword

"If I want to read some good Joyce essays, where should I start?" I wish I had a florin for every time I've been asked this question: students badly need a sense of the history of Joyce studies, and there is nothing currently available as comprehensive in its outlook as the present anthology. Not only is Gillespie's book a valuable guide to the best that has been thought and said in Joycean culture, its taxonomies divide the field in such a way that the book becomes a gate of entry to many different ways of reading and thinking about Joyce. Most Joyceans (myself included) affect a spectacular indifference to earlier scholarship, and I suspect that only a handful of these essays are discussed with any regularity by even the most assiduous researchers. By reintroducing these seminal essays to the light of day, Michael Patrick Gillespie performs a critical service to the Joyce community, and reminds us all that we are standing on the shoulders of giants.

The goal of restoring scholarly memory is a vital and necessary one. One is always struck by the role that personal memory plays in Joyce's characters, and in the whole modernist project, which amounts to a reclamation of the past, from the child's drawings in Bloom's desk drawer in "Ithaca" to Minta Doyle's grandmother's brooch in *To the Lighthouse* to the columns of St. Magnus the Martyr ("Inexplicable splendour of Ionian white and gold") in *The Waste Land*. These objects have a four-dimensional space, the fourth dimension, as Proust says, being time. In the same way, the articles here, from David Hayman's essay on one sentence in Book III of *Finnegans Wake* to S. L. Goldberg's reading of detachment and the dramatic art in *Stephen Hero*, are richly encrusted with the work of the literary generations that followed them. "The dead writers are remote from us because we *know* so much more than they did," says an anonymous voice in "Tradition and the Individual Talent," to which Eliot provides the resounding rejoinder: "Precisely, and they are that which we know." Many of these writers in *Foundational Essays in James Joyce Studies* are very much alive, but to all but specialists in the particular fields their work has been largely forgotten. Michael Patrick Gillespie has brought these essays back for us to measure more accurately the distance that we have traveled, and how much further we have still to go.

Sebastian D. G. Knowles
Series Editor

Acknowledgments

I am very grateful to a number of individuals whose advice, encouragement, and enthusiasm greatly enhanced this project. I would like in particular to acknowledge the help of the following.

Joyce Community: Derek Attridge, Murray Beja, Lucia Boldrini, Sheldon Brivic, Vincent Cheng, Kevin Dettmar, Edmund Epstein, A. Nicholas Fargnoli, Kate Flint, Andrew Gibson, Amy Gorelick, Michael Groden, Clive Hart, Cheryl Herr, Phillip Herring, Carol Kealiher, Sebastian Knowles, Sean Latham, Vicki Mahaffey, Patrick McCarthy, Patrick McGee, Timothy Martin, Michael Molino, Ira Nadel, Christine O'Neill, Barry Qualls, John Paul Riquelme, James Silas Rogers, Fritz Senn, Sam Slote, Robert Spoo, Thomas Staley, Erwin Steinberg, Weldon Thornton, Joseph Valente, Robert Wininger.

At Marquette University: Jarrold Hurlburd, Tim Machan, Krista Ratcliffe, Albert Rivero, Abby Vande Walle.

At Florida International University: Philip Marcus, Asher Milbauer, James Sutton.

At the University Press of Florida: Michele Fiyak-Burkley, Amy Gorelick, Sebastian Knowles, Ann Marlowe.

I am grateful for permission to reprint the articles appearing in this volume.

Introduction

A Retrospective Arrangement

Professors of English thrive on invoking, often haphazardly, their literary antecedents. Most of us can hardly get through conversations with colleagues and certainly cannot conduct classes without injecting apocryphal biographical anecdotes, garbled fragments of obscure poems, and knowing allusions to works of justifiably ignored authors. While for a few academics these tidbits represent the summation of their contact with the canon, for most of us this is simply an idiosyncratic indulgence. We in fact do take the trouble to read and reread the primary works in our field and make an effort to keep abreast of current critical debates.

I also believe that a majority of us deeply esteem the critical studies of the scholars whose ideas shaped our notions of the methods and concepts necessary for responding to the literature to which we have dedicated our lives. However, despite our best intentions to remain engaged with the foundational views that informed our own sensibilities, conflicting demands often overwhelm us. Our field is dominated by assimilation and progression. We work in a profession that demands familiarity with the most current theories and pushes for the continual production of new ideas. These imperatives inevitably privilege the most recent views and methods over long-established approaches. Academic expectations also pressure us to produce within highly specific areas of interest at a pace that makes it difficult for even the most conscientious scholars to follow all of the other developments in the field we claim as our specialty.

Over time, compression and selectivity characterize the pace of academic reading. At the beginning of a career, one strives mightily to become aware of the diverse critical views. Within a relatively short time, however, one finds that practical considerations preclude venturing beyond engaging the ideas of those whose works have the most immediate impact on one's own research. Pragmatism dictates concentrating one's attention on recent relevant arguments. That often leaves little time to consider the intellectual antecedents whose works led to those views, and reading outside one's area of interest is almost out of the question. As careers progress, it is not uncommon that habituation and perhaps an element of lethargy prevent much expansion of these horizons. We become comfortable in our area, and hesitate to venture beyond it.

In this respect, scholars in Joyce studies prove to be no different from colleagues in any other area of literature. A quick survey of a recent *James Joyce Quarterly* will provide ample evidence of essays attentive to a wide range of current critical opinions while showing also that only rarely do contemporary examinations evince any interest in material written beyond the past ten or twenty years. For further evidence of this process, take up any recent book-length publication on Joyce's writings and scan the Works Cited section. Imposing an implicit "past its sell-by date" on any interpretive effort of a certain age has become a routine feature of our literary studies. And the idea that a scholar might offer a useful elucidation based upon views or systems of expression more than a few years old simply does not occur to many of us. In fact, reference to an interpretive tradition will evoke a sense in many of us that goes back no further than the preceding decade.

Material circumstances reinforce this tendency toward the erasure of our critical heritage.[1] Availability, even in a digitizing age, remains a significant issue. Despite the awe and admiration that certain scholars may have evoked fifty years ago, in all but a few cases one now finds their writings relegated to back issues of journals that are buried in archives, or in books that have been sitting undisturbed on library shelves for decades. Inertia raises the risk of their fading completely from public awareness.

At the same time, the influence of early writings by individuals like Edmund L. Epstein, A. Walton Litz, Florence Walzl, and the other authors considered in this volume remains a vital if often implicit element in readers' approaches to Joyce's works. These scholars are responsible for establishing interpretative perspectives now taken as critical commonplaces or for initiating methodological practices now imbedded in our analytical assumptions. In every instance, their insights, whether acknowledged or not, have had a profound effect, enhancing immediate understanding and acting as catalysts goading readers to extend those initial insights.

Despite these achievements, one might legitimately question the need to return to early ideas if these points have been incorporated, developed, and enlarged in contemporary critical positions. The simple response is that mere awareness of the latest iteration of this critical thinking is not enough for complete understanding of the existing analytic matrix that informs Joyce studies. Reading the works of Shakespeare, in addition to the inherent pleasure the plays give, presents one with a far sharper sense of both our dramatic heritage and the creative logic permeating the construction of contemporary dramas. Likewise, having a firsthand understanding of the interpretive discoveries of the pioneering men and women of the Joyce industry will give current students a far more sophisticated grasp of the nuances of epistemological developments and of the actual mutability still part of numerous current assumptions now seemingly resolved into fixed points of view.

Some recent projects have already demonstrated the efficacy of this sentiment. While the general trend toward privileging contemporary analysis has not abated, over the past two decades a movement to recognize prior critical achievements has been under way. In the early 1990s, Janet Dunleavy asked a number of scholars to write responses to individual works by eminent Joyceans from the 1930s to the midcentury. Her collection examined the achievements of Stuart Gilbert, Adaline Glasheen, Harry Levin, Hugh Kenner, William Noon, and others.[2] A decade later, Paula Gillespie and I took a look at more diverse interpretive approaches to a narrower topic, surveying the prominent critical trends in readings of *Ulysses* that arose over the previous three decades, though admittedly this very focus underscores the tendency to privilege more recent works as representative of the critical heritage.[3] Six years later, Nicholas Fargnoli and I extended the scope of that project beyond the thirty year limit, and in the process acknowledged the difficulties confronting scholars seeking to engage what is already a dauntingly diverse and wide-ranging field. We edited a collection of essays that sought to assess the evolution of interpretations of *Ulysses* grounded in clearly defined methodologies like feminism, cultural studies, psychoanalysis, textual criticism, and other distinctly delineated hermeneutic areas.[4] (Five years earlier, Fargnoli had compiled a volume included in the Gale Dictionary of Literary Biography series that, while highlighting excerpts from Joyce's writing, also incorporated an invaluable collection of contemporary responses to Joyce's published works that neatly complements the studies noted above.[5]) Each of these books establishes a sense of distance, provides background for a general understanding of specific elements of Joyce criticism, places readers at one remove from the works discussed, and, except in the case of the volume edited by Fargnoli, offers summaries and assessments of the material rather than presenting reproductions of primary sources.

While demonstrating in various measures the importance of retrospection, these recent efforts, intentionally or not, can create the impression among contemporary Joyce scholars that pioneering essays have now been relegated to the category of historical artifacts. In fact, the impulse implicitly driving these collections, to move beyond antecedents while simultaneously acknowledging them, attests to the conflicting demands of acquiring a broad knowledge of the criticism in the field while managing the finite amount of time that one has to engage that ever increasing pool of analytical studies. In this light, the inclination to revere the pioneers while turning to summaries of their works rather than to their original efforts stands as perfectly comprehensible, but one cannot expect such précis to provide the fullest possible understanding.

At the same time, engaging essays of a half century ago proves to be less straightforward than it might initially seem. If we articulate a sense of these studies as simply forming the first stages of an evolving cultural heritage, one need not have more than a general awareness of their content. If, as I believe, they occupy a position of importance equal to other, more recent works, they assume roles as integral parts of a dynamic and reciprocal critical enterprise. This in turn means that anyone seeking the fullest interpretive response to Joyce's canon must examine them in the same detail as that afforded any contemporary study.

Though this is admittedly time consuming, ample evidence exists to support the merit of cultivating a balanced sense of past and present critical insights. The misconceptions that impaired many of the opinions voiced in the mid-1980s after the appearance of Hans Walter Gabler's edition of *Ulysses*, for instance, offer a stark example of the problems created by readers relying upon a partial or imperfect knowledge of the critical tradition. While a great number of individuals participated in the debate over the efficacy of Gabler's version, too many involved had no direct knowledge of the evolution of the textual criticism of Joyce's novel or of the fundamental interpretive issues that this long process of analysis had identified.[6] Instead, they based their opinions upon summaries, often highly selective, of what had been done on Joyce's prepublication material and upon synopses, often highly subjective, of accepted practices of textual analysis.

In consequence, the critiques to Gabler's work made by John Kidd and the support tendered by a number of readers to his often tenuous claims regarding editorial practice consistently ignored key elements in Joyce's creative process and showed a stunning lack of awareness of what previous scholarship had established regarding editorial cruxes in his work. The misunderstandings that resulted and the distorted conclusions that some reached clearly underscore the problems that can accrue when contemporary commentators offer interpretive judgments without the benefit of reading and comprehending pioneering studies—in this case the groundbreaking work published in the 1950s and 1960s by A. Walton Litz still esteemed by serious textual critics—and their impact on subsequent understanding.[7]

The process of engaging our interpretive heritage, of course, involves more than simply reverential reference to beatified titles from the past in a secular variation of the Litany of the Saints. Contemporary scholars not only need to understand and apply accurately the insights and discoveries of their intellectual forebears, they have the obligation to reexamine long accepted assumptions based on the work of the past. To continue my religious metaphors, this means that even for true believers the critical ideas that have shaped the way contemporary readers have come to understand Joyce's canon do not enjoy the same presumption of infallibility that many Catholic faithful assign to encyclicals of the popes. The early essays on Joyce need periodic review to reaffirm or overturn their efficacy. Just as a familiarity with A. Walton Litz's early textual criticism would have obviated a number of errors that crept into mid-1980s Gabler-Kidd debates, rigorous reassessments of other early works would have forestalled inhibitive interpretive views that have become critical commonplaces.

Along these lines, a still popular approach to the structure of *Finnegans Wake*, now more than seventy years old, illustrates how unexamined assumptions can exert an inhibitive influence on subsequent readings. Edmund Wilson's essay "The Dream of H. C. Earwicker" offered a speculative view that quickly became a prevalent belief. Asserting unequivocally that Joyce constructed *Finnegans Wake* around the sleeping reveries of its central character, Wilson claimed that all subsequent understanding needed to be based on that assumption. The extremely popular early book-length study of Joyce's last work, Campbell and Robinson's *A Skeleton Key to "Finnegans Wake,"* which appeared just a few years after the publication of Wilson's essay, picked up the idea that it chronicles Earwicker dreaming.[8] Campbell and Robinson's endorsement legitimized the notion, and within a relatively short time many Joyceans had come to consider this opinion an irrefutable fact.

Their reaction is not surprising. Like any effective hermeneutic generalization, the concept of *Finnegans Wake* articulating the dreams of a single individual relieved a great deal of interpretive stress that readers otherwise had to engage. For all of us, accustomed to cause-and-effect analysis, it offered the comfort of imposing a manageable linear direction on an aggressively chaotic, nonlinear narrative, and in doing so provided a sturdy foundation for a number of subsequent traditional analytic approaches.

Inevitably, this theory imposed strict causal limits on the kinds of interpretations that one could adduce from Joyce's final work, and it threatened one of the most experimental pieces of writing with a plethora of reductive responses. Several contemporary scholars—Nicholas Fargnoli, Derek Attridge, and Bernard Benstock, to name just a few—have vigorously challenged the validity of Wilson's theory of the dream and dreamer. They have suggested that one can discern far more sophisticated readings by acknowledging the narrative's dreamlike conditions without embracing the prescriptive roles of dream and dreamer.[9] Over the past decade, their resulting counterarguments have gained traction and have expanded our ability to come to grips with the text of *Finnegans Wake* by once again opening options for nonlinear readings.[10] These results underscore my point about reassessing foundational pieces of our interpretive heritage: the more often this scrutiny takes place, the greater the integrity of the critical canon.

While both refamiliarization and reassessment stand as important reasons for the retrospective arrangement offered here, nonetheless, as with the decoration of the sleeping quarters of Edward VII mentioned in the Cyclops chapter of *Ulysses*, considerations of space force us to proceed selectively. This collection returns attention to some heretofore neglected essays upon which important tenets of our current understanding of Joyce's writing are based. Laying them before readers presents the opportunity to grasp key critical concepts in their original form with greater specificity than what one sees when only the consequences or the summations of their views appear in subsequent iterations.

With a nod toward the linearity that I rather cavalierly dismissed a few paragraphs ago when speaking of *Finnegans Wake* criticism, I have split the collection into four parts, each devoted to one of Joyce's major writings, and each containing three essays dealing with various interpretive cruxes or scholarly issues of the work under consideration. At the beginning of each part, I have commented briefly on the essays' epistemological impact. To this end, I have contextualized these early efforts, making some mention of the critical achievements that preceded them. Then, looking ahead to their subsequent influence, I link them with prominent contemporary studies that grew out of their findings.

From a chronological and hermeneutic perspective, *Dubliners* offers a propitious starting point for a collection of this sort. It represents Joyce's earliest published fictional work, with initial versions of some of the stories appearing in 1904 and the collection being published as a book in 1914. It also has proved to have an enormous attraction for a wide range of literary critics, including many who have not devoted themselves to a close study of Joyce's other writing. This anomaly, at least for Joyce studies, has produced an interpretive tradition noticeably distinct from analyses of *A Portrait of the Artist as a Young Man, Ulysses,* or *Finnegans Wake.* Doubtless, many readers turn to *Dubliners* because of the nonspecialists who have contributed so much to its rich and accessible critical tradition. These writers inculcated into this heritage general assumptions about the work that have provided eminently sound fundamental concepts upon which to build securely more specifically focused observations. As a consequence, one finds sophisticated commentators, and well-known Joyceans, like Margot Norris and Garry Leonard, who have adeptly adopted poststructuralist thinking to illuminate Joyce's text, working out of a tradition inflected by a range of views from scholars with distinctly different literary backgrounds.

Florence Walzl's "The Liturgy of the Epiphany Season and the Epiphanies of Joyce" demonstrates wonderfully how insights from half a century ago remain at the core of our understandings of Joyce's stories. Her essay presents an urbane explication showing the complexity of issues that, when treated by lesser readers' hands, had led to, and unfortunately continue to lead to, hackneyed applications of clichéd principles in a fashion that actually subverts understanding of certain pivotal features of Joyce's short stories. In shining contrast, Walzl's reading reminds us of the profound intricacy of Joyce's literary application of the liturgical.

A glance at the title of Thomas Staley's "Moral Responsibility in Joyce's 'Clay'" might draw one to the hasty assumption that he is offering one of the narrow religious-based explications referenced above for which a secular-minded critic would have no sympathy or use. That would be a mistake. Despite the unease that some contemporary readers may feel when confronted with Joyce's Catholic tradition, its theology permeates his stories, and its sophisticated application cries out for equally sophisticated explications. Current readers still engage the moral decisions that inform the lives of Joyce's characters, and they see contemporary connections because of the contextualization of pre–Vatican II Catholicism that comes from Staley's four-decades-old essay.

Robert Scholes's "Semiotic Approaches to a Fictional Text: Joyce's 'Eveline'" was written a number of years after most of the other essays in the collection first appeared. Nonetheless, reading his careful elaboration of one of Joyce's least examined short stories and seeing the way Scholes applies linguistic methods that had only recently come to the awareness of the American academy affords a revelatory glimpse at the beginnings of a radical shift in Joycean interpretations. It captures wonderfully for us this paradigm shift that both connects with and reconfigures all that came before it.

The works of such pioneering critics have established a body of analytical suppositions that now make the short stories in *Dubliners* seem readily accessible even to those unaware of the rich interpretive tradition that has unpacked many of its cruxes. And, again in a condition unique to this area of Joyce criticism, they developed through instances of complementary thinking not found elsewhere. In contrast, early responses to *A Portrait of the Artist as a Young Man* struggled with differing though equally challenging views. Due in no small part to the suggestion of autobiographical resonances in its title, boundaries between fact and fiction were for some readers easily blurred, and the impulse to explain both fact and fiction by collapsing events in Joyce's life into the narrative of his first published novel threatened to overwhelm more sophisticated interpretations.

That view has doubtless been fostered by Richard Ellmann's biography of Joyce, as a careful examination of his footnotes demonstrates. To be sure, the felicity of Ellmann's prose style and the intimate access that

Ellmann enjoyed to Stanislaus Joyce and his family have produced a justifiable measure of admiration for the account of the life of a complex and contradictory author. At the same time, it also led to an unfortunate assumption of impeccable objectivity and unswerving accuracy. As critics have already documented, such a perspective can distort events in Joyce's life and lead to significant misunderstandings of his fiction.[11]

Certainly, a fine line exists between the world of Joyce's Dublin and the world he created for Stephen Dedalus, and a number of early critics have illuminated the convergent and divergent features of these worlds. As the section on *A Portrait of the Artist as a Young Man* will demonstrate, contemporary readers can now move with confidence to engaging very specific cruxes knowing or at least sensing that the fundamental issues of origin have been laid to rest. One sees this amply illustrated in the articles—cultural studies, postcolonialism, psychoanalysis, feminism—that Brandy Kershner chose as background to his edition of *Portrait* and those—emphasizing gender, sexuality, and national identity—that John Paul Riquelme chose for his.[12]

A good example of this appears in James Thrane's essay on the source of the hellfire sermon of chapter 3, which profoundly reorients one's sense of what occurs there. Thrane's scholarship calls attention to the universalities within the Catholic retreat experience that seem unique and highly fictional to many first-time readers, particularly those with little awareness of Catholic liturgy before the great reforms of Pope John XXIII.

In a similar fashion, S. L. Goldberg presents a cogent overview of the aesthetics of the novel. Admittedly, Goldberg's prose has a contentious tone not common in more recent criticism, but the concepts continue to engage readers' imaginations. As a result, the issues that had been daunting to earlier readers have now become resolved as a matter of course in the minds of contemporary students of the novel.

Finally, Thomas F. Van Laan's essay on the way that the *Spiritual Exercises* of St. Ignatius frames the narrative consciousness of the novel introduces one to the structure providing an intellectual discipline for the myriad-minded creator of the novel. As with Staley's work on *Dubliners*, Van Laan clarifies the structure for Joyce's analytical thinking rather than presenting in didactic fashion a view of what is under consideration. In the process, his essay establishes a background essential to understanding the point of view of the discourse yet quite distant from contemporary awareness.

Each of these essays delineates important interpretive areas in *A Portrait of the Artist as a Young Man*. Beyond that, each points to a different way of engaging its narrative. When taken together, they remind us not simply of the diversity of Joyce's narrative but also of the very different novels that readers are free to construct from the text. Combining a sense of these studies with the impressions from readings of *Dubliners* provides a wonderful basis for comprehending the critical heritage of *Ulysses*.

Such guidance is needed because a survey of methods for reading *Ulysses* shows far greater diversity than one finds for any of Joyce's preceding works. The novel's structure makes this inevitable. Because of the narrative's encyclopedic quality, its celebration of digression, and its stylistic innovations, the complexity of *Ulysses* offers unique interpretive dispensations for readers. Since its publication these polymorphous attractions have conveyed a sense of liberation from any imperative to reconcile apparent disunities into a broad impression of the work, and instead readers have felt free to concentrate on mastery of very specific concepts. While the novel's rich critical heritage bears out the range of interpretive freedom one can enjoy in approaching the work, this scholarship also highlights the complex analytical systems that have come to support such diversity. Recognizing the epistemological connections is even more complicated here than it was for the earlier works. Contemporary readers may be well aware of critics from the 1970s and 1980s who have seemingly made these leaps possible; in fact, the insights of commentators from that era—like Phillip Herring, Michael Groden, and Karen Lawrence—rest squarely on the achievements of writings from an even earlier period. Some brief references will make this point clearer.

Since the mid-1980s much has been made of the composition process that shaped *Ulysses*. However, it was a scholar from a much earlier period, A. Walton Litz, who first brought readers to an awareness of its complexity. Doing research on Joyce's notes and drafts at the British Museum in the mid-1950s, Litz offered marvelous insights into the impact of prepublication material on the final version of the novel.

Likewise, readers now feel comfortable moving through the antinomies of Joyce's narrative. That is because early studies, like Edmund Epstein's reprinted here, domesticated the unfamiliar not by presenting definitive interpretations but rather by showing us how to live with the ambiguities.

Readers have been aware of the need for cultural examinations of diverse aspects of *Ulysses* from its initial appearance. Richard M. Kain made some attempt to address this concern just after World War II.[13] Still, it was not until more sophisticated critics began work in the 1950s that readers came to see the full potential of this area of inquiry.

One sees this amply illustrated in the evolution of assessments of Joyce's use of Judaism in his writing. Since the 1980s, diverse critics have examined significant aspects of the topic. At the same time, their research owes a great deal to the study of anti-Semitic depictions in *Ulysses* published by Marvin Magalaner in the early 1950s. While Magalaner certainly did not present a definitive examination of the topic, he did bring forward questions of representation that became the anchor for subsequent studies of representations of anti-Semitism in *Ulysses* and for approaches to a range of other cultural topics embedded in the narrative.

Indeed, all of the essays in this section follow the paradigm laid down by commentators on Joyce's earlier writings, not simply presenting specific interpretations but delineating areas of inquiry central to understanding *Ulysses*. Because of the elaborate revision process that distinguished the preparations for the publications of *Ulysses*—first through the serialization of early versions of the first half of the novel and then through Joyce's corrections and expansions on the multiple page proofs provided by his printer, Maurice Darantière—understanding the accretive process that produced the narrative remains an essential part of any interpretation of the work. Likewise, the novel's intense referentiality makes it crucial to have some overriding sense of how to engage its cultural allusiveness. Finally, the highly charged emotions and compressed nature of the action force an even sharper awareness of the fictional and biographical distinctions than one needs for *A Portrait of the Artist as a Young Man*.

By the time one approaches the criticism of *Finnegans Wake*, the diversity of earlier interpretive approaches has given readers some sense of Joyce's hermeneutic potential, but the complexity of his last work makes the challenge of comprehending the interpretive opportunities the greatest of all. An impressive number of contemporary critics—commentators like Danis Rose and John O'Hanlan, John Gordon, Roland McHugh, and Kimberly Devlin—have provided us with sturdy guides. Yet these yeoman efforts draw heavily on stunning preliminary work done up to half a century ago, and, for all the explicative skill that contemporary critics evince, one comprehends their interpretations more clearly with this earlier work in mind.

The paraphrasing efforts of Campbell and Robinson in the mid-1940s and the musing of Edmund Wilson a decade earlier, whatever their weaknesses, made readers aware of the possibility of understanding *Finnegans Wake*. Nonetheless, it was not until David Hayman's pioneering essay that critics began to see how a careful analysis of the compositional process could greatly clarify the sinuousness of Joyce's prose.

Clive Hart took Hayman's model of explication in a different direction. He articulated a reasoned explanation (which he would subsequently expand to a book-length study) of the structure that supported Joyce's narrative. This in turn gave us a form to apply to the polymorphic and polyphonic discourse.

Robert Boyle, with his Jesuit training and his playfully digressive style, may have been the most Joyce-like of the early *Wake* critics, at least in his writing style. In the essay reprinted here, focused on a single paragraph, he offers a thematic view neatly counterpointing Hayman's stylistic interests. Here and in his subsequent work, Boyle demonstrates with impressive skill how familiar literary techniques, applied by an ingenious reader, could yield spectacular understanding not only of a specific passage but of the entire work.

Despite the justly celebratory tone applied to the works in this collection, I think it important to close by acknowledging the clear limitations of this project. While the essays reprinted here establish the range of early work done in Joyce studies, this volume stands as evocative and representative rather than definitive and exhaustive. I have omitted many essays that in a perfect world would have been included, and I have only alluded to a number of distinguished critics who certainly share in the great critical tradition that this volume celebrates. Important works like Hugh Kenner's much anthologized essay "*Portrait* in Perspective" are excluded, as are essays by such widely published authors as Fritz Senn. Focusing instead on works not readily available outside the archives of university libraries, *Foundational Essays in James Joyce Studies* aims to expand the reader's sense of the critical heritage. I firmly believe that making the essays republished here more accessible not only will lead to a fuller understanding of how interpretations of Joyce have evolved but will encourage additional foraging in back issues of scholarly journals for other important contributions.[14]

Notes

1. For many Joyceans, the term "critical heritage" will have a very specific meaning, evoking Robert H. Deming's magisterial *James Joyce: The Critical Heritage* (London: Routledge and Kegan Paul, 1970). This two-volume compilation is an essential work for anyone seeking a sound overview of the evolution of Joyce's canon and its criticism. I do not mean to co-opt it but rather hope to exemplify specifically the broad views that Deming propounded.

2. Janet Egleson Dunleavy, ed., *Re-viewing Classics of Joyce Criticism* (Urbana: University of Illinois Press, 1991).

3. Michael Patrick Gillespie and Paula F. Gillespie, *Recent Criticism of James Joyce's "Ulysses": An Analytical Review* (Rochester, N.Y.: Boydell and Brewer, 2000).

4. Michael Patrick Gillespie and A. Nicholas Fargnoli, eds., *"Ulysses" in Critical Perspective* (Gainesville: University Press of Florida, 2006).

5. A. Nicholas Fargnoli, ed., *James Joyce: A Documentary Volume* (Detroit: Gale Group, 2001).

6. For a survey of the arguments, see *Assessing the 1984 "Ulysses,"* ed. C. George Sandulescu and Clive Hart (Totowa, N.J.: Barnes and Noble, 1986). The best summaries of the fallacies in the arguments against Gabler appear in Michael Groden's "Foostering over Those Changes: The New *Ulysses,*" *James Joyce Quarterly* 22 (Winter 1985): 137–159, and his "A Response to John Kidd's 'An Inquiry into *Ulysses: The Corrected Text,*'" *James Joyce Quarterly* 28 (Fall 1990): 81–110.

7. See, for example, the reprint in this volume of Litz's "Early Vestiges of Joyce's *Ulysses*" and his book-length examination *The Art of James Joyce: Method and Design in "Ulysses" and "Finnegans Wake"* (Oxford: Oxford University Press, 1961). For examples of the range of responses made to Gabler, particularly of assessments that would have been enhanced by a greater familiarity with Litz's achievements, see *Studies in the Novel* 22 (Summer 1990), a special edition devoted to the topic and edited by Charles Rossman, at the time an uncritical supporter of Kidd.

8. Edmund Wilson, "The Dream of H. C. Earwicker," *New Republic* 91 (July 12, 1939): 270–274; Joseph Campbell and Henry Morton Robinson, *A Skeleton Key to "Finnegans Wake"* (New York: Harcourt, Brace, 1944).

9. See A. Nicholas Fargnoli in *Critical Companion to James Joyce: A Literary Reference to His Life and Work* (New York: Facts on File, 2006), 91. See also Derek Attridge, "Finnegans Awake: The Dream of Interpretation," *James Joyce Quarterly* 27 (Fall 1989): 11–29, and Bernard Benstock, *Joyce-Again's Wake: An Analysis of "Finnegans Wake"* (Seattle: University of Washington Press, 1965).

10. For an example of the effectiveness of nonlinearity, see Thomas Jackson Rice's "*Finnegans Wake*: The Complexity of Artificial Life" in his *Joyce, Chaos, and Complexity* (Urbana: University of Illinois Press, 1997), 112–140. See also my "Reading on the Edge of Chaos: *Finnegans Wake* and the Burden of Linearity" in *The Aesthetics of Chaos: Nonlinear Thinking and Contemporary Literary Criticism* (Gainesville: University Press of Florida, 2003), 29–42.

11. A very good summary of the critiques of the biographical distortions and

interpretive misconceptions that arise from this close association can be found in Ira Nadel's "The Incomplete Joyce," *Joyce Studies Annual* 2 (1991): 86–100.

12. *A Portrait of the Artist as a Young Man,* ed. R. B. Kershner (Boston: Bedford, 1993); *A Portrait of the Artist as a Young Man: Authoritative Text, Backgrounds and Contexts, Criticism,* ed. John Paul Riquelme (New York: W. W. Norton, 2005).

13. Richard M. Kain, *Fabulous Voyager: James Joyce's "Ulysses"* (Chicago: University of Chicago Press, 1947).

14. In the essays that follow I have retained the authors' footnoting styles and have silently corrected any typos.

I

Engaging *Dubliners*

Dubliners attracts the attention of more non-Joyceans—that is to say, readers with no broad concern for other Joyce works or for the critical history of this one—than any of his other writings. This fact underscores the accessibility that Joyce's short stories have for general readers. At the same time, for those interested in the analytic legacy that informs current understandings, it raises the issue of how the cumulative impact of a number of commentators who may not have a complete awareness of the broader hermeneutic tradition of these stories will affect the development of interpretations of that collection.

Asking this question does not automatically dismiss the achievements of individuals who have written on Joyce only occasionally and then only on this portion of Joyce's canon, nor does it suggest a litmus test of membership in the Joyce community as the validating feature of any analysis of the short stories. However, approaching *Dubliners* without an awareness of the achievements of previous scholars runs the risk of rediscovering the same insights every decade or so. (The career of Florence Walzl aptly illustrates my point. I can find no evidence that she ever wrote on any work other than *Dubliners*, but in her writing and her lectures she showed a profound awareness not only of the criticism of this work but of the scholarly examinations of Joyce's entire oeuvre.)

The significant point remains that the diverse scholarly backgrounds of those who choose to work on *Dubliners* provide a range of perspectives that might not otherwise be brought to bear. These varied credentials make it all the more important to consider how a rich critical tradition of studies of the short stories has provided sound fundamental concepts upon which to build more specifically focused observations. Exploring these sources, or returning to them in the case of experienced Joyce scholars, renews and enriches understanding of the achievements by pioneering critics that now inform the assumptions upon which contemporary interpretations are based.

Before the 1950s, little scholarly work on *Dubliners* had appeared.[1] Joyce's friend Padraic Colum had published an article in the 1920s that later became the introduction for an edition of *Dubliners*.[2] Harry Levin's 1941 book on Joyce's works touched repeatedly on the short stories.[3] In 1944 Richard Levin and Charles Shattuck published a close reading of the collection that linked individual stories to sections from *The Odyssey* and to chapters from *Ulysses*.[4] A few short pieces appeared in the *Explicator*. And a number of critics would occasionally make passing reference to the work in studies of other authors or topics.

The 1950s brought a flood of interest in *Dubliners*. For some scholars it was spurred by the desire to apply New Critical approaches, then very much in vogue at many universities, to works that seemed particularly suited to those methods of interpretation. Other respondents took interest in recently published biographical evidence—memoirs, a collection of Joyce's letters, and sketches from the Ellmann biography—that offered clues to understanding hitherto problematic cultural, historical, and social allusions in the short stories.[5] Still other scholars began to examine prepublication textual material like the early versions of some stories published in the *Irish Homestead* to trace the development of the creative process informing the final product.

The primary factor, however, in that sudden outpouring of interpretive works on *Dubliners* relates less to theories than to personalities. (This will also have an impact on scholarship of Joyce's other writings.) In the period just after World War II a number of young scholars began to publish examinations that offered profound insights into Joyce's work. Hugh Kenner's book *Dublin's Joyce* announced the arrival of a brilliant critical mind who would set the standard for understanding the canon for the next half century.[6] Richard Ellmann, in the processing of bringing out his magisterial biography based to a large extent upon the recollections of Joyce's brother Stanislaus and other close friends, initiated a larger critical project that would continue for as long as he remained in Joyce studies, linking people and events in Joyce's life to incidents in his writing. Marvin Magalaner showed that Joyce's early work was eminently worthy of book-length studies.[7] And Robert Scholes previewed the pioneering textual work that would appear in an edition of *Dubliners* that he was editing with A. Walton Litz with two stunning examinations of the textual makeup of the collection exemplified in its final story.[8] These works did more than illustrate alternative ways of reading the short stories. They announced the presence of rigorous critical minds who would engage Joyce's writings from imaginative points of view which set down paradigms for understanding them that would obtain for decades to come.

Kenner, Ellmann, Magalaner, Litz, and Scholes were by no means the only critics to emerge during this period to shape the way generations of subsequent readers, knowingly or not, approached *Dubliners*. Confirming my earlier observation on the attraction that the short stories held for nonspecialists, several prominent figures not otherwise associated with Joyce studies stand out among the scholars whose works, for reasons of space, are not collected in this volume. In the 1950s, to cite just two examples, the Irish poet, playwright, and jurist Donagh MacDonagh published studies of several of the short stories, and the American poet Brewster Ghiselin offered a fine overview of the collection.[9]

Throughout the 1950s a steady stream of fundamentally synoptic and explicative criticism appeared.[10] By and large the body of work presented close readings and summations of the narrative framework of the sort rarely seen in print today, but it formed an essential step in the establishment of a broad sense of the narrative direction of each of the stories and of the collection as a whole. Some of this material has been absorbed into the critical consciousness, and other studies have become justifiably neglected. While an awareness of these examinations remains important in attaining a grasp of how we understand *Dubliners,* looking more closely at groundbreaking studies that grew immediately out of this explosion of interest offers a more sophisticated overall comprehension of the interpretive evolution.

The three essays reprinted here underscore several fundamental hermeneutic shifts that reconfigured intellectual engagement with Joyce's short stories. Two of the essays delineate the interpretive direction that readings of *Dubliners* would take for the next decade and a half. The third work, though written by a critic who played an integral part in developing the heightened concern for Joyce's short stories that occurred in the early 1960s, comes from a later period and ushers in a significant epistemological shift in approaches to the collection.

The first essay in this section highlights the achievements of the doyen of *Dubliners* studies. For a quarter century, no one articulated more clearly than Florence Walzl the subtle dimensions that informed the narratives of Joyce's short stories.[11] Indeed, Walzl's pioneering writings did much to shift the view of the collection as apprentice pieces to the sense that *Dubliners* announced the abilities of an artist whose creative skills would only be elaborated in the narratives that would follow. By pointing out the refined imaginative subtleties in the collection that make Joyce's genius already apparent, Walzl's writings highlighted perspectives that adumbrated the thematic and stylistic achievements so apparent in *A Portrait of the Artist as a Young Man*, *Ulysses*, and *Finnegans Wake*.

From the mid-1950s onward, a great deal of critical attention was given over to Joyce's accounts of "moments of shining forth." O. A. Silverman's edition of Joyce's *Epiphanies* references Joyce's habit, elaborated upon in the Ellmann biography, of recording incidents that offered an instance of enlightenment, and the examples of this found in the Kain and Scholes transcription of Joyce's early prepublication material led to a great deal of speculation on the function of the epiphanic form in the short stories.[12] While a number of critics presented useful insights into the way ordinary anecdotes functioned as turning points in Joyce's stories, a danger arose that this approach would take on programmatic tendencies. Walzl's essay reprinted here, "The Liturgy of the Epiphany Season and the Epiphanies of Joyce," singlehandedly forestalled that possibility, presenting a paradigmatic example of the critical acumen and insightful understanding that continues to inform serious studies of *Dubliners*.

While the essay showed Walzl fully aware of Joyce's habits of composition, her meticulous scholarship offered a more sophisticated understanding of the dynamics behind his approach than heretofore realized. By presenting an overview of the liturgical connotations that would have shaped Joyce's conceptions of epiphany, Walzl provided a rich cultural context for the creative process that more mechanistic identification of the pattern ignored. This elaboration proved to be particularly relevant in the post–Vatican II world where Catholics and non-Catholics alike lack specific knowledge of the forms of centuries-old religious celebrations and have no clear understanding of the religious influence on daily lives that would have been a commonplace feature of Joyce's youth in Ireland.

Although critics like William Noon and Robert Boyle have endeavored to underscore the lifelong influence of Catholicism on Joyce's creative process, many readers, from Richard Ellmann onward, have shown, to offer the most charitable construction, an unease at dealing with it.[13]

Nonetheless, despite the discomfort that some contemporary readers may feel when confronted with Joyce's Catholic tradition, the influence of its theology undeniably permeates his stories. No matter his or her personal beliefs, an Irish man or woman of Joyce's time had a consciousness steeped in Catholic tradition. Without slipping into polemics, Walzl's writing showed a sophisticated understanding of this condition as she deftly outlined the liturgical landscape of Joyce's world and traced its impact on the spiritual lives of his characters.

As Walzl's exposition subtly illustrated, for a full understanding of the collection, current readers still need to engage the moral decisions that shape the lives of Joyce's characters, and they can do so with confidence because of the illumination by early critics like Walzl of the petit bourgeois Dublin morality that most of us would not be able to comprehend on our own. Later studies of the sociological forces influencing Joyce's imagination could draw upon her insights to develop further the complex interrelationship between the cultural institutions of late nineteenth- and early twentieth-century Dublin and the creative process that they informed.[14]

Thomas Staley's article "Moral Responsibility in Joyce's 'Clay'" appeared a year after the Walzl essay reprinted here. Despite the apparent similarities in titles, Staley's study did not recapitulate religious ideas already examined by Walzl. Instead, in a gesture rare in the usually timid world of literary studies, Staley quarreled with Marvin Magalaner and William York Tindall, extremely influential figures in Joyce criticism at the time, and he lamented the fact that Hugh Kenner had not yet received the attention he deserved.

Staley's article did all this in a surprisingly compressed fashion. After a fairly detailed synopsis of the story, which now reminds us that forty-five years ago *Dubliners* did not enjoy the widespread familiarity with readers that it has today, Staley took meticulous care in highlighting the criticism of William Noon and in questioning not only Magalaner and Tindall but two other scholars whose work is now long forgotten. While his correctives would have been welcome at any time, what stood out as of greater significance in terms of Joyce studies was the willingness of an individual, then only beginning in the profession, to call received ideas into question and to feel so confident in the openness and mutual respect already developing among Joyceans that he could challenge the critical conclusions of several prominent colleagues. It is Staley's object lesson in intellectual rigor rather than his specific interpretations that makes the article of continuing importance to us. While the field of Joyce studies has long been known for its acceptance and collegiality, Staley's work reminds us that these attitudes do not preclude close scrutiny of anyone's ideas.

By the late 1960s a critical mass of material on *Dubliners* had accumulated. Collections of essays and book-length studies began to appear, and interpretive approaches became both more specialized and more diverse.[15] At the same time, an increasing number of responses to Joyce's short stories came to be circumscribed by either/or theoretical dispositions that would not accommodate alternative points of view, much less sustain simultaneously a variety of responses to the works.

That commitment to linearity may itself seem dated to current readers. Nonetheless, when Robert Scholes published his exploration of hermeneutic multiplicity, "Semiotic Approaches to a Fictional Text: Joyce's 'Eveline,'" in 1979, he was offering, at least for many American readers, a radical new way of seeing a text. Indeed, he was making many of those readers aware for the first time that the term "text" itself could have any special significance.

As with Staley's critique of literary scholars, reviewing Scholes's exposition of the theories of Todorov, Genette, and Barthes may now seem closer to a nostalgic recollection than to a representation of cutting-edge interpretations. However, that perception misses the crucial supposition underlying his approach. Scholes understood even then the ongoing need to reinvigorate habitual critical approaches. With that in mind he offered a tutorial on some of the most significant advances in literary theory of the time. This commitment to revitalization, rather than the specific course of action advocated, makes the Scholes essay an important reference point in our approach to *Dubliners*.

In a manner that both reminds one of the diversity of intellectually eclectic readers like Hugh Kenner and prefigures the multiplicity of the styles of criticism that would dominate the last quarter of the twentieth century, Scholes illustrated a dependable process for creating a full reading, no matter the epistemology applied to it. He based his approach on assumptions that drew upon a range of methodologies, while deftly avoiding prescriptive adherence to any. Instead, he showed us how to move easily back and forth between the approaches of three complex theorists and formed his own interpretive strategy from an amalgamation of their views.

Further, as with the Staley essay, the focus on one story has illustrative repercussions that apply to the entire collection. In his careful reading of "Eveline," Scholes did not so much lay down a pattern for interpreting them all. Rather, he showed the rich and varied results that can come from what at the time of his writing must have seemed to many other readers like a straightforward narrative. A penetrating understanding of Joyce's writing and a confident grasp of sophisticated theoretical methodologies allowed Scholes to offer the promise of renewal for all of the works in the collection.

While his article stood out as an illustrative rather than a paradigmatic essay, it highlighted the possibilities of Joyce's text rather than delimiting them. And it privileged alternatives rather than seeking closure.

Scholes certainly would not claim to be solely responsible for the burgeoning of diverse critical approaches to the short stories. At the same time, one can hardly ignore the link between his pioneering efforts and the subsequent achievements of scholars who, over the next three decades, employed the very techniques, if not necessarily the same theoretical assumptions, that he introduced in his essay. Donald T. Torchiana's *Backgrounds for Joyce's "Dubliners,"* for example, seems to move as far as possible from the Continental epistemologies advocated by Scholes, but it nonetheless takes up in its digressive pursuit of cultural context the spirit of diversity that Scholes foregrounds.[16] Garry M. Leonard's *Reading "Dubliners" Again: A Lacanian Perspective* offers a much more obvious theoretical link to Scholes, but I think its real debt is to the open attitude to unanticipated readings that Scholes establishes and legitimizes.[17] And most recently, Margot Norris in Suspicious Readings of Joyce's "Dubliners" returns to the topic of narratology so thoughtfully introduced by Scholes and brings to bear on it a sophisticated sense of the changes in theoretical perspective that have accrued in the quarter century that has elapsed between the two projects.[18]

Of course, the essays in this section do not completely encompass the critical arc of Dubliners studies. Nonetheless, they call attention to an integral element of all sophisticated readings that will become familiar in the subsequent segments devoted to Joyce's other writings. Groundbreaking criticism stands out both for the specific insights it offers and for the encouragement given to subsequent writers. The articles by Walzl, Staley, and Scholes succeed at doing both, and in the process they remind us of the catalytic imaginative power of Joyce's short story collection.

Notes

1. For a detailed accounting of *Dubliners* criticism, and indeed interpretive examinations of all of Joyce's works, through the mid-1970s, see Robert H. Deming's *A Bibliography of James Joyce Studies*, 2nd ed. (Boston: G. K. Hall, 1977).

2. Padraic Colum, "Dublin in Literature," *Bookman* (London) 63 (July 1926): 555–561.

3. Harry Levin, *James Joyce: A Critical Introduction* (Norfolk, Conn.: New Directions, 1941).

4. Richard Levin and Charles Shattuck, "First Flight to Ithaca: A New Reading of Joyce's *Dubliners*," *Accent* 4 (Winter 1944): 75–99.

5. Stuart Gilbert, ed., *Letters of James Joyce*, vol. 1 (New York: Viking, 1957); Richard Ellmann, "Backgrounds of 'The Dead,'" *Kenyon Review* 20 (August 1958): 507–528, and *James Joyce* (New York: Oxford University Press, 1959). Ellmann's contact with Joyce's brother led directly to Stanislaus's own scholarly efforts—e.g., "The Background to *Dubliners*," *Listener* 51 (March 1954): 526–527—as well as to the biographical accounts *My Brother's Keeper*, ed. Richard Ellmann (New York: Viking, 1958) and *Dublin Diary*, ed. George Harris Healy (Ithaca, N.Y.: Cornell University Press, 1962), expanded in 1971 as *The Complete Dublin Diary of Stanislaus Joyce*.

6. Hugh Kenner, *Dublin's Joyce* (London: Chatto and Windus, 1955).

7. Marvin Magalaner, *Time of Apprenticeship: The Fiction of Young James Joyce* (New York: Abelard-Schuman, 1959).

8. Scholes, Robert, "Some Observations on the Text of *Dubliners*: 'The Dead,'" *Studies in Bibliography* 15 (1962): 191–205. See also his "Further Observations on the Text of *Dubliners*," *Studies in Bibliography* 17 (1964): 107–122.

9. Donagh MacDonagh, "'The Sisters' of James Joyce," *University of Kansas City Review* 18 (Summer 1952): 255–261, and "Joyce, Nietzsche, and Hauptmann in James Joyce's 'A Painful Case,'" *PMLA* 68 (March 1953): 95–102; Brewster Ghiselin, "The Unity of Joyce's *Dubliners*," *Accent* 16 (1956): 75–88, 196–231.

10. Gerhard Friedrich, "Bret Harte as a Source for James Joyce's 'The Dead,'" *Philological Quarterly* 33 (October 1954): 442–444; William T. Noon, "Joyce's 'Clay': An Interpretation," *College English* 17 (November 1955): 93–95; Gerhard Friedrich, "The Gnomic Clue to James Joyce's *Dubliners*," *Modern Language Notes* 72 (1957): 421–424; Clarice Short, "Joyce's 'A Little Cloud,'" *Modern Language Notes* 72 (April 1957): 275–278; Brendan P. O Hehir, "Structural Symbol in Joyce's 'The Dead,'" *Twentieth-Century Literature* 3 (April 1957): 3–13; Joseph L. Blotner, "Ivy Day in the Committee Room," *Perspective* 9 (Summer 1957): 210–217; James Ruoff, "'A Little Cloud': Joyce's Portrait of a Would-Be Artist," *Research Studies of the State College of Washington* 25 (September 1957): 256–271; Richard Carpenter, "The Witch Maria," *James Joyce Review* 3, nos. 1–2 (February 1959): 3–7; Michael J. O'Neill, "Joyce's Use of Memory in 'A Mother,'" *Modern Language Notes* 74 (March 1959): 226–230; George Knox, "Michael Furey: Symbol-Name in Joyce's 'The Dead,'" *Western Humanities Review* 13 (Spring 1959): 221–222; Concepcion D. Dadufalza, "The Quest of the Chalice-Bearer in James Joyce's 'Araby,'" *Diliman Review* 7 (July 1959):

317–325; C. C. Loomis Jr., "Structure and Sympathy in Joyce's 'The Dead,'" *PMLA* 75 (March 1960): 149–151.

11. Florence L. Walzl, "Patterns of Paralysis in Joyce's *Dubliner*," *College English* 22 (1961): 519–520; "Joyce's 'Clay,'" *Explicator* 20 (February 1962), item 46; "A Date in Joyce's 'The Sisters,'" *Texas Studies in Literature and Language* 2 (Summer 1962): 183–187; "The Liturgy of the Epiphany Seasons and the Epiphanies of Joyce," *PMLA* 80 (September 1965): 436–450; "Gabriel and Michael: The Conclusion of 'The Dead,'" *James Joyce Quarterly* 4 (Fall 1966): 17–31; "Joyce's 'The Sisters': A Development," *James Joyce Quarterly* 10 (Summer 1973): 375–421; "The Life Chronology of *Dubliners*," *James Joyce Quarterly* 14 (Summer 1977): 408–415; "*Dubliners*: Women in Irish Society," in *Women in Joyce*, ed. Suzette Henke and Elaine Unkeless (Urbana: University of Illinois Press, 1982), 31–56; "Joyce's 'Clay': Fact and Fiction," *Renascence* 35 (Winter 1983): 119–137.

12. James Joyce, *Epiphanies*, ed. O. A. Silverman (Buffalo: Lockwood Memorial Library, University of Buffalo, 1956); Robert Scholes and Richard M. Kain, *The Workshop of Daedalus: James Joyce and the Raw Materials for "A Portrait of the Artist as a Young Man"* (Evanston, Ill.: Northwestern University Press, 1965). For examples of the critical application of this approach, see Robert Scholes's "Joyce and Epiphany: The Key to the Labyrinth," *Sewanee Review* 72 (Winter 1964): 65–77, and Morris Beja's "James Joyce: The Bread of Everyday Life" in his *Epiphany in the Modern Novel* (Seattle: University of Washington Press, 1971), 71–111.

13. For two book-length examples of their work, see William T. Noon, *Joyce and Aquinas* (New Haven, Conn.: Yale University Press, 1957) and Robert Boyle, *James Joyce's Pauline Vision: A Catholic Exposition* (Carbondale: University of Southern Illinois Press, 1978).

14. See, for example, Cheryl Herr's *Joyce's Anatomy of Culture* (Urbana: University of Illinois Press, 1986) and R. B. Kershner's *Joyce, Bakhtin, and Popular Literature: Chronicles of Disorder* (Chapel Hill: University of North Carolina Press, 1989).

15. See, for example, Peter K. Garrett, ed., *Twentieth-Century Interpretations of "Dubliners": A Collection of Critical Essays* (Englewood Cliffs, N.J.: Prentice-Hall, 1968); James R. Baker and Thomas F. Staley, eds., *James Joyce's "Dubliners": A Critical Handbook* (Belmont, Calif.: Wadsworth, 1969); Warren Beck, *Joyce's "Dubliners": Substance, Vision, and Art* (Durham, N.C.: Duke University Press, 1969); Edward Brandabur, *A Scrupulous Meanness: A Study of Joyce's Early Work* (Urbana: University of Illinois Press, 1971).

16. Donald T. Torchiana, *Backgrounds for Joyce's "Dubliners"* (Boston: Allen and Unwin, 1986).

17. Garry M. Leonard, *Reading "Dubliners" Again: A Lacanian Perspective* (Syracuse, N.Y.: Syracuse University Press, 1993). Perhaps ironically or perhaps simply as a validation of multiplicity, three years later Earl G. Ingersoll presented an alternative view of the Lacanian approach in his *Engendered Trope in Joyce's "Dubliners"* (Carbondale: Southern Illinois University Press, 1996).

18. Margot Norris, *Suspicious Readings of Joyce's "Dubliners"* (Philadelphia: University of Pennsylvania Press, 2003).

1

The Liturgy of the Epiphany Season and the Epiphanies of Joyce

FLORENCE L. WALZL

It has long been recognized that Joyce's writing is a texture of epiphanies and that the basic pattern in most of his major works is a chronological cycle tracing man's life from childhood and youth to maturity and sometimes age. The combination of these devices largely explains the structure of *Dubliners* and *A Portrait of the Artist as a Young Man*, and both are used in conjunction with other techniques in *Ulysses* and *Finnegans Wake*. Although Joyce's use of them has been much discussed, the influences that led him to combine them have been less fully explored. The purpose of this paper is to assess the effect of the liturgy of the Epiphany season on Joyce's concept of epiphany and his use of the cycle pattern at the period he was writing *Dubliners*. Related liturgical influences on *Dubliners* will be discussed.

What Joyce meant by the term *epiphany* may be deduced etymologically. The basic meaning in Greek of ἐπιφάνεια is *appearance* or *manifestation*, and the word is related to a verb meaning *to display* or *show forth* and in the passive and middle voice *to shine forth*. In the early Christian period *epiphaneia* developed a religious denotation as a "visible manifestation of a hidden divinity either in the form of a personal appearance, or by some deed of power by which its presence is made known."[1] It also refers specifically to the feast of the Epiphany, 6 January.

That Joyce used the word in both the general and restricted senses seems indicated in *Stephen Hero*, where Stephen discusses the epiphanies he is writing and relates them to his esthetic theory. This theory developed

Florence Walzl, "The Liturgy of the Epiphany Season and the Epiphanies of Joyce," *PMLA* 80 (September 1965): 436–450. Reprinted by permission of the Modern Language Association of America. Copyright 1965.

in part from his linguistic interests, in that his concern with words as symbols led to a concern with reproducing both the reality of an event and its symbolic or spiritual meaning.[2] Joyce describes how a commonplace incident which seemed a symbol of "Irish paralysis" made Stephen "think of collecting many such moments together in a book of epiphanies."[3] "By an epiphany," Joyce continues, Stephen "meant a sudden spiritual manifestation, whether in the vulgarity of speech or of gesture or in a memorable phase of the mind itself. He believed that it was for the man of letters to record these epiphanies with extreme care, seeing that they themselves are the most delicate and evanescent of moments." This definition adopts the basic Greek meaning of *manifestation* but reflects the later sense of the word as a revelation of inner significance by means of outward appearance. When Joyce goes on to relate his epiphany to his threefold concept of art as "wholeness, symmetry and radiance," the idea of "shining forth" is also apparent: the moment an object is viewed in perspective by an artist, its "soul" leaps from its "appearance," it becomes "radiant," and is thus "epiphanised."[4] The beholder's realization of this manifestation of identity is like a flash of intellectual light. Joyce's concept of epiphany appears also to be colored by the popular association of the feast of the Epiphany with the star which symbolized the spiritual illumination that led the Magi to the Christ child. Joyce's early view of the epiphany is exemplified in the twenty-two prose epiphanies dating from this period. All bare paragraphs of less than 150 words, they recreate "evanescent . . . moments"; however, since they are entirely without a frame of reference, most seem trivial or meaningless. (It is significant that when Joyce adapted some of them for his mature fiction, he fitted them into a chronological framework.)[5] Joyce's epiphanies have largely been explained on the basis of this background.[6]

The term *epiphany* is often applied to the *Dubliners* stories. Yet it is not always noted that when Joyce planned the collection he called the pieces *epicleti*. What did he mean by this term and how did he derive it? It first appears in a comment he made on the stories for *The Irish Homestead*: "I am writing a series of epicleti—ten—for a paper. . . . I call the series *Dubliners* to betray the soul of that hemiplegia or paralysis which many consider a city."[7] This term seems either an adaptation of or a mistake for epiclesis (or epiklesis), and an invented plural.[8] The epiklesis is an invocation of the ancient Mass liturgies which besought God the Father through the Holy Spirit to transform the bread and wine into the body and blood of Jesus. The epiklesis has virtually disappeared from Western liturgy, but the Eastern Church regards it as the "essential form of the sacrament," the act effecting the transubstantiation in the Mass.[9] (It is equivalent in the Latin rite to the Words of Institution which repeat Jesus' statements at the Last Supper and represent the most solemn moment of the Mass.) Joyce's adoption of this term indicates that he believed the artist's creative act was analogous to the Eucharistic change effected by the priest. Such a view is supported by Joyce's application of priest-like names to the artist in *Stephen Hero* ("penitent," "confessor," and "mediator");[10] by his later description of Stephen in the *Portrait* as "a priest of the eternal imagination, transmuting the daily bread of experience into the radiant body of everliving life";[11] and by a conversation reported by Joyce's brother in which Joyce spoke of a resemblance between his work and the Mass, in that he aimed to give an "intellectual pleasure or spiritual enjoyment by converting the bread of everyday life into something that has a permanent artistic life."[12] The term *epicleti* thus refers to the artist's Eucharist.

Though *epicleti* and *epiphanies* are related words, they are not synonyms. The epicleti are the creative processes; the epiphanies, the resulting manifestations. Such a distinction had its probable origin in the Mass: just as the priest first effects the transubstantiation, uniting himself in communion with Divinity, and only later in distributing communion affords the laity a similar experience, so in Joyce's view the writer transforms real experience into art, having in the process godlike insights into the nature of things, as a result of which his work of art later offers a like experience to the reader.

An influence on Joyce's concept of the epiphany that has not been explored is that of the many epiphanies (i.e., the numerous manifestations of divinity in the life of Jesus) in the liturgy of the Church year. Liturgy refers primarily to the prayers of the Mass, which have both fixed and variable parts, the latter dependent on the season and the Calendar of Saints. Church liturgy also includes the prayers of the breviary (i.e., the daily prayers of the canonical hours read by priests and religious). As a sodalist Joyce was acquainted with the breviary, and in the *Portrait* (Chapter iv) he describes how the poetic beauty of Church ritual and liturgy attracted him to the priesthood.

Two aspects of liturgy which appear to have affected Joyce's writing greatly are the cyclic pattern of seasons in the Church year and its planes of symbolic meanings and correspondences. The Church year describes a cycle within which there are sub-cycles in combination. The basic cycle turns upon the seasons (Christmas, Easter, and Pentecost); this cycle is called the Proper of the Time, and upon it is superimposed the Calendar of the Saints. Each season has its special colors, motifs, and symbols; and each is divided into sub-cycles (the Christmas season, for example, includes the sub-cycles of Advent, Christmas, and Epiphany). The liturgical year is a never-ending round, each season flowing into the next, recalling in its readings and antiphons the past season and anticipating the future one; thus the Pentecostal end of the Church year emphasizes the second coming of Christ, and at the same time prepares for Advent's stress on the first coming.[13] As to the symbolic correspondences of the liturgical cycles: medieval liturgists saw not only a universal time scheme in the three Church seasons, but also a parallelism to the career of Christ (Christmas representing his youth, Easter his mission as redeemer, and Pentecost his teachings as a preparation for his second coming).[14] As to liturgy's several levels of meanings, Dr. Pius Parsch in *The Church's Year of Grace* cites "three distinct planes on which the liturgical drama is enacted": a historical plane presenting past Biblical events, especially the life of Christ, as narrative; a level of present symbolism, moral and spiritual in nature, operating to produce a Christ-like life in the individual; and, finally, a mystical eschatological level preparing the Christian for future eternal life.[15]

All Joyce's major works are time cycles with linked beginnings and endings; and it may well be that his early knowledge of these cyclic patterns of liturgy influenced his adoption of the life cycle as a fictional device (as well as his acceptance of Vico's view of human history as recurring cycles, a theory basic to *Finnegans Wake*). Further, Joyce's works are all multileveled, a characteristic usually attributed to Dante's influence. However, long before Joyce learned Italian at the University, he was familiar with Church liturgy; and liturgy is probably the prior and predisposing influence.

A section of liturgy which had a particularly important influence on Joyce is the sequence of services in the Epiphany sub-cycle, consisting of the Feast of the Epiphany, the six Sundays following, and two related feast days, each of which presents an epiphany of Christ's divinity. In all liturgy this is the part most intimately associated with the term *epiphany*, and its influence on *Dubliners* is apparent in several respects: first, it provided a structural model for the work; second, it influenced Joyce's concept of the literary epiphany and as a result his narrative technique; third, it affected his mode of characterization; and fourth, it offered him various liturgical motifs and symbols that he paralleled or inverted in individual stories as best suited his purposes. Analysis of the Epiphany season liturgy will clarify the nature of these influences.

The Epiphany sub-cycle consists of nine feasts that make a thematic and structural unit: as a cycle it opens and closes with feasts (Epiphany and Candlemas) that are symbolically linked; as a sequence it consists of related epiphanies organized into two groups. The great feast of 6 January needs special comment as it introduces all the major themes and itself commemorates the three most important epiphanies of the sub-cycle (the Magi, Baptism, and Cana manifestations). The Epiphany is an ancient feast originating in the Eastern Church. It was believed that Jesus was born on 6 January and that as a young man he was baptized on his birthday. Later some churchmen assigned the miracle of the water turned into wine at Cana to this date. Hence all three events became associated with the feast; for example, the present liturgy of the Western Church illustrates this triple commemoration, one edition of the missal noting that the Epiphany presents "three manifestations of our Lord: to the Gentiles in the persons of the Magi; to the Jews at His baptism in the Jordan; and to the disciples at the marriage feast in Cana of Galilee."[16] At different periods, however, one or another of these manifestations was chiefly commemorated. In the early Church baptism of worshippers was the event primarily celebrated and lights were carried to symbolize the spiritual illumination of baptism.[17] Later the Epiphany became the prime Nativity festival of the Eastern Church and some Western rites. In most of the Western Church the feast is popularly associated with the visit of the Magi. The spiritual significance of these three epiphanies is largely conveyed by use of symbolic imagery appropriate to the season. The entire Christmas liturgy is pervaded by symbolism of light and the coming of a king. Parsch shows that the "symbol of sun and light . . . gives this season its unity," dawning in Advent, "growing in brilliance like the sun at Christmas, reaching zenith at Epiphany, and finally setting at Candlemas";[18] and that Jesus is imaged as the true sun of the world, the light of lights. Imagery of the coming of a king-god to his city or kingdom colors this liturgy also in prayers of preparation for the king's coming in Advent, arrival at Christmas, and revelation of himself at Epiphany. It gains symbolic significance from the related imagery of the mystical marriage of Christ, i.e., the king's coming to his bride the Church (and all individuals in it). The theme of mystical union is recurrent both in the feast and the following season. For example, the Benedictus of the Epiphany illustrates the imagery in relation to the three epiphanies celebrated on 6 January.

> This day the Church is joined to her heavenly Spouse, for Christ has cleansed away her crimes in the Jordan; with gifts the Magi hasten to the royal nuptials, and the guests are gladdened with wine made from water.[19]

The feast of the Epiphany thus showed Joyce the use of linked epiphanies and the value of symbolic imagery in conveying spiritual meanings.

Especially important as a structural influence on *Dubliners* is the arrangement of epiphanies comprising the entire Epiphany sub-cycle, extending from 6 January to 2 February, Candlemas.[20] This sequence of Sundays and feast days falls into two distinct groups, each with its own pattern: the first presenting a series of epiphanies in Jesus' early life, which progress chronologically from infancy to early manhood; the second, a set of contrasting epiphanies exemplifying the powers and functions of Christ as mature teacher in his public ministry.

The first group, comprising four Masses in the Proper of the Seasons, traces Jesus' career to the start of his public life at thirty. On 6 January, though three epiphanies are commemorated, the emphasis is on the visit of the Magi, the gospel telling the story according to Matthew (ii.1–12), the collect begging illumination from the Father who by "a star didst on this day manifest" his Son "to the Gentiles," and the antiphons rejoicing in the coming of a king into his kingdom. The Mass is characteristic in that the gospel presents the epiphany and the variable prayers employ relevant symbolism. The three following Masses continue the chronology. The First Sunday after Epiphany gives the story of Christ's visit to the Temple at twelve (Luke ii.42–52), which Parsch describes as an epiphany of godhead "in the person of the boy Jesus."[21] Next the Octave of the Epiphany on 13 January celebrates the baptism of Jesus in early manhood (John i.29–34).[22] Finally, the Second Sunday after Epiphany commemorates the miracle at Cana (John ii.1–11), the event traditionally regarded as concluding Jesus' private life and opening his public career, and with it the chronological epiphanies end. As a group they give manifestations of Jesus' power in early life and cover a childhood-youth-manhood pattern.

On the succeeding Sundays comprising the second part of the Epiphany cycle, the character of the gospels changes. Parsch explains, "the liturgy chooses certain miracles and discourses . . . without regard to their chronological order. However, the Mass formularies are still highly influenced by Epiphany themes. Thus, on successive Sundays Christ appears in His kingdom as the divine Physician (third Sunday), as Conqueror (fourth Sunday), as Judge (fifth Sunday), and as Sower of God's kingdom (sixth Sunday)." Each gospel presents "a manifestation of His power and activity" and a different aspect of Jesus' mature ministry.[23] In order, the gospels narrate the cures of the leper and servant of the Centurion (Matthew viii.1–13), the calming of the sea (Matthew viii.23–27), the parable of the good and evil sowers (Matthew xiii.24–30), and finally, the parables of the mustard seed and the leaven (Matthew xiii.31–35). As a group they show symbolically the nature of the kingdom Christ is founding: the miracles of physical salvation illustrate the reviving power of the new society and the parables of growth its vital life.

The season of Epiphany ends with Candlemas, commemorating the purification of the Virgin and the presentation of the infant Jesus in the Temple, a feast restating the various motifs of the season. The gospel gives Simeon's prophecy of Jesus as "a light" and "revelation" (Luke ii.22–32), and the candlelight processional proper to the feast symbolizes the welcome of a newborn king and Christ as light of the world. Thus these seasonal symbols conclude the Christmas cycle as they began it, and the homage of Simeon thematically repeats that of the Magi. To summarize: thematically the Epiphany cycle pictures the development of a Messiah in manifestations of power; structurally it consists of a series of linked epiphanies arranged in two patterns, one chronological, the other typal; symbolically it develops a major life-light theme through its imagery.

Joyce was undoubtedly attracted to this section of liturgy sometime after 1900 when he was working out his concept of the literary epiphany. At this period also he began developing the pattern for his fiction and was apparently interested in the structure of this sequence. The newspaper versions of the first *Dubliners* stories ("The Sisters," "Eveline," and "After the Race") show little evidence of a unified schematic plan for the collection. However, Joyce eventually produced fifteen stories in an intricately structured four-part arrangement of balancing groups of tales, in which commentators have noted symbolic correspondences, literary parallels, and patterns of vices and virtues.[24] The organization is extraordinarily complex: each tale can be read independently and yet the book is a study of a whole society; the stories progress from pictures of individuals to those of groups; and the work develops a paralysis-death motif throughout.

The integration is such that Joyce insisted that the omission of even one story would be an almost "mortal mutilation" of the work.[25] Yet despite its complexity, the basic structure of *Dubliners* is simple—it consists of epiphanies placed in chronological and symbolic arrangements.

The Epiphany cycle gave Joyce this model. Its two-part internal division offered a design readily adaptable to *Dubliners*. Though Joyce divided *Dubliners* into four parts and his proportions are different, the basic plan is similar. His division of the stories into "childhood, adolescence, maturity and public life"[26] follows the order of the liturgical epiphanies. The first eleven tales deal with boys, young people, and mature men and women; and these make a chronology of life in Ireland. At this point the chronology is dropped and the four final stories are epiphanies of Irish society. Each tale presents a different aspect of contemporary culture and illustrates respectively and typically politics, art, religion, and social relationships. In short, the order and the essential divisions are those of the liturgical epiphanies.

If Joyce had used only a life cycle in *Dubliners*, it would be plausible that his structure had been suggested by purely fictional prototypes. However, the complex internal patterning in which two series, one chronological and the other typal, are matched with a concomitant progression from private and individual manifestations to increasingly public and social ones parallels closely the liturgy.

Moreover, a strength of *Dubliners* is that like the Epiphany sequence there is a correspondence of structural and thematic patterns. In both, the manifestations taken in sequence make a greater and more significant revelation. Each liturgical epiphany is an individual manifestation of Christ's power, but the whole series is a revelation of divinity. Each story in *Dubliners* is a manifestation of the paralysis of an individual or group, but the whole collection is a death pattern for an entire society.[27]

This structural similarity highlights a difference: thematically the series are opposites. Joyce consciously inverts the Epiphany season motifs of divine power and action and, using a hemiplegic imagery, makes *Dubliners* a study of human impotence and inaction. This ironic inversion reflects Joyce's moral purpose. His aim was "to write a chapter of the moral history" of Ireland by means of stories that would "betray the soul of that . . . paralysis" characteristic of Dublin.[28] Like the liturgy, epiphany and parable join in these tales, but unlike it the themes are decay and death, not growth and life. This inversion of theme involves a concomitant reversal of the Epiphany season symbols of light and King's coming (i.e., mystical union). In *Dubliners* symbols of darkness and betrayal prevail.

The Epiphany sequence also influenced Joyce's concept of the literary epiphany and as a result his short story technique. The linked gospels of the season have a recognizable narrative pattern: usually a sequence of details in a simply told story effects a sudden revelation of spiritual or moral meaning. This illumination is produced by a distinctive act which may be a miracle but may also be an apparently commonplace event or statement. The revelation usually illuminates symbolism in earlier details. For example, on 6 January, the significance of the Magi's journey becomes clear when the star "came and stood" over the "place where the child was" (Matthew ii.9), thus indicating the homage of all creation to the Messiah; and in the narrative of Jesus among the doctors of the Temple the enigmatic statement of the twelve-year-old that he is doing his "father's business" (Luke ii.49) is itself the "theophany" of godhead.[29] In the final gospels, all homely parables, the entire effect depends on inherent symbolism, and epiphany here is essentially apologue.

In these gospels, even those describing great miracles, there is a contrast between the simplicity of the narrative level and the significance of the symbolic. Liturgical commentators have remarked on this difference. For example, incorporated into the Divine Office of this season until recently was the reflection of St. John Chrysostom on the story of the Magi: "Entering the house the Magi saw the Child and Mary His mother. And prostrating, they adored Him. . . . What, one wonders, moved them to adore the Child? Outwardly, there was nothing unusual about the Virgin; and the house, too, was far from impressive . . . there was nothing to fill them with wonder or impel them to adoration." In fact, St. John observes that all seemed "very commonplace." What "appeared to their senses was of no importance outwardly, the crib, the hut, a poor mother"; yet they adored and brought gifts such as are proffered "not to a man but only to God." What inspired their behavior, he states, was "the star and the enlightenment imparted" that gave them "perfect understanding."[30] In this epiphany spiritual light illuminates the commonplace and reveals a special meaning in ordinary experience.

This contrast between the apparent triviality of outward events and the importance of inner meaning is reflected in Joyce's well-known definition of the epiphany in *Stephen Hero*: it is "a sudden spiritual manifestation" which derives from a "vulgarity of speech or of gesture" or from a "phase of the mind itself." In fact, the example he cites illustrates this point precisely. A "trivial incident" of the Dublin streets is shown as revealing the spiritual inadequacy of love in Ireland. On an evening of "misty Irish spring" Joyce observes a boy and girl flirting before one of those "brown brick houses which seem the very incarnation of Irish paralysis." A fragment of their inane dialogue reveals to him suddenly, not only the inanity of their emotions, but also by projection—since all the details suggest symbolism—the superficiality of romantic love in Ireland.[31] This example illustrates a narrative process in which symbolic details clustering about a simple episode result in a suggested meaning of greater significance than the event itself. The narrative pattern of the early Joycean epiphany, is, therefore, like the liturgical one.

The illumination in Joyce is also similar to the liturgical epiphany, both in the means by which it is achieved and the nature of the revelation itself. Both in liturgy and Joyce the epiphany is a process of enlightenment. The Epiphany season Masses indicate it to be a sudden spiritual illumination: for example, on 6 January, the Lesson from Isaiah (lx.1–6) opens: "Arise, be enlightened, O Jerusalem: for thy light is come. . . . Lift up thine eyes round about, and see: . . ."; the Collect prays that man be brought to a right "contemplation"; and the Preface exults that Christ's coming has restored man by the "new light" of his immortality. Throughout the entire season a seeking for spiritual enlightenment is enjoined upon the worshipper. Significantly Joyce describes the process of epiphany as a seeking for spiritual perspective or light. It is "the gropings of a spiritual eye which seeks to adjust its vision to an exact focus," and "the moment the focus is reached the object is epiphanised." Thence is derived the "sudden spiritual manifestation," which is the epiphany.[32]

The nature of the revelation in Joyce also recalls the liturgy. The liturgical epiphanies are basically manifestations of divinity. For example, the Epiphany season gospels all manifest Jesus' identity as God. These epiphanies are often called theophanies (i.e., visible manifestations of God, or a god, usually by appearance in physical form). In the early Church the term *theophany* was used interchangeably with *epiphany* for those manifestations deriving from the events in the life of Jesus that illumined his divine nature to his disciples.[33] The epiphany is then a revelation of the divine personality of Jesus, who was not only true man with a true human nature but also true God, one in essence or nature with the Father. The association of these two terms, both referring to manifestations of

Being, may have contributed (in conjunction with Thomistic influences) to Joyce's identification of *quidditas* with *claritas* as the main elements in the literary epiphany.[34]

In both *Stephen Hero* and the *Portrait* Joyce describes an esthetic theory based on St. Thomas Aquinas that he called "applied Aquinas."[35] He adopts the view of St. Thomas that the three requisites of beauty are *integritas* (wholeness), *consonantia* (symmetry), and *claritas* (radiance). What is especially interesting is the next step in his reasoning, his identification of *claritas* with another scholastic quality, *quidditas*. In both discussions, he indicates he had been puzzled by the meaning of *claritas* in St. Thomas, but adds that the identification of *radiance* and *quiddity* has "solved" his difficulty. In *Stephen Hero* he writes "*Claritas* is *quidditas*. . . . This is the moment which I call epiphany. First we recognize that the object is *one* integral thing [*integritas*], then we recognize that it is an organized composite structure, a *thing* in fact [*consonantia*]: finally, when the relation of the parts is exquisite, when the parts are adjusted to the special point, we recognize that it is *that* thing which it is. Its soul, its whatness, leaps to us from the vestment of its appearance. The soul of the commonest object, the structure of which is so adjusted, seems to us radiant [*claritas*]. The object achieves its epiphany."[36] This identification of *claritas* and *quidditas*, which is described as *epiphany* in *Stephen Hero*, though not in the *Portrait*, seems an instantaneous apprehension of the essential being or nature of the object, an apprehension which acts as an illumination for the beholder. No matter how humble or commonplace the object, a realization of its quiddity constitutes an epiphany. Even the Ballast Office clock, Joyce said in *Stephen Hero*, was thus "capable of an epiphany." Though Stephen passes it repeatedly as a mere item of "Dublin's street furniture," some day he may really "see it" and "know at once what it is: epiphany."[37] In this early definition apprehending "what it is" is the essence of the epiphany. Its origin seems liturgical.

The fact that Joyce abandoned use of the term *epiphany* in the *Portrait* needs comment. A comparison of the esthetic discussions in *Stephen Hero* and the *Portrait* shows that the definitions of beauty are virtually identical to the point where Joyce identifies *claritas* with *quidditas*. Then a significant difference occurs: in the *Portrait* this synthesis is not called *epiphany* and the discussion is different. The *claritas-quidditas* synthesis is described as the creative insight of the artist. "The radiance . . . is the scholastic *quidditas*, the *whatness* of a thing." It is "felt by the artist when the esthetic image is first conceived in his imagination" and is a "luminous silent stasis of esthetic pleasure" in which the "radiance of the esthetic image" is "apprehended luminously by the mind" which has already apprehended its "wholeness" and "harmony."[38] A shift in viewpoint is evident. Earlier the *claritas-quidditas* synthesis was described as a manifestation usually deriving from outside experience. In Joyce's illustrations it tended to result from an observation of life (i.e., the Ballast Office clock) and in his early work was manifest to a person (Joyce in his twenty-two prose epiphanies), or to a character (Stephen Hero observing the young couple flirting), or to the reader (as in such stories as "Ivy Day in the Committee Room" or "Grace" in *Dubliners*). In contrast, in the *Portrait* the *claritas-quidditas* synthesis is a moment of creative insight in the artist's consciousness when he perceives how, by verbal and imagistic manipulations, he may create a character or situation or setting that will in turn give a revelation of life. In short, it seems essentially an artist's epiphany. It may involve a manifestation to the reader, but secondarily, as a later result of the artist's insight and creativity.

Significant as these differences are, they represent not so much a change of viewpoint as a shift in emphasis from one to another of the "twin faculties" of the creative process, the equation of which Joyce had said in *Stephen Hero* was the "secret of artistic success." The first was "a selective faculty" by means of which the artist must "disentangle the subtle soul of the image from its mesh of defining circumstances"; the second "a reproductive faculty" by which he would "re-embody it in artistic circumstances chosen as the most exact for it."[39] In his early esthetic in *Stephen Hero* he put emphasis on the first, the selective faculty which gave an illumination of the "soul of the image," called this experience epiphany, and related it to radiance and quiddity. Later in the *Portrait* he emphasized the reproductive faculty, avoided naming this experience epiphany, but identified it with *claritas* and *quidditas*.

This shift is consonant with Joyce's developing technique and his theory of the impersonality of art. *Epiphany* in the earlier sense fits well the type of revelations in his early work, such as the epiphanies "on green oval leaves," the lyrics, or *Stephen Hero*; it becomes progressively less appropriate for the dramatic objectification Joyce was moving toward in his fiction, even by the time he completed *Dubliners* and was writing the *Portrait*.[40]

In *Ulysses* and *Finnegans Wake* the subjective consciousness of the artist largely disappears, and meaning is conveyed more and more by verbal symbolization. Hence the *claritas-quidditas* experience became more and more for Joyce the artist's creative insight. Symptomatic of Joyce's own dissatisfaction or uncertainty with the term *epiphany* may be the fact that as early as 1904 he called the *Dubliners* stories *epicleti*, a term associated with the transubstantiation.

In the main, in *Dubliners*, the narratives resemble the liturgical epiphanies. The typical story presents a single episode in which prosaic details forward the slight action. The effect is cumulative and near the end some detail, act, or speech will effect a sudden revelation of the inner reality of the situation or character.[41] There is a marked contrast between the outer stylistic realism and inner moral symbolism.

Essentially the story is planned as a manifestation, and every detail is directed to produce the illumination. As a result, little happens externally; events are repetitively commonplace and trivial. In typical stories a child goes uneasily to the wake of a priest, a boy skips school and has a disappointing day, a man gets drunk after a hard day at the office and comes home belligerent, a clerk meets a former classmate and makes the inevitable comparisons, and a group of politicians discuss candidates. The most dramatic events involve a girl who decides she cannot elope, a young man who is pressured into marriage, and a husband who discovers that his wife cherishes the memory of a dead boy. Yet the stories prove striking revelations of character and penetrating cross-sections of Irish society. The revelation invariably illuminates symbolic meanings in earlier details.

As in some of the religious epiphanies, the moment of illumination may be effected by a commonplace detail, such as a banal remark about a corpse, a good-morning greeting after a night of gambling, the crying of a child, the forgetting of a song, or the sound of snow falling. However, the detail is only the final psychological spark for an illumination that has been artfully prepared. This structure is most apparent in stories of self-revelation like "Araby" where a boy sees in the mere act of lights being turned out a projection of his psychological blindness, or "Eveline" where a girl envisions in the bars leading to a ship's gangplank the cage in which she is caught by circumstance and weakness, or "A Painful Case" where a lonely man perceives in the wormlike shape made by the lights of a departing train an image of his own deathly isolation. However, this basic pattern of narrative is perceptible even in the complex, multi-leveled stories, such as "The Sisters," "Two Gallants," and "Clay," which Joyce wrote or revised last.

Joyce's handling of character reflects the liturgical epiphany in another way. The Joycean protagonist is both individual and type, an approach to character Joyce could observe in the liturgy. Both the Mass and Divine Office present Jesus as man and Messiah and maintain a constant awareness of the Messianic type and antitype (i.e., the original of the type). Jesus is shown as the antitype of Messiah, fulfilling Israel's concept of Deliverer as foretold by the prophets, not merely in prophetic passages, but also in acts regarded as types or figures.[42] The liturgy thus reflects a tradition of Biblical exegesis which stresses the typological significance of the Old Testament in prefiguring the mysteries of the New. In this interpretation Adam, Noah, Moses, the prophets, and other Biblical characters are not only historical characters but types of the Messiah; and such actions as the sacrifice of the Paschal lamb and the offering of Melchisedech are prefigurations of Christ's acts. The liturgy frequently recollects these *figurae* and draws numerous analogies between the precursors and the Messiah, between Christ and the priest in the Eucharistic sacrifice, and between Jesus and the ordinary man.

These concepts, which Joyce knew intimately as part of his religious heritage, explain, in part, two unusual features of the treatment of the main characters in *Dubliners*. First, though each of the fifteen stories has a central character who is a definite individual and usually a social type, all these heroes and heroines are aspects of a single implied protagonist, a kind of antitype of Man. For example, the heroes of the first three tales are boys who are unnamed, fatherless, and in the tales successively older. The heroes are thus depersonalized and made to seem first characters, then types of boyhood, and finally representations of the antitype of universal Man which is the central figure of *Dubliners*. This everyman character is made eventually to represent both sexes, various ages, and different social levels and occupations.[43] Intricate plot patterning emphasizes this typological aspect of *Dubliners*. Similar characters may be put in like situations (the clerks of "A Little Cloud" and "Counterparts") or in opposite situations (the celibates of "Clay" and "A Painful Case"). Dissimilar characters may be contrasted in parallel plots (the young men of "Two Gallants" and

"The Boarding House"). The individual crises are so made social tragedies and the result is a composite picture of life in Ireland that reinforces the everyman concept of the work.

Moreover, Joyce's use of God, Bible, and saint analogies (or inversions) in his characterizations arises from his awareness of the liturgical types. His mind was so possessed with this dual view of man as individual and type that he rarely separated a character from the *figura* it recalled for him. As a result, *Dubliners* is full of ironic analogies: the heroes are often ironic Christ figures, the women ironic types of the Virgin or Mother Church, and the numerous priests ironic figures of God, Jesus, or the Church.

Examination of the individual stories will clarify these parallelisms and inversions of liturgy in structure, theme, and characterization. Joyce's own four-fold division offers a convenient approach for discussion.

Of all groups, the first, depicting childhood ("The Sisters," "An Encounter," and "Araby"), is most affected by the Epiphany liturgy. All three tales are private manifestations to individuals like the epiphanies of Jesus' early life, and all three present inversions of the Epiphany theme of enlightenment, in that their common theme is disillusionment in a belief of some kind—a disillusionment developed in plots depicting defective human relationships and imaged by light becoming darkness. All three tales present a search for religious values that ends in failure, and thus they seem ironic variations of the quest of the Magi for the King-God.

In this symbolism the influence of liturgy was reinforced by the example of Yeats who in "The Tables of the Law" and "The Adoration of the Magi" had used Magi-quest symbols as vehicles for his religious mysticism. In these stories Yeats dealt with the founding of religious cults that used traditional religious symbols in new meanings: for example, "The Adoration of the Magi" deals with three old Irishmen who receive a vision directing them to undertake a journey to a far country to seek a woman who will give them an annunciation. Joyce indicated that this story and "The Tables of the Law," which he actually memorized, influenced his thinking.[44] Also both stories affected revisions made in some of the earliest *Dubliners* tales.[45] These combined influences, literary and liturgical, result in an opening triad of stories in which Joyce anticipates Eliot as Yeats had anticipated both of them in use of Magi symbolism.

The three stories are all multi-leveled. At the realistic narrative level, they picture the disillusionment of innocent youths as a result of encounters with disappointment, evil, and death. On the symbolic level all are epiphanies involving religion. They are highly patterned: the heroes are all lonely, sensitive boys dissatisfied with their home and cultural environments and vaguely aspiring to something ideal; all seek meaningful relationships with figures older than themselves; and all are disappointed. There is a moral level also in that the triad represents a study in the theological virtues: the stories in order present disillusionment in faith, hope, and love.[46]

"The Sisters" opens *Dubliners* with a story of the death of an old, half-demented priest who stands symbolically for the Irish church and nation.[47] It presents a boy's first awareness of death, an emotion made more painful by an accompanying disillusionment in the cleric. In the tale, a boy, desiring knowledge, has sought out an ailing but learned priest for tutoring in Latin and in religious dogma. After the priest's death the boy, disillusioned by what he learns of the priest's past, loses faith in the values the cleric has represented. Symbols convey Joyce's meaning: ecclesiastical stagnation and decay are suggested by the paralysis and mental deterioration of the cleric, materialism by a dream-confession of simony, and failure of spiritual mission by the breaking of a chalice. In several ways the story seems an inversion of the events of the Epiphany, the original Nativity feast. It is a quest for religious belief—but one that fails. A child comes bearing gifts to a supposedly wise man who proves a moribund failure. The end of the quest is not discovery of a birth and new faith as with the Magi, but disbelief and death. The tale is suffused with darkness and decadence from the opening, with its emphasis on the words *night*, *darkened*, and *paralysis*, through the gloomy scenes of the dozing priest and candle-lit wake, to the final reminiscence of the dark confessional where the mad priest had been found. Thus "The Sisters" opens *Dubliners* with an epiphany of darkness, disillusionment, and death; in contrast, the feast of the Epiphany begins the liturgical season with the theophany of light, belief, and birth.

"An Encounter," which appears superficially to describe a realistic meeting of young boys with a pederast, presents symbolically childhood's loss of innocence.[48] The story has other levels of meaning: it is a failure in the theological virtue of hope and is also a quest for religious reality in which Magi motifs are utilized. Three boys dissatisfied with their restrictive father-dominated school society play truant to see the world and life. They plan a trip to the seashore, specifically to the Pigeon House, Dublin's light and power station on a breakwater. Of these three young "magi," one never starts at all, and the other two, distracted by meeting the pervert, do not reach their goal, the Pigeon House, which suggests the Dove or Holy Spirit and whose function seems a God-Power symbol. Instead, as the sun goes under a cloud, the old pervert in his decayed black suit gives the one remaining boy meaningless sex preachments as if "unfolding some elaborate mystery."[49] Frightened, the young hero retreats to his old dispensation—the environment and companions he had despised. The frustration of the quest is imaged by the disappearance of the sun (perhaps a pun) and by the failure to reach the illuminating powerhouse. The story is a cynical inversion of the journey of the Magi.

"Araby" is also a tale of dual meaning.[50] The outward action is slight: a boy who has fallen in love with an older girl goes to a bazaar, romantically named Araby, to buy his love a gift, but once there realizes in the unexpected tawdriness of the exhibition the unreality of his adolescent emotion. The details reveal more. The girl is a virginal figure whom the boy worships from afar. (He prostrates himself each morning to see her.) She is always illumined by light and is associated with religion and the Church by the convent retreat she attends. The youth images his devotion to her as a chalice he carries among hostile strangers and associates realization of his love with the gift he means to give her. Like the traditional Magi, on his journey to Araby he is beset with difficulties, but the similarity ends there. His quest is a blank. He arrives to find the exhibition dark and empty like a church after a service. It is ready to close and there is nothing to buy. This pilgrim has begun too late, cannot find what he seeks, and fails in his gift-giving. The conclusion offers marked inversion of Epiphany light symbolism: the Wise Men found the light of the world at the end of their journey—that is the essential meaning of the Epiphany; the youth, plunged into darkness as the lights of Araby go out, senses in his temporary blindness the vacuity of his love—a manifestation on the symbolic level of disillusionment in the theological virtue of charity, as well as in religion in general.

At the symbolic level, then, all three tales present religious pilgrimages that fail.

The next eight stories, which comprise Joyce's second and third groups, complete the chronology and markedly develop the everyman concept. Each protagonist is older than the previous one, and all the stories are in typal pairs. Joyce's second group, the stories of adolescence ("Eveline," "After the Race," "Two Gallants," and "The Boarding House"), show young men and women making the vocational and marriage (or love) choices appropriate to this age. The tales are epiphanies of paralyzed will power, since each youth facing a vital choice either avoids a decision or makes one so unwise that the result is a life trap. To illustrate: the first pair of stories "Eveline" and "After the Race" show a poor young girl and a rich young man making their vocational choices—for the girl marriage and for the man a business venture involving his patrimony.[51] Both prove too weak-willed to act purposefully. Eveline rejects a life-giving marriage for a twilight life of drudgery imaged by dust symbols, and Jimmy Doyle's empty future is forecast by his gambling away his father's money. The moment of epiphany for each is effected by blended light and eyesight imagery, a symbolism consistent with Joyce's view of the epiphany as enlightenment.[52] Doyle's "dark stupor" is contrasted to the dawn from which he shields his eyes. Eveline's unseeing eyes reflect her psychological state. Moreover, her epiphany is initiated by what seems an inversion of the Baptism of Christ epiphany. Eveline, about to elope abroad, suddenly feels immersed in the "seas of the world" and drowning.[53] What might have been her initiation into a vital new life seems death to her. Her name suggests that she may be an Eve figure. The next pair of stories have contrasting plots of betrayal: in "Two Gallants" a servant girl is betrayed by two ne'er-do-wells; in "The Boarding House" an industrious young man is trapped into marriage by two conniving women. Joyce's third group, the stories of maturity ("A Little Cloud," "Counterparts," "Clay," and "A Painful Case"), continue the typal concept and represent a progression in moral and psychological paralysis. The first pair contrast two clerks inhibited in their jobs and family life; the second pair, two celibates who perform dull work, the old maid among women in a laundry, the old bachelor among men in a bank. Darkness and death images dominate these final tales. Thus from childhood to age Joyce's chronological sequence pictures characters whose "paralyzed force" and "gestures without motion" presage only the fall of the final shadow.

In these eight tales a shift of theme is apparent. Whereas the stories of childhood had developed a faith-disillusionment theme in imagery of light and darkness, these tales in their repetitive plots of disunion, betrayal, and sterility seem ironic inversions of the Marriage of Cana manifestation and of the mystical marriage symbolism associated with the Epiphany season.

The fact that the motifs of vocation and marriage (or love) are linked in seven of the eight narratives probably reflects liturgy. Christian commentators early gave mystical interpretation to the Cana miracle, noting that Jesus' first public manifestation took place at a marriage feast and prefigured the Eucharist.[54] Symbolically Jesus was viewed in two roles, as Messiah-Teacher and as Bridegroom of the mystical marriage. The office of the Second Sunday after Epiphany quotes St. Augustine: the "whole Church" is "included in that marriage of which Christ is the Bridegroom (for all have entered into mystical nuptials with Him)." Moreover, the reason "our Lord accepted the invitation and came to the wedding was . . . to show that matrimony is a great mystery-symbol. Furthermore, the bridegroom in that marriage typified the Lord because they said to him, 'You have kept the good wine until now.' The good wine Christ has indeed kept until now, namely his Gospel."[55] Jesus as Bridegroom in union with his bride, the Church, and Christ as Teacher beginning his mission are joined in a symbolism noted apparently by Joyce.

In the light of this background, the repeated failures in vocation and love-marriage relationships in *Dubliners* undoubtedly have religious significance. Therefore, the stories of courtship, "Two Gallants" and "The Boarding House," may be expected to have anagogic elements. "Two Gallants" has been chiefly interpreted as a tale of Irish nationalism.[56] A multi-leveled story, its theme of betrayal is key to the plot. At the narrative level it pictures the betrayal of a slavey whom a bully, Corley, abetted by a parasitical follower, Lenehan, seduces and bilks of her savings. At the nationalistic level, this is the story of Ireland exploited and betrayed by conquerors. At the religious level the perfidy is pictured as a variant of the betrayal of Christ. The story is an ironic inversion of the events of Holy Thursday: Lenehan's solitary meal and anxiety paralleling the Eucharistic Last Supper and the agony in the Garden; and Corley's kiss, as he obtains the girl's money, repeating the act of Judas. The epiphany is initiated when Corley displays to the admiring "gaze of his disciple" Lenehan the "coin" of betrayal.[57] It illuminates the liturgical inversions in character. The slavey, who wears the Virgin's colors, is a debasement of the Virgin of the mystical marriage; Lenehan is a missionless Christ; and Corley, the "base betrayer," is a Judas figure. Atmospherically the veiling of the moon and final disappearance of natural light image the moral movement of the story.

"The Boarding House," the only tale in which a marriage is effected, might also be expected to have religious significance. Yet this story has been regarded as "naturalistic,"[58] and it is one of the few for which no religious explication has been proposed. Certain details, however, merit examination. The hero, Doran, is tricked into marriage by a scheming mother and daughter. Though he realizes he is being "had," he yields under the double pressure of a priest in the confessional and of the supposedly outraged mother who threatens to disclose the affair. These two figures suggest the forces of the Church and society respectively. By forcing the issue on Sunday morning just before Mass, the mother aligns herself with the moral position of the Church; and by threatening to tell Doran's employer, with the hypocritical conventionalities of the business world— actions reflecting Joyce's view of Irish society as clerically dominated and mercenary. The characterizations of the bride and groom are significant.[59] The word *reparation* is repeatedly associated with Doran (it appears five times), suggesting he is an ironic Christ figure. Polly Mooney is described as a girl of "wise innocence," a "little perverse madonna," and her actions hint that she is one of the maidens of the marriage parable of the wise and foolish virgins by which Jesus described the kingdom of heaven: the affair between the couple began when Polly, who had let her candle go out, came late one night to Doran's door for a light, thus suggesting the foolish virgins who had no oil in their lamps when they arose to meet the bridegroom in the night (Matthew xxv.1–13). The story seems an ironic inversion of the mystical marriage of Christ with his virgin bride the Church and thus a commentary on the spiritual life of the Irish family.

The stories of maturity in the next group depict characters whose work and family relationships are empty or sterile. For example, Chandler of "A Little Cloud" and Farrington of "Counterparts" are clerks frustrated by the coercive monotony of office routine and trapped by family obligations.[60] They express their resentment in outbursts affecting their children. The details of the epiphanies in these stories suggest that they are Holy Family inversions. Chandler perceives in his wife's irritation and his child's rejection of him the failure of his family relationships. When at this point the wailing child is referred to as "little lamb of the world," the analogy to Jesus and the Holy Family implies a spiritual failure beyond the literal vocational and family failures of the narrative. Farrington, after a humiliating day at the office and a drinking bout, comes home late to find the hearth fire out and his wife at chapel. As his small son kneels before him praying a *Hail Mary*, he vents his frustration in beating the child. The very posture of the characters suggests a God-the-Father irony.

"Clay" moves between the thematic poles of the feasts of All Saints and All Souls, for its heroine, Maria, is a potential Virgin Mary type whose life of emotional denial has made her a shade appropriate to the Halloween setting of the tale.[61] The mingled suggestions of saint and witch in her character mirror not only her personal frustration but the inhibition of the religious spirit in Ireland. She is paired with Mr. Duffy of "A Painful Case," whose rejection of love, unlike Maria's, is deliberate. His epiphany is a realization that since his life is devoid of love, he is already one of the dead—an illumination initiated by an apparition of the rejected woman and completed by the disappearance of lights in the chill night. As a group these tales present characters whose occupations are fruitless and whose lives lack that unity in love that is the foundation of a successful marriage, a viable society, and a meaningful Church.

The final group, the stories of "public life" ("Ivy Day in the Committee Room," "A Mother," "Grace," and "The Dead"), give contrasting pictures of Irish society. The shift from chronological to typal epiphanies at this point is a marked structural parallel to the Epiphany sequence; but except for certain motifs and symbols in the last two tales, liturgical influences are not as apparent as in earlier groups. Joyce depends on literary and historical allusions to develop ironic contrasts between vital figures of the past and his impotent groups. His method of ironic inversion is unchanged, but heroic human figures replace his Christ-Virgin-Magi parallels. For example, in "Ivy Day" venal politicians are posed against memories of Joyce's hero Parnell; in "A Mother" a banal show is contrasted with recollections of a great operatic tradition; and in "Grace" a drunkard's fall from virtue burlesques the *Divine Comedy*. ("The Dead," written later and designed to act as a coda for the whole collection, has a different plan of construction.)

The first three of these stories represented Joyce's original final group for his projected 1905 edition, and in that version they would have offered a closing triad dealing with the theological virtues of faith, hope, and charity (though in an inverse order), as did his opening group of tales.

"Ivy Day in the Committee Room" deals with betrayal of national principles and a national leader.[62] (The final act of hate at the opposite pole from love is betrayal of trust.) The plot is a set of antitheses contrasting wardheelers, ready to sell their country for a miserable handout and a drink, with the memory of a national leader who sacrificed fortune, health, and life to a patriotic cause. Details of double dealing and betrayal build up cumulatively, suggesting the episodes of Parnell's career; but near the end, an explicit reference to Jesus and Judas makes it clear that the references throughout are ambivalent. Parnell, the absentee hero of "Ivy Day," emerges as a Christ figure; the political Messiah deserted by turn-coat followers and repudiated by the Irish Church is a parallel to Jesus betrayed by Judas and condemned by the high priests. In such a reading the cynical politicians of the Committee Room, who have agreed that "Parnell is dead," contrast ironically with the disciples of the upper room expectant of a resurrection.[63] "Ivy Day," like "Two Gallants," is a triple-leveled story having an approximation to the three planes which Parsch describes as characteristic of liturgy: a narrative plane giving a realistic episode; a plane of present moral symbolism, which is nationalistic in this tale; and a spiritual plane on which the betrayal is viewed in the perspective of Christ's career.

Except that the theme of "A Mother" is failure in the virtue of hope, the story has little apparent religious symbolism.[64] In this tale a girl's ambitions for a musical career are defeated, both by her mother's materialism and by the mediocrity of the arts in Ireland. The censorious, mercenary, convent-bred Mrs. Kearney is, like Mrs. Mooney of "The Boarding House," a figure characteristic of clerically-dominated Irish society. She represents the provinciality and puritanism of its culture.

The very title of "Grace" is ironic because it is a story of lack of spirituality and repudiation of faith both by a group of businessmen making a retreat and by their worldly priest-director.[65] The tale is triple-leveled. At the narrative level, a drunkard, Mr. Kernan, is persuaded by his friends to make a retreat. The level of Dantean analogy offers satiric humor in Mr. Kernan's infernal fall down the stairs of a barroom lavatory, his purgatorial "wash[ing] the pot," and his celestial return to grace at the retreat by means of a sermon that puts heaven in cash register terms.[66] Beneath this level of ironic humor lies the essential allegory of the Dantean everyman and his life pilgrimage, exemplified in Mr. Kernan as in all the figures of *Dubliners*. This story was the original ending of *Dubliners*.

Certain details suggestive of the Epiphany season liturgy appear both in "Grace," the projected 1905 ending, and in "The Dead," the 1914 published conclusion. This is consonant with Joyce's habit of writing conclusions that round out his openings. Just as the first story, "The Sisters," has Magi symbolism reminiscent of 6 January, the opening of the Epiphany season, so "Grace" has details suggestive of Candlemas, the end of the season. The

Purification is a picturesque feast on which worshippers hold lighted candles, both in celebration of Christ, the "light to the revelation of the Gentiles," and also in recollection of their baptismal vows. (Baptismal candles are regarded as symbols of grace and the light of Christian faith.)[67] In "Grace," at the climax of the retreat, the men are to light candles while they renew their baptismal vows. However, we know in advance that Kernan has already contemptuously dismissed this "magic-lantern business." His declaration that he will "bar the candles" is a symbolic rejection of Christian faith.[68] Had Joyce succeeded in getting *Dubliners* published in 1905, the book would have ended, as it began, with candlelight imagery and portraits of decadent priests symbolic of Ireland and the Church.

As finally published, *Dubliners* ends with "The Dead," a Christmas story.[69] The setting and season of "The Dead" seem more than coincidence since they act functionally and symbolically. The scene is a holiday party—definitely not Christmas Day nor New Year's Eve but probably Twelfth Night, 6 January. The hero, Gabriel Conroy, undergoes a double epiphany: the first a revelation that his society is psychologically paralyzed and the second a realization that, because he has never lived to the full, he is one of the dead. (This realization in itself may represent a rebirth—interpretations differ.)

Thematically and symbolically the story seems to offer inversion of the three major epiphanies associated with the Feast of 6 January: the revelation to the Magi, the manifestation at Christ's baptism, and the miracle at the Marriage of Cana. The story is threaded with functional symbols, three of which seem related to these liturgical epiphanies. The first is the theme of love and romance which in "The Dead" inverts the Marriage of Cana motif. It is introduced by the bitter remarks on marriage of the maid, Lily, and developed by episodes in which the old spinster hostesses play romantic music and Gabriel discovers in himself a reawakened awareness of his wife, Gretta. It culminates in Gabriel's realization that he has never known or possessed the whole of Gretta and has never really loved anyone but himself. His marriage has not been a union of spirit, only of body. This marriage epiphany is closely related to another, the epiphany of the falling snow. There is little question that the water and snow have baptismal significance and so link this symbol with the second manifestation of the Feast of 6 January. All through the hot, stuffy evening party, Gabriel longs for the fresh, cold, moisture-laden air outside. His desire to escape from his society and to live more vitally is thus connected symbolically

with water, the natural symbol of rebirth and baptism. However, his experience with the regenerative water is in the form of the frozen, sterile
snow, which is now his natural element. Finally, light and darkness appear
prominently as symbols of enlightenment-insensitivity and birth-death in
shifting patterns of ambivalence. Ironically, at the party the lights within
seem to illuminate an Irish society of narrow provinciality and desiccated
values, chiefly concerned with the dead past; while the great darkness
outside suggests all Europe and its living culture. But later, when Gabriel,
belatedly romantic, extinguishes the candle in the bedroom, dark and
light function in their archetypal symbolism. The light that outlines man
and wife is not that of moon or star, but the ghastly flickering gaslight
from outside, suggestive of the dead youth Michael. The enlightenment
that Gabriel undergoes is a discovery of his deadness in a dead society. His
final epiphany is initiated by a vision of a winter graveyard at night with
snow falling on the living and the dead. For Gabriel it is a recognition of
his psychological paralysis. For the reader Joyce suggests, by his references
to spears, thorns, a hill, "crooked crosses," and the "last end," a more universal religious significance.[70] As a vision of darkness and death the story
seems a deliberate inversion of the Feast of the Epiphany, the manifestation of light and life in Christ that the Magi found. Thus *Dubliners* ends as
it began with darkness, paralysis, and death. Nonetheless, in Gabriel Conroy's final epiphany Joyce seems to affirm the conditions for rebirth for all
the Dubliners, conditions that recall the three great liturgical epiphanies
celebrated on 6 January, the light of mature self-understanding, the baptismal death of ego that brings new life, and that charismatic love which
is the essence of spiritual union.

In retrospect, the inversion of the Epiphany sequence that *Dubliners*
represents is clear. Contrast the nine manifestations of the Epiphany cycle
with the fifteen of *Dubliners*. Jesus is revered as a babe by the Magi, mar-
veled at as a boy by the doctors in the Temple, blessed as a youth by the
Holy Spirit at his baptism, and confirmed in the eyes of his disciples at
Cana. In his career he draws followers by miracles of physical recovery
and by discourses promising eternal life. It is a pattern of developing life
and action. In *Dubliners* children are disillusioned, youths make stultify-
ing choices of mates and vocations, mature men and women are unable to
act purposefully, and society as a whole demonstrates cultural stagnation.
The epiphany in *Dubliners* is a manifestation, not of divine power and authority, but of impotence, paralysis, and death. These thematic inversions

are heightened by inverse symbolism of the Epiphany symbols of light and king's coming. The plots of disunion and betrayal invert the motif of the mystical marriage; and the stories of blindness, decay, and death invert the light-life theme of the Epiphany season. Darkness and light function as moral opposites throughout the book: shadow, mist, dimness, night, and dust suggest evil and death; sun, moon, and candlelight suggest God, goodness, and life. Atmospherically, darkness pervades *Dubliners*: thirteen of its fifteen stories have scenes at twilight or night, and in the final tales cumulative effects of cold and darkness culminate in the night, graveyard, snow, and death imagery of "The Dead." *Dubliners* is then influenced by the Epiphany liturgy in its overall design of patterned inversion as well as in the details of many of its stories.

In conclusion, the liturgical epiphany in its meaning of a manifestation of divine power offered Joyce a term which, placed in a literary setting, could signify both *revelation* in its usual technical sense and *spiritual illumination* in psychological and symbolic senses. At the period when Joyce was developing in *Dubliners* a collection of tales which as a group made a total framework and offered a single comment, the sequences of epiphanies in the life of Jesus gave him a structural pattern which offered diversity and unity and which as a whole presented a significance greater than that of the parts. The liturgy provided him a type of hero-savior and pattern of heroic action that he could parallel and invert with ironic effect. The cyclic patterns, the multiple levels of meaning, and the anagogic imagery which Joyce derived from the Epiphany season liturgy result in a rich fabric of religious symbolism that adds dimension and depth to *Dubliners*.

Notes

1. William F. Arndt and F. Wilbur Gingrich, *A Greek-English Lexicon of the New Testament and Other Early Christian Literature* (Chicago, 1957).

2. James Joyce, *Stephen Hero* (New York, 1944), pp. 26–27.

3. Ibid., p. 211. For the biographical background of the epiphany see Richard Ellmann, *James Joyce* (New York, 1959), pp. 87–89 and 169; Oliver St. John Gogarty, *As I Was Going Down Sackville Street* (New York, 1937), p. 295; Stanislaus Joyce, *My Brother's Keeper: James Joyce's Early Years* (New York, 1958), pp. 124–127; and Joseph Prescott, "James Joyce's Epiphanies," *MLN*, LXIV (May 1949), 346.

4. *Stephen Hero*, pp. 210–213. For the epiphany as a part of Joyce's aesthetics see Maurice Beebe, "Joyce and Aquinas: The Theory of Aesthetics," *PQ*, XXXVI (January 1957),

32–34; Haskell M. Block, "The Critical Theory of James Joyce," *JAAC*, VIII (March 1950), 182–183; Rudd Fleming, "*Quidditas* in the Tragi-Comedy of Joyce," *UKCR*, XV (Summer 1949), 289–290; Irene Hendry, "Joyce's Epiphanies," in *James Joyce: Two Decades of Criticism*, ed. Seon Givens (New York, 1948), pp. 27–46; Hugh Kenner, *Dublin's Joyce* (Bloomington, Ind., 1956), pp. 144–154; and William T. Noon, *Joyce and Aquinas* (New Haven, 1957), pp. 60–85.

5. See James Joyce, *Epiphanies*, ed. O. A. Silverman (Buffalo, 1956).

6. For additional definitions and discussions see William Powell Jones, *James Joyce and the Common Reader* (Norman, Okla., 1955), pp. 11–13; Harry Levin, *James Joyce: A Critical Introduction* (Norfolk, Conn., 1941), pp. 27–32 and 73; and William York Tindall, *James Joyce: His Way of Interpreting the Modern World* (New York, 1950), pp. 120–121, and *A Reader's Guide to James Joyce* (New York, 1959), pp. 10–12.

7. James Joyce, *Letters*, ed. Stuart Gilbert (New York, 1957), p. 55.

8. Ibid., and Ellmann, p. 169.

9. Adrian Fortescue, "Epiklesis," *The Catholic Encyclopedia*, 1909, V, 502–503.

10. *Stephen Hero*, pp. 32, 77, and 202–203.

11. James Joyce, *A Portrait of the Artist as a Young Man*, Compass Edition (New York, 1956), p. 221.

12. *My Brother's Keeper*, pp. 103–104. See Ellmann, p. 169.

13. Pius Parsch, *The Church's Year of Grace*, trans. William G. Heidt (Collegeville, Minn., 1957), I, 10 and 370–378.

14. Ibid., pp. 8–10.

15. Ibid., pp. 3–4.

16. *The Catholic Missal*, ed. Charles J. Callan and John A. McHugh (New York, 1934), p. 123. Quotations from liturgy, unless otherwise indicated, will be from this work, pp. 130–147 and 733–740.

17. Cyril Martindale, "Epiphany," *The Catholic Encyclopedia*, 1909, V, 504–506; and Parsch, I, 264. Christmas, the popular festival of the West, is a later development.

18. Parsch, I, 16.

19. Ibid., pp. 265 and 17.

20. Because of the movable calendar of the Church year, not all these feasts are celebrated every year during Epiphany.

21. Parsch, I, 295–297. The Feast of the Holy Family, now celebrated on the Sunday within the octave of the Epiphany, is not considered here because it is of recent institution.

22. This octave has recently been suppressed by the Holy See. The day has now received a new name, The Commemoration of the Baptism of Our Lord (Pope John XXIII, *motu proprio, Rubricarum instructum*, 25 July 1960).

23. Parsch, I, 322 and 347.

24. See James R. Baker, "Ibsen, Joyce, and the Living-Dead: A Study of *Dubliners*," in *A James Joyce Miscellany*, Third Series, ed. Marvin Magalaner (Carbondale, Ill., 1962), pp. 19–32; David Daiches, *The Novel and the Modern World* (Chicago, 1939), pp. 83–100; Brewster Ghiselin, "The Unity of Joyce's 'Dubliners,'" *Accent*, XVI (Spring 1956), 75–88, and (Summer 1956), 196–213; Jones, pp. 9–23; Kenner, pp. 53–68; Richard Levin and

Charles Shattuck, "First Flight to Ithaca: A New Reading of Joyce's *Dubliners*," in *Two Decades of Criticism*, pp. 47–94; J. Mitchell Morse, *The Sympathetic Alien: James Joyce and Catholicism* (New York, 1959), 97–110; Tindall, *Guide*, pp. 3–8 and 11–49; and Florence L. Walzl, "Pattern of Paralysis in Joyce's *Dubliners*," *College English*, XX (January 1961), 221–228.

25. Quoted in Herbert Gorman, *James Joyce* (New York, 1939), p. 156.

26. From a letter to Grant Richards in Gorman, p. 150.

27. The *Portrait* offers a variation of this plot device in that it consists of a series of chronological epiphanies, each focusing on a significant aspect of Stephen Dedalus' development as an artist, the novel as a whole justifying flight of the artist into exile.

28. From a letter to Grant Richards in Gorman, p. 150, and a letter to Constantine P. Curran, in *Letters*, p. 55.

29. Parsch, I, 297.

30. From the third nocturne lessons on the Seventh Day after Epiphany, quoted in Parsch, I, 285.

31. *Stephen Hero*, pp. 210–211.

32. Ibid., p. 211.

33. See *The New Schaff-Herzog Encyclopedia of Religious Knowledge* (New York, 1911), XI, 403: "In the ancient Church the term *theophaneia*, the same as *epiphaneia*, was almost exclusively restricted to the manifestation of God and the divine glory in Christ." *Webster's New International Dictionary of the English Language* (1959) defines *theophany* as "a physical manifestation of the presence of God or a God to man, esp. by incarnation in a human body or appearance in human form," and *epiphany* as "a manifestation; sometimes an apparition, as of God; usually a manifestation of Christ as divine." See also *A Catholic Commentary on Holy Scripture* (London, 1953), pp. 618 and 727, and Parsch, I, 264–265.

34. See Noon, pp. 49–54 and 60–83, for the influence of St. Thomas Aquinas on Joyce's concept of the epiphany.

35. *Stephen Hero*, p. 77.

36. Ibid., p. 213. See also *Portrait*, pp. 212–213.

37. *Stephen Hero*, p. 211.

38. *Portrait*, p. 213.

39. *Stephen Hero*, pp. 77–78.

40. See James Joyce, *Ulysses*, Modern Library Edition (New York, 1946), p. 41. For discussion of Joyce's developing fictional techniques in *Dubliners*, see Marvin Magalaner, *Time of Apprenticeship: The Fiction of Young James Joyce* (New York, 1959), pp. 73–87.

41. Stories illustrating the pattern of a single episode leading directly to an epiphany are "The Sisters," "An Encounter," "Araby," "Eveline," "After the Race," "Two Gallants," and "A Painful Case." Stories varying this technique by use of parallel episodes or two or more epiphanies are "A Little Cloud," "Counterparts," "Clay," "Ivy Day in the Committee Room," and "Grace." "The Dead," written at a later date, has a more conventional short story structure, though it too ends with an epiphany.

42. See *A Catholic Commentary on Holy Scripture*, pp. 130–131: " . . . the OT led up to Christ by prophecies, or predictions in word, and by types or figures, or predictions

in act and fact. . . . The significance of these has become apparent in their fulfillment in the antitype." See also pp. 56–57 and 536–537. *A New English Dictionary* (Oxford, 1901) defines *type* as " . . . spec. in Theol. a person, object or event of Old Testament history, prefiguring some person or thing revealed in the new dispensation; correl. to *antitype*"; and *antitype* as "that which is shadowed forth or represented by the 'type' or symbol."

43. "Eveline" and "After the Race" contrast the sexes in youth; "Clay" and "A Painful Case" in later middle age. In the eleven tales comprising the life cycle each protagonist is definitely older than in the previous tale.

44. See *Stephen Hero*, pp. 176–178, and *My Brother's Keeper*, p. 180.

45. Magalaner, *Time of Apprenticeship*, p. 78.

46. See Ghiselin, pp. 81 and 196–199, and Walzl, pp. 227–228.

47. See Stanislaus Joyce, *Recollections of James Joyce* [1941], trans. Ellsworth Mason (New York, 1950), p. 21. For explications citing religious motifs in this story, see Ghiselin, pp. 196–198; Julian B. Kaye, "Simony, the Three Simons, and Joycean Myth," in *A James Joyce Miscellany*, ed. Marvin Magalaner (New York, 1957), pp. 21–23; Kenner, pp. 50–53; Magalaner, *Time of Apprenticeship*, pp. 73–78; Marvin Magalaner and Richard M. Kain, *Joyce: The Man, the Work, the Reputation* (New York, 1956), pp. 71–75; Fritz Senn, "'He Was Too Scrupulous Always': Joyce's 'The Sisters,'" *James Joyce Quarterly*, II (Winter 1965), 66–72; Tindall, *Guide*, pp. 13–17; and Florence L. Walzl, "A Date in Joyce's 'The Sisters,'" *Texas Studies in Lit. and Lang.*, IV (Summer 1962), 183–187.

48. For explications citing religious motifs, see Julian B. Kaye, "The Wings of Daedalus: Two Stories in 'Dubliners,'" *MFS*, IV (Spring 1958), 31–37; Sidney Feshbach, "Death in 'An Encounter,'" *James Joyce Quarterly*, II (Winter 1965), 82–89; and Tindall, *Guide*, pp. 17–19.

49. James Joyce, *Dubliners*, Compass Edition (New York, 1958), p. 27.

50. For explications citing religious motifs, see Ghiselin, p. 199; Magalaner and Kain, pp. 77–79; William Bysshe Stein, "Joyce's 'Araby': Paradise Lost," *Perspective*, XII (Spring 1962), 215–222; and Tindall, *Guide*, pp. 19–21. Stein notes Advent-Christmas symbolism in certain details.

51. For explications citing religious motifs, see Ghiselin, pp. 199–200; William Bysshe Stein, "The Effects of Eden in Joyce's 'Eveline,'" *Renascence*, XV (Spring 1963), 124–127; and Tindall, *Guide*, pp. 21–22.

52. Eye imagery is employed in the conclusions of "Araby," "Eveline," "After the Race," "Two Gallants," "The Boarding House," "A Little Cloud," "Clay," and "The Dead." For a discussion of eye imagery in relationship to radiance, see Robert S. Ryf, *A New Approach to Joyce: The Portrait of the Artist as a Guidebook* (Berkeley, Calif., 1962), pp. 149–152.

53. *Dubliners*, p. 41.

54. Parsch, I, 308–317.

55. Ibid., p. 309. See St. Augustine, Homily viii on John ii.1–4 and Homily ix on John ii.1–11.

56. For explications citing religious motifs, see Robert Boyle, "'Two Gallants' and 'Ivy Day in the Committee Room,'" *James Joyce Quarterly*, I (Fall 1963), 3–9; Ghiselin, pp. 200–201; Noon, pp. 83–84; Tindall, *Guide*, pp. 23–25; and Florence L. Walzl, "Symbolism in Joyce's 'Two Gallants,'" *James Joyce Quarterly*, II (Winter 1965), 73–81.

57. *Dubliners*, p. 60.

58. Tindall, *Guide*, p. 26.

59. *Dubliners*, pp. 62–65 and 67.

60. For explications citing religious motifs, see Harold Brodbar, "A Religious Allegory: Joyce's 'A Little Cloud,'" *Midwest Quarterly*, II (Spring 1961), 221–227; and William Bysshe Stein, "'Counterparts': A Swine Song," *James Joyce Quarterly*, I (Winter 1964), 30–32.

61. For explications citing religious motifs, see Baker, pp. 27–28; Richard Carpenter and Daniel Leary, "The Witch Maria," *James Joyce Review*, III, i–ii (1959), 3–7; Magalaner and Kain, pp. 84–91; William T. Noon, "Joyce's 'Clay': An Interpretation," *College English*, XVII (November 1955), 93–95; Tindall, *Guide*, pp. 29–31; and Florence L. Walzl, "Joyce's 'Clay,'" *Explicator*, XX (February 1962), Item 46.

62. For explications citing religious motifs, see Joseph L. Blotner, "'Ivy Day in the Committee Room': Death without Resurrection," *Perspective*, IX (Summer 1957), 210–217, and Magalaner and Kain, pp. 79–84. Blotner details the Jesus-disciple analogies fully.

63. *Dubliners*, p. 132.

64. For an interpretation of Mrs. Kearney as a Mother-Church figure, see Tindall, *Guide*, pp. 36–38.

65. For explications citing religious motifs, see Ghiselin, pp. 206–207; Kaye, "Simony, the Three Simons and Joycean Myth," pp. 23–24; and Tindall, *Guide*, pp. 38–41.

66. *Dubliners*, p. 163.

67. Parsch, I, 372 and 378.

68. *Dubliners*, p. 171.

69. For an explication of "The Dead" as an Epiphany story, see Kaye, "The Wings of Daedalus: Two Stories in *Dubliners*," pp. 37–41. For other religious motifs, see Gerhard Friedrich, "Bret Harte as a Source for James Joyce's 'The Dead,'" *PQ*, XXXIII (October 1954), 442–444; and William York Tindall, *The Literary Symbol* (New York, 1955), pp. 224–228.

70. *Dubliners*, pp. 223–224.

2

Moral Responsibility in Joyce's "Clay"

THOMAS F. STALEY

Most of the critical exegesis of Joyce's "Clay" reveals a great deal of dexterity on the part of the nearly dozen critics who have written on the popular story. Since Marvin Magalaner, in 1953, first suggested the dual level of symbolism (that of Maria as witch on the one hand and the Blessed Virgin on the other) the explications of the story have focused on the interlocking symbolic levels and have seen the story as Joyce's attempt to handle apparently paradoxical symbolic elements simultaneously.[1]

This aspect of the story offers interesting opportunities for the interpreter to exhibit his perception of symbolic structures in a literary work, but with "Clay" the conclusions that have been drawn are a little short of absurd. The preoccupation with the symbolism has warped the usually perceptive Magalaner's vision and, more seriously, led those who have followed him into a phantasmagoria which adds nothing to the story and seriously misinterprets it.[2] As is so often the case with interpretations of Joyce's work, Hugh Kenner, although he has been patently ignored by most Joyce critics, tells us what "Clay" is about: "Maria is 'Clay' as humanity itself, as susceptible to molding, and as death in life. Joe's wife, another Mrs. Mooney, has eased her into the laundry and one may suspect will soon ease her into a convent; and Maria, one is sure, will never quite realize how she got there."[3]

Let us start from the beginning—an unmarried, middle-aged woman named Maria works in the "Dublin by Lamplight" laundry and on All Hallows Eve she sets out to visit Joe Donnelly and his family. She takes the tram, stopping at a bakery for a slice of plumcake. On the second tram she

Thomas Staley, "Moral Responsibility in Joyce's 'Clay,'" *Renascence* 18 (1966): 124–128. Reprinted with permission of *Renascence*. Copyright 1966.

encounters a gentleman who makes room for her to sit down and talks to her. Upon arriving at Joe's, she discovers that she has lost the plumcake. Maria is urged to take part in a Hallows Eve game which predicts one's future; she is blindfolded, led to a table where she touches the clay which one of the neighbor girls has substituted for water (the death for life substitute as the symbolists would validly read it). The second time she plays the game she gets the prayer-book. After the game is over Maria seems content again and is asked to sing the song "I Dreamt that I Dwelt," the second verse of which she leaves out and repeats the first verse.

The structure of the story is based upon Maria's recognition of the hypocrisy of her existence through a series of encounters with her fellow Dubliners. When the story opens we meet a Maria who is totally unaware of the world around her; she is the adult product of the paralysis that is Dublin—unaware of the disintegration of community, never cognizant of the meaning of her existence. The Donnelly family for which she once worked as nursemaid had broken up, and she has been shunted off to a laundry to work. Joe and his brother Alphy, whom Maria cared for, no longer speak—the Dubliners have grown up. Even in the laundry the employees fight among themselves; Maria, the most impassive of Dubliners, wanders in the midst of this social chaos trying to keep peace.

Each social relationship in the story enforces the theme of disintegration of human understanding and love, the dominant theme throughout *Dubliners*. Until the last scene of the story, Maria is unaware of her plight, unable to recognize the essential inhumanity of the people who make up her world. Lizzie Fleming, her fellow worker, establishes the relationships for the evening when, with the same irony as the narrator uses, she suggests that Maria will surely get the ring. Maria delays her decision as to which kind of cake to buy and the saleslady, annoyed, asks her if she wants a wedding cake. The irony of the girl's words passes completely over Maria and she blushes.

The boys on the tram make no motion to give Maria a seat on the bus; however, an elderly gentleman makes room for her. Slightly inebriated, he makes conversation, but, as she finds out when she reaches Joe's, he has perhaps played the Halloween trick of stealing her plumcake. Visibly disturbed for the first time in the story, Maria asks the children if they had eaten it. Remembering the scene on the tram with the gentleman, Maria is not only irritated but disappointed. The moral degeneration of Dublin is beginning to touch Maria's consciousness. In her conversation with Joe, she mentions Alphy, and Joe spills his venom on his brother. Maria, momentarily upset, still appears undaunted by the hatred and lack of love, even among brothers, which surround her.

Finally, coerced into playing the Hallows Eve game, Maria touches the clay. A bit bewildered, she at least "understood that it was wrong that time and so she [would have] to do it over again." Once more things seem to subside, but during the quiet conversation self-awareness is beginning to dawn on Maria. As she and Joe and his wife talk of the past much like the guests at the Sisters Morkan party in "The Dead," we become aware that these people are dead souls who must constantly draw on the mundane past to give any vitality to the present.

Mrs. Donnelly asks Maria to sing a song before she leaves, and Maria sings in a tiny quavering voice "I Dreamt that I Dwelt." She does not sing the second verse with its references to marriage and happiness, because, for the first time, she sees her life for what it is. All the encounters of the evening, climaxed with the trick played on her by the children in the substitution of the clay for the water, have slowly but emphatically brought her to self-awareness. The clay incident is the most dramatic moment in the story, hence the title. The denouement, however, takes place in the singing of the song where Maria confronts for the first time with open eyes the sham and hypocrisy of her world, the great separation between dream and reality. The epiphany in the story is not, as Professor Tindall suggests, Joe's but Maria's. Joe, filled with tears, still yearns sentimentally for the past; he has not changed nor been led to any discovery by the events in the story. In their paralysis the Donnelly family is deluded into thinking that Maria has forgotten the second verse, but she knows it all too well. The discovery is solely Maria's; it is she who is aware of her predicament for the first time. Unwittingly, Maria in her journey through the streets of Dublin has completed her unwilling quest and reached an understanding of herself and is for the first time confronted with the terrible emptiness of her life.[4]

Magalaner's interpretation has led him to suggest that Joyce "seems uncertain where to place the emphasis," that too many motifs "deflect from the central point of the narrative."[5] In light of my reading, I think that the centrality and essential unity of the story is clear; that there is no conflict of focus between the touching of the clay and the song: the episode with the clay is the dramatic climax of a series of events which gradually lead Maria from ignorance to self-awareness. Had the game with the clay not been played or had she not encountered all the circumstances during the evening Maria would never have realized that she lived in a world where she, like clay, has been molded and from which she cannot escape.

One further point should be mentioned, and this concerns the undue emphasis placed upon the Blessed Virgin and witch connections. What is Maria? Witch or Blessed Virgin, or both? The absurdity of these sugges- tions is only momentary. William T. Noon, S.J., in the best detailed study of "Clay" which has come to my attention, strongly suggested a moral consideration of the story, but, unfortunately, at the time he wrote his es- say the witch/Virgin controversy had not come to his attention.[6]

Richard Carpenter and Daniel Leary have clearly traced the witch-like overtones suggested by Maria, and they see her as being "predestined, in a witchlike fashion, to bring discord to those she most desires to share happiness with."[7] In their version she becomes "an unintentional spirit of discord" who is like the "queen in Snow White, at the mirror on the wall."[8] Without trying to refute each allusion to Maria's "witchishness" suggested by these writers, it should be noted that all of these descriptions in the story can also be read as indications of her lack of self-knowledge, her unawareness of the world around her; even the physical descriptions such as the four references to the tip of her nose reaching the tip of her chin ironically suggest her simple mindedness and vacant thought. Irony is Joyce's mode in this story.[9] The allusion by Joyce to Hallows Eve which is All Saints Day, a feast of the Church, reveals as much as anything else the hollow remnant of a once meaningful feast day. This is substantiated not only by the actions of the characters, but by the ironic juxtaposition of past and present which Joyce was later to use in "The Dead" and, of course, in *Ulysses*. A day which commemorates those dead who lived lives of meaningful existence is set against a modern day life of social strife and meaninglessness.

The analogy of the Blessed Virgin seems even more tenuous. The vari- ant of the name Mary is the first of many analogies cited by Magalaner. Maria's role as a "peace-maker," her being unmarried and a virgin, the offering of the barmbracks (seen as communion with the raisins in the bread suggesting wine), being referred to as "Mother" by Joe, Lizzie Flem- ing seen in relation to the Biblical parallels of Elizabeth announcing to Mary that she is to be the Mother of Christ, all point to the Blessed Virgin analogy. Several other points are also offered by Magalaner. All of these possible associations are quite interesting and perhaps contribute some understanding to the story. As it has been pointed out time and again, we must take every possibility into consideration when we read Joyce.

If, however, we see this analogy in light of the Nausicaa episode of *Ulysses*, we are able to view the extension of meaning in another light. In Nausicaa, Joyce's comments on the "Cult of Mary" are an indictment against those who see Mary as a female God who becomes their supplication of grace, and who feel that in their reverence to her they can negate their moral responsibilities. So to see in "Clay" Maria as analogous to the Blessed Virgin Mary who is ignored by contemporary Dublin seems to present a conflict. According to Joyce, his Dubliners would be only too content to praise in litanies and act out meaningless rituals to the Blessed Virgin rather than accept the responsibilities of humanity needed to carry on in the image of Christ in the Gospels.

As Leopold Bloom was later to say in *Ulysses*, the nuns may eat well in the convents of Dublin, but it is a perversion of the Christian sense of religious vocation if becoming a nun is merely a retreat from life and not a vital mission in the world. Therefore, when Maria finally touches the prayer-book, Mrs. Donnelly predicts that she will enter the convent within a year, and she says this with no understanding of Maria's wants and needs but merely as a way of shuffling off the last remnant of a world where people like Maria exist; a world where a person such as Maria loves someone like Joe Donnelly without motive and without reason, simply because he is another human being. Maria is shunted off, out of the world where she can pray for Joe and his family, but they will not have any human responsibility toward her. This is why Maria is unable to sing the second stanza of the song; her journey on this night has awakened her; she realized the gigantic gap between reality and dream, between what human responsibility really is and how it manifests itself in the modern world.

In "Clay" Joyce has given us a glimpse of the great moral theme of *Ulysses*: man's lack of a sense of responsibility to himself and to his fellow man.

Notes

1. Marvin Magalaner from "The Other Side of James Joyce," *Arizona Quarterly*, IX (Spring, 1953), pp. 5–16.

2. Unable to reconcile the symbolic extensions which he has suggested, Magalaner concludes his interpretation by saying that "Joyce was a very young writer when he wrote 'Clay.'" Marvin Magalaner and Richard M. Kain, *Joyce: The Man, the Work, the*

Reputation (New York, 1956), p. 89. William York Tindall follows the symbolic overtones that Magalaner has suggested and gives them further extension. William York Tindall, *A Reader's Guide to James Joyce* (New York, 1959), p. 29.

3. Hugh Kenner, *Dublin's Joyce* (Bloomington, 1956), pp. 57–58.

4. The structure of the story can be seen as Joyce's rather ironic use of the Journey archetype; in Maria's case the journey leads unknowingly to self-understanding. She is the reluctant adventurer who is called but refuses or is unable, at first, to recognize the meaning of the signs until she has been initiated and is reborn. But a thorough reading of the story in this light would be the subject of another essay, for mythological symbols have to be followed through all their implications to make the analogy worthwhile. To stress the dichotomous symbols of witch and Virgin surrounding Maria places the emphasis exclusively on her symbolic function in the story rather than on her vital thematic functions, and this accounts for Magalaner's confusion of the structure guiding the narrative level. Joyce's characters are not symbols in any artificial or contrived sense. It is in her quest and journey that Maria achieves symbolic stature, but this must be seen in its entirety to have validity.

5. Marvin Magalaner and Richard M. Kain, *op. cit.*, p. 89.

6. William T. Noon, "Joyce's 'Clay': An Interpretation," *College English*, XVII (November, 1955).

7. Richard Carpenter and Daniel Leary, "The Witch Maria," *The James Joyce Review*, vol. 3, nos. 1–2 (1959), p. 3.

8. *Ibid.*, p. 7.

9. To read Maria as a witch also requires one to ignore several incidents where she does prevent discord, such as the acceptance of the wine at Joe's insistence, her settling of arguments at the laundry, and her comment that she didn't like nuts anyway to prevent an argument over the lost nutcracker.

3

Semiotic Approaches to a Fictional Text

Joyce's "Eveline"

ROBERT SCHOLES

The purpose of this discourse is a simple one. I wish to argue, and to demonstrate as well as possible, that certain semiotic approaches to fictional texts, each incomplete in itself, can be combined in a manner that facilitates the practical criticism of fiction. The three approaches I wish to combine into a single methodology are the following:

1. That of Tzvetan Todorov, as illustrated in his *Grammaire du Décameron.*
2. That of Gérard Genette in "Discours du récit" from *Figures III.*
3. That of Roland Barthes in *S/Z.*

In each of these cases the critic has attempted to generate a method of analysis appropriate to the specific material under immediate consideration and to test the method on the material. But in every case the method, it is suggested, may have wider application as well. My thesis in this discourse is that all three of these methods do indeed have wider applications, that they complement one another in addressing the fictional text from different angles, and further, that they even suggest a sequence of use, each of them presenting itself as a segment in a meta-method in which they function as units of a syntagmatic process, units whose order should always be the same. The meta-method I wish to illustrate consists of approaching the text via Todorov, Genette, and Barthes in that order. The illustration will be based upon Joyce's "Eveline."

The three critics actually examine different levels or features of the

Robert Scholes, "Semiotic Approaches to a Fictional Text: Joyce's 'Eveline,'" *James Joyce Quarterly* 16 (Winter 1979): 65–80. Reprinted with permission from *James Joyce Quarterly.* Copyright 1979.

text, though their work naturally overlaps at certain points. Todorov, who based his method on the hundred tales of Boccaccio's *Decameron*, calls his study a "grammar." Genette, who illustrates his system on Proust's *Recherche*, is interested in "figures" that operate at the "rhetorical" level of the text. Barthes, working with a novella of Balzac, is more completely semiotic, as he seeks to codify all the ways in which a fictional text generates its significations. These three writers, then, offer us a grammar, a rhetoric, and finally a semiotic of fiction. This is true—with certain qualifications, which will emerge from the following discussion.

Todorov's grammar has two main features. He reduces fictions to plot structures that can be represented by a simple symbolic logic, and he codes the semantic features of his symbolic notations so that they reveal the principal thematic concerns of the action in any story. Todorov's method calls for a summary of the story's action to be made first, and then for the reduction of the summary to symbolic form. But this procedure has two large faults. First, the summary must be intuitive, governed by no explicit system, and second, the resulting notation has a spurious exactitude, based upon its resemblance to the summary rather than to the fiction itself. Working with stories as simple and sharply delineated as Boccaccio's, the problem is not so great, but when we seek to move to modern fiction it becomes acute.

The critic of modern fictional texts must employ Todorov's approach as a heuristic tool, a way of focusing interpretation upon features of all fictional texts. Our perception of fictions depends in part upon our understanding of what Barthes calls the code of actions. We recognize a story as a story because we perceive in it a causal/chronological system that has, as Aristotle pointed out, a beginning, middle and end. Todorov offers us a way of isolating the major action in any work of fiction so as to bring it to the foreground of our attention. Using his system of notation, we seek the story within any work of fiction. Obviously, most fictions are more than stories, especially modern fictions; and some fictions are anti-stories, pseudo-stories, in which the idea of story itself is parodied or denied for some ideological or thematic purpose. Todorov offers us a way to seek the story in any fiction and to record the results of that search. If we find no story, or a partial story, that, too, is a significant result.

But what *is* a story? Todorov will help us be precise in answering that question. A story is a certain kind of sequence of propositions. Fictional propositions are of two kinds: attribution and actions. The most fundamental fictional sequence is attribution, action, attribution—beginning, middle, end. Let me illustrate. If characters are nouns, attributes are adjectives, and actions are verbs, we can present a simple story in the following way:

$$X\text{-}A + (XA)\text{opt}X \to Xa \to XA$$

Where

$$
\begin{aligned}
X &= \text{Boy} \\
A &= \text{love, to be loved by someone} \\
a &= \text{to seek love, to woo} \\
\text{opt } X &= \text{Boy (X) wishes (opt)} \\
\text{-} &= \text{negation of attribute: -A is to lack love, to be unloved}
\end{aligned}
$$

Thus the sequence reads Boy lacks love plus Boy wants to be loved which yields Boy seeks love which yields Boy is loved. We know this is a story because it is a sequence of propositions involving the same subject, in which the last proposition is a transformation of the first. An unhappy ending might be a simple repetition of the first proposition: X-A. A very unhappy ending might be X-A!, Boy lacks love with vengeance.

But happy or unhappy, what makes the sequence a story is the return to the opening proposition at the end. Stories are about the successful or unsuccessful transformation of attributes.

In applying Todorov's method to modern stories, the first problem is often to isolate the major sequences of actions, to find the master story. "Eveline" is rather simple in this respect, but other stories in *Dubliners* are much more difficult. To find a story in "Ivy Day" is not so easy. But even "Eveline" presents problems of another sort. The chain of symbols representing the syntax of a story is just one aspect of its "grammar." The other aspect is lexical or semantic. We must reduce the complex of qualities associated with the characters (what Barthes calls connotative code) to a few summary features which are activated by the story itself. This semantic summarizing is the most crucial aspect of the interpretive process at this level of analysis. In actual practice, the interpreter must simply try out attributions until they seem incapable of further refinement. The method here requires the skill of the interpreter, and it will display any lack of such skill mercilessly—but the method cannot provide it.

Here is a version of the story "Eveline":

$$XA + XB \to X\text{-}C + YaX + (X\text{-}A + X\text{-}B \to XC)\ \text{pred}X \to (XbY)\ \text{pred}X + XA! \to X\text{not}bY \to (XB + X\text{-}C)!\ \text{imp}$$

X   Eveline
Y   Frank
A   a Dubliner
B   celibate
C   happy—respected, secure
a   to offer elopement
b   to accept elopement
-     negative of attribute
not   negative of verb
pred predicts or expects
imp   is implied by discourse

The annotation may be read as follows: Eveline is a Dubliner—literally a resident of Dublin, but figuratively much more. This attribute, built up over the whole sequence of stories, is in fact what the stories are about, as the title of the book indicates. This story, like most of the others, marks most heavily such features as isolation, deprivation, and repression, combined with an inability to act so as to change this condition of life. Eveline is also celibate. Dubliners tend to be either celibate or unhappily married, and celibacy is usually marked in the stories as a negative attribute, connotating incompletion, frustration, isolation. The third proposition indicates that Eveline is unhappy with her life. This is less than explicit, but can be inferred from her reaction to Frank's proposal and other descriptions of her home life. The action of the story starts with Frank's proposal of elopement, which leads Eveline to imagine that her situation will change for the better, signified by the reversal of sign on the attributes in the fifth proposition. Her prediction of the elopement itself in the sixth proposition is, in fact, bound up with the changes she predicts in the fifth. All this is quite explicit in the text. But Eveline *is* a Dubliner! She finally refuses the elopement, and the story closes with the strong implication that her original condition resumes, only intensified by her having missed this chance to leave Dublin and change her life. This is a simple story, which could easily be coded as the negation of the one of Vladimir Propp's Russian fairy tales. The prince comes to rescue the princess from the villain's dungeon, but she decides finally that the dungeon is less frightening than the thought of leaving it, and sends the hero home empty-handed. Naturalism sometimes generates its "authenticity" by the inversion of romance. But let us return to the process of notation and what it reveals.

Looking simply at the syntactic configuration here we see that the three attributive propositions which constitute the "situation" of "Eveline" are repeated with emphasis at or near the close of the narration. And though this repetition is more a matter of implication than of statement, the implications are quite clear. We can see also that the attributes remain unchanged; an essentially unhappy situation finally persists, even intensifies. This, in fact, is the rule of *Dubliners*. The grammar of these stories tends toward the persistence of unpleasant conditions—from bad to worse. A few stories show a change from better to worse. Only one shows any improvement of an opening situation, and that is "Two Gallants" in which the impecunious Lenehan is finally likely to benefit by sponging off his friend Corley, who has just received a gold coin from a servant girl in exchange for his sexual favors. But behind this "happy" ending the portrait of Lenehan as an aging sponger who is trapped in his Dublinesque existence becomes clearer and clearer. His real condition improves no more than Eveline's.

The point of this discussion is that Todorovian notation forces us to focus on questions of attribution, forces us to thematize the work. When applied to a body of works by a single author, such as the *Dubliners* stories, it brings to our attention recurrent features of syntactic and semantic coding, raising questions about such matters as why so many of these stories turn on celibacy and its various alternatives, and finally about the ultimate attribution, the state of being a Dubliner. This method is relatively crude, examining only two gross features of the text—action and attribution—but its usefulness for the analyst and the teacher is very real indeed.

The most elaborate and systematic apparatus yet developed for the study of fictional texts is that proposed by Gérard Genette in his "Discours du Récit" from *Figures III*. In the course of an extended discussion of Proust's *Recherche*, Genette presents a method for analyzing a fictional text according to its tense, mood, and voice—thus borrowing his terminology from the traditional grammar of the verb, on the grounds that all fiction can be seen as "the expansion of a verb." Genette begins by distinguishing three aspects of fictional texts which enable us to recognize them as fictional, and also provide us with points of departure for their study. Every fictional text comes to us in the form of a *récit* or narrative discourse—a text in fact. And this discourse informs us of a set of fictional events which can be distinguished from the text itself. Every fictional discourse conveys to us a story, which exists in a different spatio-temporal situation from the discourse itself, and from its own production or our reading of it. In addition to this, every narrative text also conveys explicitly or implicitly some circumstances of narration, some explanation for its own existence as a text, both in relation to the events narrated and to some *narrataire* or audience. When the narrative situation of a text is examined closely, the narrator and *narrataire* virtually never correspond exactly with author and reader, nor do the circumstances of narration agree with those of a book's actual writing and reading.

Keeping in mind these three elements of all fictional texts (the discourse, the story, and the narration), Genette begins his study of narrative by examining aspects of what he calls fictional "tense." In the temporal arrangements of fiction he discerns three major areas for investigation: order, duration, and frequency. *Order* is the arrangement of events expressed as a relationship between story and *récit*, the chronology of the story as opposed to the way the text arranges this chronology and presents it to us. (This is close to the Russian formalist distinction between story and plot.) *Duration* is a relationship between the temporal extension of events in the story and the attention devoted to them by the *discourse*. This is a matter of speed or velocity, which may be expressed as a ratio between the hours, days, and years of story time and the words and pages of the printed text. The third temporal aspect of a fictional text, *frequency*, involves the ways in which events may be repeated either in the story itself (the same thing happening more than once) or in the *discourse* (the same event described more than one time).

Within these three main aspects of tense Genette makes many further discriminations, only some of which we will attend to here, as not all are significant for a study of "Eveline." The order of presentation of the events in "Eveline" is both simple and complex. The base time of the narrative is the evening of Eveline's projected departure from Dublin. Joyce presents these events in two scenes: the first begins with darkness falling as Eveline sits by her window, and ends with her standing up. The second scene begins after the ellipsis dots. The time is that same night (though we must infer this) and the scene continues until the end of the story. Within this simple, chronological scheme, however, this story moves through an extraordinary complexity of temporal arrangement. Confining ourselves for the moment to fairly large and readily distinguishable blocks of time, we can discern a temporal movement in the story something like this:

A Base time (beginning, into second paragraph)

B Childhood (mid second paragraph)

C Base Time (end second paragraph and beginning of third)

D (A complex section to be scrutinized more closely later on)

E Recent past (Miss Gavan and the Stores)

F Future ("She would not cry many tears . . .")

G Recent past (Saturday night, etc.)

H Future ("She was about to explore another life . . .")

I Recent past (Eveline's relationship with Frank)

J Earlier past (Frank's history)

K Base time (—the "evening deepened")

L Earlier past (Eveline's mother's illness and death)

M Base time mixed with future (end of first section)

N Ellipsis in base time

O Base time (whole second scene, with only a hint of future)

Even ignoring many minor temporal shifts we can discern, then, fifteen distinct sections ranging over at least six separate periods of time in the life of Eveline, extending from her childhood to her possible future with Frank. But because of the way that Joyce has handled the perspective of this story, all these times are contained within the base time of the two scenes. They are all presented to us as aspects of Eveline's thought in a base time which is very close to "present" tense, even though narrated in a conventional past. Even the ellipsis indicates a present and dramatic passage of time. Since Genette discusses perspective as an aspect of "mood," we shall return to it after examining more closely certain aspects of tense that we have thus far set aside.

The fourth temporal unit that we noted above is so complicated temporally that I refrained from specifying its location in time. Now let us look at it more closely. The third section has brought us back to base time, with "Now" and "Home," as Eveline looks around her darkening room. Let us watch closely the temporal movement within a couple of sentences here:

She looked [base time] around the room, reviewing [base time] all its familiar objects, which she had dusted [past, iterative] once a week for so many years, wondering [past, iterative] where on earth all the dust came from. Perhaps she would never see again [future, conditional, negative] those familiar objects from which she had never dreamed [past, negative, subordinated within future] of being divided [future, within past negative, within future] (*D* 37).

What we have here is a rapid oscillation between the past seen as iterative, a familiar round of repeated events, dull but comforting, and a future dimly perceived as the absence of these familiar surroundings. The future as absence ("never see again") is a frightening prospect. Because she is trying to "weigh each side of the question," Eveline's thoughts continually move from the past to the future. But for her the future is at worst negative (never) and at best conditional: "she *would* be married . . . People *would* treat her with respect then. She *would* not be treated as her mother had been . . ." (italics added). And the future inevitably leads her back to the past. She can see it only dimly, negatively, conditionally. It has no reality for her, no more than Buenos Ayres as a place has more reality than the Melbourne of her father's "casual" expression. When she begins to think of herself as wife, she fatally concludes by thinking of her mother. We should note in this respect that her future, if she should remain home, is a subject that eludes her even more completely than her future in Buenos Ayres, while she is weighing "each side of the question." We know that she has "palpitations" and we know that "latterly" her father has begun to threaten her with physical violence. And we can infer that her mother had been physically abused in the past. Eveline almost admits this thought to consciousness when she reflects that she would not be "treated as her mother had been" and then moves in the next sentence to thoughts of her father's violence. There is much in both the past and the future that is unexpressed in Eveline's revery.

In developing these considerations I have been led from thoughts of tense into questions of voice and perspective. As Genette points out, this kind of thing is inevitable in analysis, since we are arbitrarily dividing for discussion a thing which is indivisible, because we cannot hope to say everything about a text at once. But this analysis will take us even further into the concerns of the story if we let it. Time, as we are seeing, is not simply a feature of the structure of this narrative, it is a major element of Eveline's situation, "Her time was running out" the narrator tells us, and she knows it. She is facing a moment of terrible choice between a future she cannot conceive and one that she will not admit. Human beings are distinguished from other animals by their ability to project, to reach, through language and vision, into the future. But Eveline is so trapped in the past—in her promise to her dead mother, in the ritual of her church—that she not only fears the future but finally retreats from present awareness altogether: "Moving her lips in silent fervent prayer" she has finally lost the gift of speech and all ability to perceive and communicate. She becomes "passive, like a helpless animal."

Turning from the temporal order of a text to its duration, Genette distinguishes four basic speeds of narration:

1. The ellipsis—infinitely rapid
2. The summary—relatively rapid
3. The scene—relatively slow
4. The descriptive pause—zero degree of progress

The basic novelistic rhythm, he indicates, is an alteration between undramatic summaries which provide connective delays and dramatic scenes in which the decisive action takes place. In "Eveline" we have all four varieties of duration: an ellipsis between the two sections of the narrative; a summary of Eveline's and Frank's past lives; the dramatic scene at the quay; and even some description, though so little as to make virtually no pause in the story. But we need to notice some peculiar aspects of Joyce's employment of these techniques. First of all, he manages things so that all description and summarizing are presented as aspects of Eveline's thought, and hence function as drama or scene. The narrative segments set in base time do in fact constitute a scene of extended duration, in which a relatively short time in the story occupies a long part of the text. And the first scene, with all its temporal oscillation, gives us a sense of base time passing very slowly. Then the second scene, after the ellipsis, by stretching time out even more, emphasizes the passing of seconds, as the inexorable process of the ship's departure (time and tide wait for no man) brings the future and present to a point of congruity, whereupon Eveline, no longer able to weigh past against future, is driven out of human time altogether into the frozen present of animal existence.

Genette's treatment of fictional mood also provides a useful way into Joyce's story. Genette divides mood into two aspects: distance and perspective. Narrative distance is a function of the amount and precision of detail provided in any discourse. The more detail given, the closer we come to scenic description. Some details may be present gratuitously, as it were, to give "the effect of the real," of something named only because it is "really there." In "Eveline" such items as the "odour of dusty cretonne," or the "coloured print of the promises made to the Blessed Margaret Mary

Alacoque" seem to function in this "gratuitous" way, as mere bits of "life," but in the hands of Joyce in particular, these informational bits are likely to carry meanings in more than one code. In this respect Genette's approach needs to be supplemented by that of Roland Barthes, as I shall suggest more extensively below.

In his discussion of distance and perspective Genette considers the critical debate on "showing" versus "telling" in fiction and the modernist emphasis on "showing," which he defines as a preference for scene over summary, with an attendant effacement of the narrator. Joyce, it is clear, is a perfect example of this tendency, at least in "Eveline," where scene reaches out to include all summary and where we have to exercise considerable ingenuity to detect a narrative persona manipulating Eveline's voice and perspective. Genette also insists on the analyst's observing a distinction between perspective and voice in critical study. The eyes we see through and the voice we hear are not necessarily the same in narrative, though in "Eveline" there seems to be little significant difference.

The various perspectives adoptable in fiction are matters of focus. Certain aspects of the events in any story may be clarified by the narrative focus, while others may be hidden or obscured, temporarily or permanently. Focus determines how far into the life of a character we may be allowed to penetrate, and how many characters will be open to interior scrutiny. "The type of focus is not fixed for a whole work, necessarily," Genette observes, "but for a determined segment of narrative which may be very brief." He develops a terminology for a number of varieties of perspective—internal, external, fixed, variable, multiple, and unfocused—but like their counterparts in American discussions of fictional point-of-view these terms may not have sufficient analytical value to justify their taxonomic complexity. The shifts in narrative focus that really count may function at a level where linguistic sensitivity and intuition count for more than apparatus. Even here, however, Genette gives us some interesting leads. He points to the tendency of fictions to employ strategies he calls "paralipse" and "paralepse": that is, the withholding from the reader of information which he "ought"—according to the prevailing focus—to receive; and the presenting to the reader of information which the prevailing level of focalization "ought" to render inaccessible. Joyce, it seems to me, is a highly paraleptic writer, in "Eveline" and in other works as well. In this story he chooses what Genette calls a fixed internal focus, all thoughts being filtered through the mind of Eveline herself, and presented in language much like her own in both syntax and diction (though this is technically a matter of voice rather than perspective—or rather *her* language is a matter of perspective, *his*, the narrator's, is a matter of voice). In choosing Eveline as a focus, Joyce—as in many other stories—has selected a central intelligence who is not very intelligent. Here is where he differs most from both Proust and Henry James, who preferred an intelligence much like their own at the center of their work. (There are some exceptions to this, as in *What Maisie Knew*, but it can be argued that even Maisie is potentially a Jamesian intelligence, and she is certainly enveloped in a rich, Jamesian voice.) But Joyce favored, in the *Dubliners* stories, an internal perspective fixed in a mind which is not only deprived of certain knowledge about the events of the story but which is absolutely limited in education and intelligence. These limited minds trying to cope with painful situations, more than anything else, give the stories their ironic and naturalistic flavor. And this method posed for Joyce an esthetic problem that he delighted in solving—the problem of paralepse, of conveying to the reader more information than the code required by his perspective "ought" to convey.

Rhetorically speaking, whenever we encounter paralipse or paralepse we are in the presence of irony. In the case of "Eveline" we have already noted how Eveline suppresses certain thoughts about her future in Dublin, and the way in which she links associatively the ideas of her father's brutality and her mother's insanity and death without acknowledging the logical connection between them. In these instances Joyce is leading us to make inferences that result in our helping to "construct" the story we are reading. We, by an act of inference, piece together some of Eveline's situation, and at the same time are enabled to make the further inference that she is suppressing precisely the matter that we have inferred. This takes Joyce in the direction of what Roland Barthes calls the *scriptible* text, a modernist fiction which forces the reader to participate in the creation of its events and meanings. But I would argue that he stops well short of giving us liberty to construct what meanings we please. Our inferences are guided, unobtrusively but firmly, in ways that we have been investigating and will continue to investigate.

This discussion is taking us beyond the range of Genette's system of fictional analysis, but for a very good reason. His treatment of fictional voice, which is illuminating with respect to Proust, is simply not very helpful when we turn to Joyce, though Joyce is one of the most vocalic of writers. This is because Genette considers under voice only matters involving the relationship between distinguishable narrators and the tales they relate. Joyce's kind of ventriloqual effect, in which he narrates in the voice of a character while seeing the character as a third person, limiting himself to saying what the character might perceive but using this saying to convey the views of an invisible narrator—this possibility is just not sufficiently regarded by Genette, perhaps because it involves an interacting between perspective and voice, which he has been at such pains to separate. It is actually Roland Barthes who comes closest to offering us what we need to complete the analysis of a text like "Eveline."

In *S/Z*, his book-length analysis of Balzac's story "Sarrasine," Barthes works his way through the text, a few phrases or sentences at a time, interpreting these "lexias," as he calls them, according to the ways they generate meanings in five signifying systems or codes. His five codes are as follows:

1. The proairetic code or code of actions, which he calls "the main armature of the readerly text"—by which he means, among other things, all texts which are in fact narrative. Where most traditional critics, such as Aristotle and Todorov, would look only for major actions or plots, Barthes (in theory) sees all actions as codable, from the most trivial opening of a door to a romantic adventure. In practice, he applies some principles of selectivity. We recognize actions because we are able to name them. In most fiction (Barthes' readerly texts) we expect actions begun to be completed, thus the principle action becomes the main armature of such a text. (Todorovian notation seeks to isolate this main armature for study.)

2. The hermeneutic code or code of puzzles plays on the reader's desire for "truth," for the answers to questions raised by the text. In examining "Sarrasine," Barthes names ten phases of hermeneutic coding, from the initial posing of a question or thematization of a subject that will become enigmatic to the ultimate disclosure and decipherment of what has been withheld. Like the code of action, the code of enigmas is a principal structuring agent of traditional narrative. Between the posing of a riddle and its solution in narrative, Barthes locates eight different ways of keeping the riddle alive without revealing its solution, including equivocations,

snares, partial answers, etc. In certain kinds of fiction, such as detective stories, the hermeneutic code dominates the entire discourse. Together with the code of actions it is responsible for narrative suspense, for the reader's desire to complete, to finish the text.

3. The cultural codes. There are many of these. They constitute the text's references to things already "known" and codified by a culture. Barthes sees traditional realism as defined by its reference to what is already known. Flaubert's "Dictionary of Accepted Ideas" is a realist's Bible. The axioms and proverbs of a culture or a subculture constitute already coded bits upon which novelists may rely. Balzac's work is heavily coded in this way.

4. The connotative codes. Under this rubric we find not one code but many. In reading, the reader "thematizes" the text. He notes that certain connotations of words and phrases in the text may be grouped with similar connotations of other words and phrases. As we recognize a "common nucleus" of connotations we locate a theme in the text. As clusters of connotation cling to a particular proper name we recognize a character with certain attributes. (It is worth noting that Barthes considers denotation as simply the "last" and strongest of connotations.)

5. The symbolic field. This is the aspect of fictional coding which is most specifically "structuralist" in Barthes' presentation. It is based on the notion that meaning comes from some initial binary opposition or differentiation, whether at the level of sounds becoming phonemes in the production of speech; or at the level of psycho-sexual opposition, through which a child learns that mother and father are different from one another and that this difference also makes the child the same as one of them and different from the other; or at the level of primitive cultural separation of the world into opposing forces or values which may be coded mythologically. In a verbal text this kind of symbolic opposition may be encoded in rhetorical figures such as antithesis, which is a privileged figure in Barthes' symbolic system.

Since the space and time for a Barthesian amble through the lexias of "Eveline" are not available, I shall invert his procedure and simply locate some elements of each code as found in Joyce's text.

1. Code of Actions (proairetic). In "Eveline" these range from the relatively trivial "She sat," completed four pages later by "She stood up," to the more consequential action of her leaving Dublin for good, which of course never occurs. This is a story of paralysis, which is a major connotative code in all the *Dubliners* stories. Significantly, we never see Eveline move a single step. Even in the last climactic scene her actions are described as "She stood . . . She gripped . . . She set her face." This increasing rigidity thematizes the connotative code of paralysis.

2. Code of Enigmas (hermeneutic). Joyce does not rely heavily on this code. Above all, he does not feel a need to complete it. We begin with some questions about who Eveline is, why she is tired, and the like, but there is no mystery about this. Frank is an enigma, of course. The discourse tells us something about him, but only gives us Eveline's thoughts about Frank's version of his life. There is also some mystery attached to Eveline's mother, the cause of her death, and the mysterious phrase she uttered which no one can decipher. But the discourse does not complete or "solve" these mysteries. Like the priest who went to Melbourne, they suggest a world not completely fathomable, beyond the comfortable realism of Balzacian discourse. The final enigma, the reason for Eveline's refusal, forces us back into the text, and out to the other *Dubliners* stories to find solutions that will never have the assurance of discursive "truth."

3. Cultural Codes. Cultural coding in this tale is not so much the property of any narrative voice, or of the discourse itself, as it is something in the minds of the characters. Eveline's father sees Frank under a code of cynical parental wisdom: "I know these sailor chaps." Eveline sees him as codified by romantic fiction: "Frank was very kind, manly, openhearted." The discourse ratifies neither view. It avoids the cultural codes of Dublin, which so dominate the characters' lives. Of these, the most powerful is the code of Irish Catholicism, which would classify Eveline's action as a sin.

4. Connotative Codes. The dominant code is the code of paralysis, which is a major element in Eveline's character as well as in the world around her. It is connoted by Eveline's motionlessness throughout the story. It is even conveyed by the dreary,

monotonous sentence structure—subject, verb, predicate, over and over again. And it is signified by such details as the promises made to the Blessed Margaret Mary Alacoque, who was paralyzed until she vowed to dedicate herself to a religious life. The way in which this saintly lady's life comments on Eveline's own introduces another level of connotation, the ironic. Through its ironic combination of signs, the discourse paraleptically leads us to a view of Eveline's situation beyond her own perception of it. She sees herself as weighing evidence and deciding. But the discourse ironically indicates that she has no choice. She is already inscribed as a Dubliner in Joyce's code, and a Dubliner never decides, never escapes. As Diderot's *Jacques le fataliste* would have it, *il est écrit en haut*, it is written above—in Joyce's text.

5. The Symbolic Code. For Joyce in *Dubliners* the primal opposition is not male vs. female but sexed vs. unsexed, usually presented as celibate vs. profligate, an opposition that is almost unmediated by any linking term. Only the dead are fruitful or potent in Joyce's wasteland. In "Eveline," the sailor Frank is set in opposition to the father as rival for Eveline, who is filling her mother's role in the household. In this symbolic opposition Frank is associated with water, freedom, the unknown, the future, and potency. The father's house is dusty, Eveline is a slave in it, but it is known, rooted in the past, and fruitless. As her father's slave/wife, Eveline will be sterile, impotent, celibate, a kind of nun, a Dubliner. This symbolic opposition emerges most powerfully from the clash of connotations in a single sentence in the final scene, when Eveline sees "the black mass of the boat lying in beside the quay." This "black mass" is an innocent descriptive phrase which also connotes the sacrilegious power of the act Eveline is contemplating here. To board that boat, leave the land and enter upon the sea, would be to leave what is known, safe, already coded. It would be above all to flout the teachings of the church, to sin. The virgin, the nun, a celibate safely within the cultural codification of ritual is opposed to the defiled woman upon whose belly the black mass is blasphemously consummated. But look more closely. In that other harmless descriptive phrase, "lying in," another terror is connoted. To "lie in" is to be delivered of child, to be fruitful, to be uncelibate, not to play the mother's role for the father, but

to displace her and the father both, sending them into the past. It is to accept life—and the danger of death. These connotations activate the symbolic level of the text by their juxtaposition of its antitheses. And in that extraordinary figure, "All the seas of the world tumbled about her heart," the discourse connotes both the heart surrounded by amniotic fluid ready to burst with life, and also the fear of drowning in life itself, lured beyond her depth by a person she can no longer allow herself to recognize. Our final vision of Eveline is of a creature in a state of symbolic deprivation. If the symbolic code is rooted in the fundamental processes of cognition and articulation, what is signified in that code at the end of "Eveline" is a creature who has lost those fundamental processes, not only at the level of speech and language but even the more fundamental semiotic functions of gesture and facial signals: "She set her white face to him, passive, like a helpless animal. Her eyes gave him no sign of love or farewell or recognition." However we interpret the story, we are surely intended to regard with pity and fear the situation of this young woman absolutely incommunicado, capable of giving "no sign."

Maturing Views of *A Portrait of the Artist as a Young Man*

In the introduction to the *Dubliners* section, I alluded to wide-ranging analytical approaches to the collection, often by individuals with little other
involvement in Joyce studies. I made a distinction between the works of
critics who centered their attention on a specific story and its interpretive
heritage and the productions of those who felt able to write without the
need for such awareness. My point was simple but central: problems inevitably arise when commentators (and by extension readers for scholarly
presses) believe that one can understand the short stories without coming
to grips with the scholarly examinations that have grown up around them.
When this occurs, those unaware of the rich interpretive heritage that has
already unpacked many of the cruxes run the risk of offering reductive
analyses that simply miss many crucial elements within the narratives
or, worse, make assertions that scholarly studies have long shown to be
without merit or foundation.[1] A study of the range of critical responses to
A Portrait of the Artist as a Young Man reveals the persistence of different though equally challenging assumptions endangering the clarity of a
number of approaches.

With no prompting necessary beyond the title, many early readers felt
invited to pursue autobiographical connections between the author and
his characters, and by the mid-1920s, as interest in the work's author grew,
the public was being made increasingly aware of the parallels between fact
and fiction by studies correlating events in Joyce's life with those in the
novel. Herbert Gorman's 1926 biography, written with Joyce's help, called
attention to the similarities between incidents in the lives of James Joyce
and of Stephen Dedalus.[2] A decade later Oliver St. John Gogarty added a

series of anecdotes, often grounded on dubious authority and written with malicious intent, to the information published by Gorman.[3]

Some critics quickly took up these accounts to bolster their explorations of interpretive connections between events in Joyce's life and those represented in his fiction. In one of the first academic examinations of *A Portrait of the Artist as a Young Man*, J. W. Campbell began his address to the Sydney University Literary Society by stating confidently that the book "is indubitably a semi-autobiographical work."[4] A 1939 essay by Joseph Prescott, after a lengthy summary of the narrative, presents a sweeping interpretation of the novel that blithely conflates Joyce and Stephen. In the following year David Daiches published an essay, seasoned with the patronizing tones of an English critic examining the efforts of the provincial Irish, that was equally confident about linking Joyce and Stephen.[5]

This inclination toward amalgamation of fact and fiction continued through the 1950s, with a number of prominent critics offering interpretations based upon perceived echoes of Joyce's life in his fiction.[6] Before going any further, let me be clear that I am not dismissing such efforts out of hand. The social and cultural contexts of the middle-class and lower-middle-class worlds inhabited by Joyce and his family in the late nineteenth and early twentieth centuries did much to inform that author's fiction, and no complete understanding of Stephen's world could come without a clear sense of Joyce's. A number of early critics did a commendable job illuminating the convergent and divergent features of these worlds. However, contemporary readers wishing to move with confidence to the examination of very specific textual issues need assurance that the fundamental questions of origin have been given no more or less than the attention they deserve. For this, readers must turn to critics who exercise careful attention to the distinction between fact and fiction.

Early in his biography Richard Ellmann, eschewing any qualification, makes a too easily misinterpreted statement regarding Joyce's integration of his life into his art: "His relations appear in his books under thin disguises. In general, those who bear the Joyce name appear to better advantage than those who bear the name of Murray, his mother's family. In this treatment Joyce follows the prejudices of his father."[7] At first glance, Ellmann's remark may seem simply a straightforward scholarly presentation of carefully researched connections between life and art. In fact, it implicitly endorses a tenuous connection between fact and fiction that, no matter how carefully documented the research might be, would not obtain in analogous situations. (For example, what would historians say to someone who suggested reading selections from *War and Peace* for insights into the Battle of Borodino?) In such a situation, when rigorous distinctions are not maintained, confusion inevitably results, as when Ellmann two pages later describes incidents in the life of William O'Connell, granduncle of James Joyce, and references pages from *A Portrait of the Artist as a Young Man* as support for these observations.[8]

Ellmann is by no means the only reader who used Joyce's fiction to find confirmation of supposed events in the author's life. Indeed, a number of memoirs and other recollections, intentionally or not, provided additional fuel for this method of reading.[9] However, the popularity of Ellmann's biography makes his application of such an approach particularly dangerous.

The impulse to use events in Joyce's life to interpret the narrative of his first published novel has produced a long line of scholarship that tilts too easily toward misleading interpretations. As recently as 1991, in his introduction to the Everyman's Library edition of *A Portrait of the Artist as a Young Man*, Richard Brown acknowledged the continuing difficulty readers have in avoiding reductive biographical interpretations: "the title represents the conundrum of a self-fulfilling prophecy: that the novel is indeed an autobiographical portrait of the novelist who produced it and indeed the 'young man' (Stephen) may have become the 'artist' (Joyce) by the very act of painting his own 'portrait.'"[10] I have no doubt that Brown, a very fine Joyce critic, sees a sharper distinction between Joyce and Stephen that this passage implies, but the association he makes here can create a damaging perception for less astute readers.

At the same time, while Joyce's biography became a heuristic for a number of early critics, others adopted far different scholarly approaches. In 1948 two important essays signaled areas that would remain central to understanding Joyce's first published novel for decades to come. Mark Schorer's examination of style in five works from *Moll Flanders* to *A Portrait of the Artist as a Young Man* underscored and contextualized the innovative techniques, now recognized as a paradigm for modernism, that Joyce highlighted in his composition.[11] Even more significant, Hugh Kenner's masterly explication refuted those readers who approached *A Portrait of the Artist as a Young Man* with an overzealous biographical bent for understanding the novel. In a stunning exploration of the ironic features of Stephen Dedalus, he elaborated on the distance between character and author.[12]

Kenner's insightful reading, though widely anthologized, needs to be introduced to each new generation of Joyceans, for over the years a surprising number of critics have continued to resist its implications, despite the cogency and sophistication of his argument. More than a decade after it appeared, for example, a reader like Wayne Booth, with a prose style as evasive as the one he critiques, can still feel dissatisfied with approaches that identify the narrative and narrator as standing at an ironic remove from the central character.[13] Instead, in the voice of a carping pedant Booth prefers to see *A Portrait of the Artist as a Young Man* as a creative failure, or at least as a work less successful than one might have hoped:

> Even if we were now to do our homework like dutiful students, even if we were to study all of Joyce's work, even if we were to spend the lifetime that Joyce playfully said his novels demand, presumably we should never come to as rich, as refined, and as varied a conception of the quality of Stephen's last days in Ireland as Joyce had in mind. For some of us the air of detachment and objectivity may still be worth the price, but we must never pretend that a price was not paid.[14]

Robert Scholes, while never completely embracing Kenner's views, offers a sure sense of Joyce's discourse that answers the fretting of Booth with a sound view of the complexity of Stephen's character as it is elaborated within the narrative.[15] Each of these contrasting readings distinguishes itself with nimble logic, but taken together they underscore for me the need to see the narrative in the broadest context imaginable.

Although such significant intratextual questions remained a central aspect of the critical debate surrounding the novel, its cultural ambience, outside the strict biographical readings advocated by Ellmann and others, was from an early stage also an important concern. Prefiguring a trend that would encompass detailed studies of all of the major social institutions that inform the context of *A Portrait of the Artist as a Young Man*, Chester Anderson in 1952 reminded readers of the centrality of Catholic iconography in the narrative.[16] Anderson's essay remains significant for its specific interpretive achievements, but it also merits attention for its more far-reaching accomplishment: foregrounding the necessity of comprehending connections between the creative forces and the spiritual impulses in Joyce's work.

Over the next few years this issue received extended attention from scholars interested in discerning the imaginative elements delineating the creative framework of *A Portrait of the Artist as a Young Man*. In 1957 Maurice Beebe deftly summarized observations on the impact of the scholastic approach to knowledge underlying the Jesuit instruction that Joyce received and speculated on its subsequent influence on the composition of his first published novel.[17] J. Mitchell Morse, taking extratextuality much further than any of the others, and certainly with greater truculence and less tolerance than Beebe evinced, extended the discussion beyond the philosophy of St. Thomas Aquinas to include the views of St. Augustine.[18] After a long introduction to the thinking of St. Augustine, including a vigorous effort to underscore its classical and secular foundations, Morse linked these views to Stephen's approach to creativity.

While this background is important, it remains in a secondary position of critical relevance. Extratextual scholarship that ranges as far afield as Anderson's, Beebe's, and Morse's can significantly enhance already soundly developed readings, but fundamental understanding of *A Portrait of the Artist as a Young Man* requires more direct engagement with the discourse. Even the most dazzling hermeneutic digressions of contemporary readers must rest on the solid critical insights relating directly to narrative development if they are to achieve any significance. The trio of essays collected in this section exemplify the importance of comprehending seemingly elemental textual features in all of their complexity. To that end our three critics use principles of theology, aesthetics, and philosophy to outline conceptions central to Joyce's discourse and to lay down interpretive paradigms that can guide even the most discursive analyses back to the text.

Early discussions of Joyce's aesthetics brought out important issues relating to intellectual perspective. However, those examinations also moved the emphasis from the work to ancillary material that Joyce may or may not have employed in the same fashion as the critics who invoked it. This was clearly not the case with James Thrane's "Joyce's Sermon on Hell: Its Sources and Backgrounds," which offered an analysis of Father Arnall's hellfire sermon of chapter 3. It presented an early rebuttal of any inclination to understand the account of the flamboyant exhortations of Father Arnall as nothing more than a burlesque of Catholic liturgy. By showing how Farther Arnall's preaching came directly out of a long traditional of homilies prescribed for such retreats, Thrane profoundly reoriented a reader's sense of Joyce's spiritual tradition and of his motives for incorporating the retreat experience into the narrative.[19]

Furthermore, Thrane's research paved the way for later critics whose work on cultural context became so important to a fuller understanding of the novel.[20] In particular, it underscored the universality of the series of sermons heard by Stephen and his classmates that might otherwise seem a highly imaginative fictional creation to many readers, particularly those with little awareness of the makeup of Catholic liturgy before the great reforms of the Second Vatican Council. Instead of identifying a surrealistic quality, like that which a contemporary reader might be inclined to overlay on Father Arnall's talks, Thrane's exposition demarcated the paradigmatic features of the sermon and clarified the familiarity that Father Arnall's audiences in the chapel would have had with this standard approach.

Thrane's research profoundly affects the assumptions one makes about the expectations that the Belvedere students would bring to such an experience and the consequences of their hearing this sort of preaching. Taken a step further, it reminds readers of the tension that always exists within Joyce's narratives. The irony so brilliantly highlighted by Hugh Kenner coexists quite effectively with a straightforward narration of events. This juxtaposition, often without stylistic distinction, heightens both the challenge and the pleasure of reading the novel.

Along these lines, S. L. Goldberg's essay "Joyce and the Artist's Fingernails" presented a cogent overview of the aesthetics of the novel, one ranging back and forth through Joyce's fiction from *Stephen Hero* to *Finnegans Wake*, to clarify many of the ontological and epistemological issues raised by Stephen that had seemed so daunting to early readers. In a painstaking fashion Goldberg parsed the logic of Stephen's disquisition and integrated what for many had been a digressive and even idiosyncratic discourse into the mainstream of the narrative.

Admittedly, Goldberg's patronizing attitude toward any mind but his own and his intolerance of any ideas to which he did not subscribe will test the patience of many contemporary critics, but his careful application of the aesthetic principles that so many readers of chapter 5 tend to ignore continues to present profoundly useful insights into Joyce's creative process and more than repays a willingness to endure Goldberg's imperious tone. When he directed his attention to the structure of the aesthetic theory, Goldberg presented a clear and lucid overview, and he made useful connections between the theory of chapter 5 and contrasting examples of its application in *Stephen Hero* and *Ulysses*. As a result, one comes to a more precise understanding of what Stephen says to Lynch as well as to a finer sense of the form of the latter work. From this vantage, readers can discern for themselves the relation of Stephen's creative theories to Joyce's.

Finally, Thomas F. Van Laan's essay on the way that the *Spiritual Exercises* of St. Ignatius frame the narrative consciousness of the novel, "The Meditative Structure of Joyce's *Portrait*," presents a useful counterpoint to Goldberg's outline of Joyce's and Stephen's creative, imaginative, and spiritual dispositions. While a great number of early critics turned to autobiography to understand the complexities of Joyce's narrative, many of these scholars, and Ellmann stands as a prime example, had so little comprehension of and in some cases so little sympathy for the impact of Catholicism, particularly as represented to Joyce through his Jesuit education, that they failed to account for the most meaningful if the most subtle features that inform the author's worldview and by extension his writing.

Without enmeshing itself in issues of Stephen's or, more dangerously, Joyce's system of beliefs, Van Laan's study laid out the metaphysical context in which both author and fictional hero came to intellectual maturity. Van Laan summarized an ontological background essential to understanding the point of view of the discourse that continues to stand at quite a distance from contemporary awareness, and his examination made important connections between the spiritual and the creative development of Stephen's consciousness. In the process, Van Laan went beyond Goldberg's concentration on aesthetic values to provide a brilliant analysis of the structure of Stephen's imaginative development.

The three authors represented here by no means establish definitive views or prescriptive readings of Joyce's novel. Indeed, a great many accounts of aspects of the narrative, both complementary and diverse, have come to the foreground in the years immediately following the appearance of these works.[21] Paradoxically, the range and specificity of these subsequent studies underscore the liberating effect of the essays reprinted here. The investigations that followed them had their foundational ideas of the novel established in the foreground of the general consciousness, and so could develop more specific topics with greater confidence.

One finds evidence of this effect in the outpouring over the past four decades of book-length studies on the novel. Case studies and essay collections had been available from the mid-1950s through the 1960s.[22] After the groundbreaking work profiled here, a range of more sophisticated critical tools began to appear in the form of draft material, word counts, and reference guides.[23] Near the end of the decade, *James Joyce Quarterly* devoted a special issue to the novel.[24] More important, however, Chester Anderson's aforementioned Viking Critical Edition appeared, not only assuring a widespread use of *A Portrait of the Artist as a Young Man* in high school and college courses but also introducing a sophisticated representation of accessible readings of that work to a broad general audience.[25]

Beginning in the 1970s a range of book-length critical studies of Joyce's novel appeared. Though only a few matched the first in this series, Edmund Epstein's *The Ordeal of Stephen Dedalus*, all evinced an intellectual freedom derived directly from the pioneering authors mentioned here.[26] Work continues to be published on *A Portrait of the Artist as a Young Man*, but, as the abbreviated overview offered in this section indicates, the most essential feature of ongoing progress remains a thorough knowledge of the achievements of our predecessors.

Notes

1. For a good critique of the problems that arise from an insufficient attention to the critical tradition, see John Whittier-Ferguson's review of Daniel R. Schwarz's edition of *The Dead* in *James Joyce Quarterly* 33 (Summer 1996): 641–646.

2. Herbert S. Gorman, *James Joyce: His First Forty Years* (London: Geoffrey Bles, 1926).

3. Oliver St. John Gogarty, *As I Was Going down Sackville Street* (London: Rich and Cowan, 1937).

4. J. W. Campbell, *"A Portrait of the Artist as a Young Man": An Appreciation* (Sydney: Sydney University Literary Society, 1933), 3.

5. Joseph Prescott, "James Joyce: A Study in Words," *PMLA* 54 (March 1939): 304–315; David Daiches, "James Joyce: The Artist in Exile," *College English* 2 (December 1940): 197–206.

6. For some early instances of autobiographical approaches to the novel, see Daiches, "James Joyce: The Artist as Exile"; Robert G. Kelly, "James Joyce: A Partial Explanation," *PMLA* 64 (March 1949): 26–39; Marvin Magalaner, "James Mangan and Joyce's Dedalus

Family," *Philological Quarterly* 31 (October 1952): 363–371; Dorothy Van Ghent, "On *A Portrait of the Artist as a Young Man*," in *The English Novel: Form and Function* (New York: Rinehart, 1953), 263–276; John V. Kelleher, "The Perceptions of James Joyce," *Atlantic Monthly* 201 (March 1958): 89–90; Roy Pascal, "The Autobiographical Novel and the Autobiography," *Essays in Criticism* 9 (April 1959): 134–150.

7. Richard Ellmann, *James Joyce*, rev. ed. (Oxford: Oxford University Press, 1982), 11.

8. Ibid., 13, 746n9.

9. J. F. Byrne, *Silent Years: An Autobiography with Memoirs of James Joyce and Our Ireland* (New York: Farrar, Straus and Young, 1953); Stanislaus Joyce, *My Brother's Keeper* (New York: Viking, 1958); Mary Colum and Padraic Colum, *Our Friend James Joyce* (Garden City, N.Y.: Doubleday, 1958); Constantine Curran, *James Joyce Remembered* (Oxford: Oxford University Press, 1968).

10. James Joyce, *A Portrait of the Artist as a Young Man*, ed. Richard Brown (New York: Alfred A. Knopf, 1991), v. For a good discussion of the distinctions between Joyce's life and Stephen's, see R. B. Kershner's introduction to his edition of *A Portrait of the Artist as a Young Man* (Boston: Bedford, 1993), 6–12.

11. Mark Schorer, "Technique as Discovery," *Hudson Review* 1 (1948): 67–87.

12. Hugh Kenner, "The *Portrait* in Perspective," in *James Joyce: Two Decades of Criticism*, ed. Seon Givens (1948; New York: Vanguard, 1963), 132–174. See also William T. Noon, *Joyce and Aquinas* (New Haven, Conn.: Yale University Press, 1957), 34–35, 66–67.

13. Wayne Booth, "The Problem of Distance in *A Portrait*," in *The Rhetoric of Fiction* (Chicago: University of Chicago Press, 1961), 323–336.

14. Ibid., 336.

15. Robert Scholes, "Stephen Dedalus: Poet or Esthete?" *PMLA* 79 (1964): 484–489. Chester Anderson reprints Booth's and Scholes's essays back to back in his edition of *A Portrait of the Artist as a Young Man* (New York: Viking, 1968), 455–480.

16. Chester G. Anderson, "The Sacrificial Butter," *Accent* 12 (1952): 3–13.

17. Maurice Beebe, "Joyce and Aquinas: The Theory of Aesthetics," *Philological Quarterly* 36 (January 1957): 20–35. As noted earlier, Fr. William Noon published a book-length study of Joyce and Aquinas in the same year, though his scope was far broader than that of the Beebe article.

18. J. Mitchell Morse, "Augustine's Theodicy and Joyce's Aesthetics," *ELH* 24 (March 1957): 30–43.

19. It is also useful to recall an essay that appeared nearly simultaneously with Thrane's, Elizabeth F. Boyd's "Joyce's Hell Fire Sermons," *Modern Language Notes* 75 (1960): 561–571, and also James Doherty's "Joyce and *Hell Opened to Christians*: The Edition He Used for His Hell Sermons," *Modern Philology* 61 (1963): 110–119.

20. One finds a good cross-section of such approaches in R. B. Kershner Jr.'s edition *A Portrait of the Artist as a Young Man: Complete, Authoritative Text with Biographical, Historical, and Cultural Contexts, Critical History, and Essays from Contemporary Critical Perspectives*, 2nd ed. (Boston: Bedford, 2006).

21. See, for example, Robert Scholes, "Joyce and Epiphany: The Key to the Labyrinth," *Sewanee Review* 72 (Winter 1964): 65–77; Kenneth Burke, "Fact, Inference, and Proof in

the Analysis of Literary Symbolism," in Burke, *Terms for Order*, ed. Stanley Edgar Hyman (Bloomington: Indiana University Press, 1964), 145–172; Bernard Benstock, "A Covey of Clerics in Joyce and O'Casey," *James Joyce Quarterly* 2 (Fall 1964): 18–32; Thomas E. Connolly, "Kinesis and Stasis: Structural Rhythm in Joyce's *Portrait of the Artist*," *Dublin University Review* 3 (1966): 21–30; James Naremore, "Style as Meaning in *A Portrait of the Artist*," *James Joyce Quarterly* 4 (Summer 1967): 331–342; Hans Walter Gabler, "The Seven Lost Years of *A Portrait of the Artist as a Young Man*," in *Approaches to Joyce's "Portrait": Ten Essays*, ed. Thomas F. Staley and Bernard Benstock (Pittsburgh: University of Pittsburgh Press, 1976), 25–60, and "The Christmas Dinner Scene, Parnell's Death, and the Genesis of *A Portrait of the Artist as a Young Man*," *James Joyce Quarterly* 13 (1975): 27–38.

22. See, for example, Joseph Feehan, ed., *Dedalus on Crete: Essays on the Implications of Joyce's "Portrait"* (Los Angeles: St. Thomas More Guild, Immaculate Heart College, 1957); Thomas E. Connolly, ed., *Joyce's "Portrait": Criticisms and Critiques* (New York: Appleton-Century-Crofts, 1962); William E. Morris and Clifford A. Nault Jr., eds., *Portraits of an Artist: A Casebook on James Joyce's "A Portrait of the Artist as a Young Man"* (New York: Odyssey, 1962); Robert S. Ryf, *A New Approach to Joyce: The Portrait of the Artist as a Guidebook* (Berkeley and Los Angeles: University of California Press, 1962).

23. Robert Scholes and Richard M. Kain, eds., *The Workshop of Daedalus: James Joyce and the Raw Materials for "A Portrait of the Artist as a Young Man"* (Evanston, Ill.: Northwestern University Press, 1965); Leslie Hancock, *Word Index to James Joyce's "Portrait of the Artist"* (Carbondale: Southern Illinois University Press, 1967); Don Gifford and Robert J. Seidman, *Joyce Annotated: Notes for "Dubliners" and "A Portrait of the Artist as a Young Man*," 2nd ed. (Berkeley and Los Angeles: University of California Press, 1982).

24. *James Joyce Quarterly* 4, no. 4 (Summer 1967), ed. Richard M. Kain.

25. Chester G. Anderson, ed., *A Portrait of the Artist as a Young Man: Text, Criticism, and Notes* (New York: Viking, 1968).

26. Edmund L. Epstein, *The Ordeal of Stephen Dedalus: The Conflict of the Generations in James Joyce's "A Portrait of the Artist as a Young Man"* (Carbondale: Southern Illinois University Press, 1971); Homer Obed Brown, *James Joyce's Early Fiction: The Biography of a Form* (Cleveland: Press of Case Western Reserve University, 1972); Morris Beja, ed., *James Joyce: "Dubliners" and "A Portrait of the Artist as a Young Man": A Casebook* (London: Macmillan, 1973); John Bristow Smith, *Imagery and the Mind of Stephen Dedalus: A Computer-Assisted Study of Joyce's "A Portrait of the Artist as a Young Man"* (Lewisburg, Pa.: Bucknell University Press, 1980); Bruce Bidwell and Linda Heffer, *The Joycean Way: A Topographic Guide to "Dubliners" and "A Portrait of the Artist as a Young Man"* (Baltimore: Johns Hopkins University Press, 1982); Joseph A. Buttigieg, *A Portrait of the Artist in Different Perspective* (Athens: Ohio University Press, 1987); Weldon Thornton, *The Antimodernism of Joyce's "Portrait of the Artist as a Young Man"* (Syracuse, N.Y.: Syracuse University Press, 1994); Julienne H. Empric, *The Woman in the Portrait: The Transforming Female in James Joyce's "A Portrait of the Artist as a Young Man"* (San Bernardino, Calif.: Borgo, 1997); Roy Gottfried, *Joyce's Comic Portrait* (Gainesville: University Press of Florida, 2000); Gerald Doherty, *Pathologies of Desire: The Vicissitudes of the Self in James Joyce's "A Portrait of the Artist as a Young Man"* (New York: Peter Lang, 2008).

4

Joyce's Sermon on Hell

Its Source and Its Backgrounds

JAMES R. THRANE

Stephen's effort, in Joyce's *A Portrait of the Artist as a Young Man,* to impose a romantic order upon the adolescent tumult within him and the Dublin commonplaceness without is soon exhausted, like his pot of pink paint.[1] The phantom of Dumas's Mercedes is made flesh in Nighttown, and soon, deep in mortal sin, Stephen sits in the chapel of Belvedere College on a gloomy December day while the retreat master remorselessly expounds the spectacles and torments of hell. Overwhelmed by fear and remorse, Stephen confesses his sins and once more sets about ordering his life—no longer by outworn configurations of romance but by the admonitory consciousness of death, judgment, hell, and heaven. However, when he is urged to ask himself whether he has a vocation, his long-standing dissatisfactions with a church that has too much of the Dublin earth about it assume definite form, and he concludes that his freedom must remain inviolate, that "self-doomed, unafraid," he must learn wisdom "apart from others . . . wandering among the snares of the world."

The reactions of most readers to Father Arnall's depiction of eternal tortures have been less extreme than Stephen's. Farrell calls it "one of the most magnificently written passages in all of Joyce's work," comparable with Dante, and all have granted its dramatic effectiveness. But few readers can judge the sermon and the phase of development that it opens apart from their own assumptions and commitments: Father Arnall's words produce something like awe, amusement, or scorn (and little more) in Magalaner, Tindall, and Kenner. Catholic writers, with no hostile bias,

James Thrane, "Joyce's Sermon on Hell: Its Source and Its Background," *Modern Philology* 57 (1960): 172–198. Reprinted with permission from the Copyright Clearing Center. Copyright 1960.

nevertheless have objected to the sermon, one critic, Father Noon, holding that it is not a "comprehensive or characteristic Catholic account."[2] Kevin Sullivan's recent study of *Joyce among the Jesuits* contains a somewhat more thorough study than these of the sermon as well as of Stephen's short-lived effort to live remembering the four last things only. Pointing out the retreat's relationship to St. Ignatius' *Spiritual Exercises,* Sullivan also examines Stephen's new rule of life in relation to the manual of the Belvedere College sodality of which Joyce was prefect for two years. He concludes that this manual, compiled by Father James A. Cullen, S.J., was "the primary, if not the exclusive, source" of the plan by which Stephen lays out his life in devotional areas.[3] This is possible, although, as Sullivan says, many books of devotion treat such topics similarly. However, he goes on to suggest, on the basis of eight passages containing more or less similar phrases, that the manual was also the source of the sermon on hell. This is an error. The primary—probably the sole—printed source of this sermon was, as I will show, the English version of an Italian tract called in translation *Hell Opened to Christians, To Caution Them from Entering into It,* written by Giovanni Pietro Pinamonti, a seventeenth-century Jesuit. This title is not entirely new to Joyce students: J. F. Byrne recalls that *"Hell Open* [sic] *to Christians"* was displayed (not inappropriately) with the Deadwood Dicks in Josh Strong's bookshop at 26, Wellington Quay, where Mr. Bloom hopefully selects Molly's reading; and there is also assistant town clerk Henry's peevish complaint ("Hell open to christians they were having . . . about their damned Irish language") in the Wandering Rocks section of *Ulysses* (p. 243), which may indicate that the title had a sort of proverbial status in the gray inferno of Joyce's Dublin. At least, so Byrne uses it, fifty years later.[4]

Father Pinamonti (1632–1703), born in Pistoia of a noble family, entered the Society of Jesus in 1647. Illness forcing him to lay aside his studies, he gave up a teaching career in favor of rural mission work, in which for twenty-six years he was the companion of the famed preacher Paolo Segneri. His own preaching brought Pinamonti the friendship of Cosimo III, grand duke of Tuscany, and other notables, and such works as *La Religiosa in solitudine* (1695) and *Il Direttore* (posth. 1705) carried his fame beyond Italy. *L'Inferno aperto al cristiano perchè non v'entri: Considerazioni delle pene infernali proposte a meditarsi per evitarle,* first published anonymously at Bologna in 1688, went through many editions and was translated into Latin, French, German, Spanish, and Portuguese. It first appeared in English, anonymously translated, at London(?) in 1715, and passed through at least six more editions in the next hundred-odd years. The two editions of Victorian times that concern us appeared at Derby in 1844, probably as one of the Derby Catholic Book Society's numerous publications, and at Dublin in 1868, from the well-known firm of James Duffy, Wellington Quay. The text of the latter edition, which I have used and which corresponds so closely with the *Portrait* sermon, is probably the one used in all earlier printings; the extracts given by Dearmer from the 1753 edition (Dublin) differ only in punctuation and spelling.[5] At any rate, aside from a few omitted phrases and errors in biblical references, the translation is accurate and fairly literal, although not enough so as to make it at all probable that Joyce ever saw the Italian original.[6] Like the others, this 1868 edition, a badly printed forty-eight-page pamphlet, is illustrated with seven grotesque woodcuts showing fettered sinners tormented by the everlasting fire of Matthew, chapter 25, and the undying worm of Mark, chapter 9. These pictures have had much to do with the notoriety accorded the tract since the late nineteenth century; in one influential Victorian commentator they evoked a guilt "which called for the performance of a lustration."[7]

Hell Opened to Christians, following a traditional pattern in devotional literature, consists of seven daily "Considerations" or meditations, each analyzed, somewhat arbitrarily, under three points and concluding with a short prayer to a different sacred personage. (Joyce has not used the prayers or the sermon "On the Joys of Heaven"—evidently not by Pinamonti—that concludes the 1868 version.) The considerations themselves analyze the twofold punishment of mortal sin, the first three examining the *poena sensus* or pain of sense:[8] (1) The Prison of Hell (its straitness, darkness, and stench); (2) The Fire (its quality, quantity, and intenseness); and (3) The Company of the Damned (the damned themselves, the devils, and the accomplices in sin). Father Arnall's Friday-morning sermon comprises these points in this order, save that it treats as one topic the lost souls and the accomplices of the third consideration. His afternoon sermon is based, nearly as closely, on Pinamonti's remaining four considerations, which set forth the *poena damni* or pains consequent on the eternal loss of the beatific vision: (4) The Pain of Loss (it is infinite, most painful, and retributive); (5) The Sting of Conscience (memory of past pleasures, fruitless remorse, and good occasions neglected); (6) The Pain of Extension (despair from the infiniteness and intensity of spiritual pangs and from the damned souls' comparison of their lot with that of the saints); and (7) Eternity (pain is endless, unchangeable, and just).[9]

Or, in Maurice Daedalus' laconic précis, "Stink in the morning and pain of loss in the evening" (*Stephen Hero*, p. 57).

Resemblance, of course, does not necessarily mean indebtedness. This plan of organization is common in a tradition of devotional literature that has long flourished, especially during the seventeenth century. The sermon has, in fact, so many affinities with this tradition that they need separate consideration. This—along with the scarceness of Pinamonti's tract—is why I have printed below most of the sermon's passages together with their equivalents in *Hell Opened to Christians* (1868 ed.). The obvious correspondences not merely in image, example, and organization but even in sequence and phrasing should leave little doubt concerning Joyce's extensive use of the Italian's work; and, as I will show, only a work that corresponds to Joyce's as closely as Pinamonti's does merits consideration as its source at all.

Hell Opened to Christians	*A Portrait of the Artist*

[Isa. 5: 14 ("Hell hath enlarged . . ."), Father Arnall's text for the morning sermon (*Portrait,* p. 370) appears in *Hell Opened* (twice, on pp. 4 and 12), as do all other texts he quotes.]

[First Consideration: The Straitness of the Prison of Hell.] Consider, that the first injustice a soul offers to God, is the . . . breaking [of] his commandments, and declaring not to be willing to serve him: "Thou saidst, I will not serve."—Jer. ii. To punish, therefore, so great a boldness, God has framed a prison in the lowest part of the universe. . . . Here

Lucifer, we are told, was . . . a radiant and mighty angel; yet he fell. . . . What his sin was we cannot say. Theologians consider that it was . . . the sinful thought conceived in an instant: *non serviam: I will not serve . . .* (370–71)

though the place itself be wide enough, the damned will not even have that relief, which . . . a poor prisoner has in walking between four walls . . . because they shall be bound up like a faggot, and heaped upon one another . . . and this by reason of the great number of the damned, to whom this great pit will become narrow and strait. . . . (7–8) Those miserable wretches will not only be straitened, but also be immoveable; and, therefore, if a blessed saint, as St. Anselm says, in his book of Similitudes, will be strong enough . . . to move the whole earth: a damned soul will be so weak, as not to be able even to remove from the eye a worm that is gnawing it. The walls of this prison are more than four thousand miles thick. . . . (8)

The straitness of this prison house is expressly designed by God to punish those who refused to be bound by His laws. In earthly prisons the poor captive has at least some liberty of movement, were it only within the four walls of his cell. . . . Not so in hell. There, by reason of the great number of the damned, the prisoners are heaped together in their awful prison, the walls of which are said to be four thousand miles thick: and the damned are so utterly bound and helpless that, as a blessed saint, Saint Anselm, writes in his book on similitudes, they are not even able to remove from the eye a worm that gnaws it (373). [Note that it is Pinamonti, not Anselm, who speaks of a worm gnawing the eye.]

Hell Opened to Christians	*A Portrait of the Artist*
Consider, that this prison will not only be extremely strait, but also extremely dark. It is true, there will be a fire, but without light. . . . That will be true . . . by a contrary miracle to what was wrought in the Babylonian furnace, for there, by the command of God, the heat was taken from the fire, but not the light of brightness: but in hell, the fire will lose its light, but not its heat. Moreover, this same fire, burning with brimstone, will have a searching flame, which being mingled with the rolling smoke of that infernal cave, will . . . raise a storm of darkness, according to what is written . . . [in] Jude xiii. . . . (8–9) Finally,	—They lie in exterior darkness. For, remember, the fire of hell gives forth no light. As, at the command of God, the fire of the Babylonian furnace lost its heat but not its light so, at the command of God, the fire of hell, while retaining the intensity of its heat, burns eternally in darkness. It is a neverending storm of darkness, dark flames and dark smoke of burning brimstone,
the same mass of bodies heaped one upon another will . . . make up a part of that dreadful night; not a glimpse of transparent air being left to the eye of the damned. . . . (9) If	amid which the bodies are heaped one upon another without even a glimpse of air.

Hell Opened to Christians	*A Portrait of the Artist*
amongst all the plagues of Egypt, darkness alone was called horrible; what name shall we give to that darkness, which is not to last for three days only, but for all eternity [?] (9)	Of all the plagues with which the land of the Pharaohs was smitten one plague alone, that of darkness, was called horrible. What name, then, shall we give to the darkness of hell which is to last not for three days alone but for all eternity?
Consider, how much the horror of this prison, so strait and obscure, must be heightened,by the addition of the greatest stench. First, thither, as to a common sewer, all the filth of the earth shall run after the fire of the last day has purged the world. Secondly, the brimstone itself continually burning in such a prodigious quantity, will cause a stench not to be borne. Thirdly, the very bodies of the damned will exhale so pestilential a stench, that if any one of them were to be placed here on earth, it would be enough, as St. Bonaventure observes, to cause a general infection (9). . . . Air, itself, being for a time closely shut up, becomes insupportable;—judge, then, what those unhappy prisoners must suffer from the collected sink [*sic*] of this eternally loathsome abyss (9).	—The horror of this strait and dark prison is (373) increased by its awful stench. All the filth of the world, all the offal and scum of the world, we are told, shall run there as to a vast reeking sewer when the terrible conflagration of the last day has purged the world. The brimstone, too, which burns there in such prodigious quantity fills all hell with its intolerable stench; and the bodies of the damned themselves exhale such a pestilential odour that as Saint Bonaventure says, one of them alone would suffice to infect the whole world. The very air of this world, that pure element, becomes foul and unbreathable when it has been long enclosed. Consider then what must be the foulness of the air of hell. . . . (374)
[Second Consideration: The Quality of the Fire.] . . . Even among men there never was found a greater torment [than fire]. (11) . . . If . . . we cannot bear ever so little awhile [*sic*] the flame of a candle, how shall we for ever be buried in flames . . . ? (12) Nevertheless, you must not think the fire of hell is like	. . . The torment of fire is the greatest torment to which the tyrant has ever subjected his fellow creatures. Place your finger for a moment in the flame of a candle and you will feel the pain of fire.

Hell Opened to Christians	*A Portrait of the Artist*
ours. . . . Our fire is created for the benefit of man, to serve him as a help in most arts, and for the maintaining of life; but the fire of hell was only created for God to revenge himself of the wicked. . . . Our fire is often applied to subjects not at all proportioned to its activity; but the fire of hell is kindled by a sulphureous and bituminous matter, which will always burn with unspeakable fury. . . . (11) Finally, our fire destroys what it burns, therefore, the more intense it is, the shorter is it[s] duration; but the fire in which the damned shall for ever be tormented, shall burn without ever consuming. . . . (12)	But our earthly fire was created by God for the benefit of man, to maintain in him the spark of life and to help him in the useful arts whereas the fire of hell is of another quality and was created by God to torture and punish the unrepentant sinner. Our earthly fire also consumes more or less rapidly according as the object which it attacks is more (374) or less combustible. . . . But the sulphurous brimstone which burns in hell is a substance which is specially designed to burn for ever and for ever with unspeakable fury. Moreover our earthly fire destroys at the same time as it burns so that the more intense it is the shorter is its duration: but the fire of hell has this property that it preserves that which it burns and though it rages with incredible intensity it rages for ever.
Consider what strength this devouring fire will have, on account of the great quantity thereof. . . . (12) [A] sea of fire, which has neither shore nor bottom. . . . (18) Who is there that can doubt, that if a whole mountain were thrown into this great furnace, but that it would melt as soon as a piece of wax? This the devil was forced to own, being asked by a soldier. . . . (12) . . . that flame, so fierce and so great, will not only afflict us without, as it happens with the fires of this world; but will penetrate our very bones, our marrow, and even the very principle of our life and being. . . . Every one	—Our earthly fire again . . . is always of a limited extent: but the lake of fire in hell is boundless, shoreless and bottomless. It is on record that the devil himself, when asked the question by a certain soldier, was obliged to confess that if a whole mountain were thrown into the burning ocean of hell it would be burned up in an instant like a piece of wax. And this terrible fire will not afflict the bodies of the damned only from without

Hell Opened to Christians	*A Portrait of the Artist*

that is damned will be like a lighted furnace, which has its own flames in itself; all that filthy blood will boil in the veins, the brains in the skull, the heart in the breast, the bowels within that unfortunate body, surrounded with an abyss of fire. . . . (13)

but each lost soul will be a hell unto itself, the boundless fire raging in its very vitals. . . . The blood seethes and boils in the veins, the brains are boiling in the skull, the heart in the breast glowing and bursting, the bowels a redhot mass of burning pulp, the tender eyes flaming like molten balls.

Consider, that whatever has been said either as to the strength, the quality, or the quantity of this infernal fire, it is nothing in comparison to the intenseness it will have as being the instrument of the Divine Justice. . . . [I]t will have its rise from the foot of the throne of God, that is to say, it will receive an incredible vigour from the omnipotency of God; working, not with its own activity, but, as an instrument, with the activity of its agent. . . .

—And yet what I have said as to the strength and quality and boundlessness of this fire is as nothing when compared to its intensity, an intensity which it has as being the instrument chosen by divine design for the punishment of soul and body alike. It is a fire which proceeds directly from the ire of God, working not of its own activity but as an instrument of divine vengeance.

(13) . . . as God makes use of material water in baptism, not only to wash the body, but to cleanse and sanctify the soul, so in hell he makes use of fire, though material, to punish her when sinful and unclean. The infernal fire then is an effect of the omnipotency of God injured by sinners; it is a visible sign of that infinite hatred which the divine goodness bears to sin, as also an invention of his wisdom to recover the honour taken from him by the wicked. . . . (13)

As the waters of baptism cleanse the soul with the body so do the fires of punishment torture the spirit with the flesh. (375–76) . . . and . . . the immortal soul is tortured eternally . . . amid the . . . glowing fires kindled in the abyss by the offended majesty of the Omnipotent God and fanned into everlasting and ever increasing fury by the breath of the anger of the Godhead.

Hell Opened to Christians	*A Portrait of the Artist*
[Third Consideration: The Company of the Damned.] Consider, what great torment will be added to the infernal habitation by the inhabitants themselves. The being in ill company is so great a pain, that one would think the very plants on earth are sensible of it, whilst	—Consider finally that the torment of this infernal prison is increased by the company of the damned themselves. Evil company on earth is so noxious that the plants, as if by instinct,
they withdraw themselves, and fly from those that are noxious or hurtful to them. (15) . . . all laws being overturned [in hell], and all	withdraw from the company of whatsoever is deadly or hurtful to them. In hell all laws are overturned—
reason banished, there will be no regard to consanguinity, parentage, country, or to any tie or motive which might mitigate their desperate	there is no thought of family or country, of ties, of relationships. . . . All sense of humanity is forgotten.
rage against each other. . . . their very howlings and groans will make them intolerable. (16)	The yells of the suffering sinners fill the remotest corners of the vast abyss. The mouths of the damned are full
Consider, that the company of the accomplices in sin will be painful above all imagination. . . . (17) Who can conceive the curses, blasphemies and execrations they will spit out . . . ? (18) The punishment assigned for parricides was to be shut up in a sack with a cock, a serpent, and a monkey, and so to be thrown into the sea: but how little do the lawgivers among men understand what pain is! The divine justice has found out other sort of company wherewith to punish criminals; a place full of executioners and condemned persons . . . in the middle of a sea of fire. . . . (18) . . . those friends for whose sake you turned your backs on God, will be the cruelest furies . . . no devil will torment you so much as the	of blasphemies against God and of hatred for their fellow sufferers and of curses against those souls which were their accomplices in sin. In olden times it was the custom to punish the parricide . . . by casting him into the depths of the sea in a sack in which were placed a cock, a monkey and a serpent. . . . The intention of those lawgivers . . . was to punish the criminal. . . . But what is the (376) fury of those dumb beasts compared with the fury of execration which bursts from the parched lips . . . of the damned in hell when they behold . . . those who aided and abetted them in sin . . . those whose immodest suggestions led them on to sin,

Hell Opened to Christians	A Portrait of the Artist

person you disordinately loved. . . . Those eyes which are now your stars, shall then send forth darts more piercing than the very lightning. (17–18)

Consider, the company of the devils will prove far more tormenting than would be that of our greatest enemies. . . . They will afflict the damned two different ways, by their sight and by reproaches. (16) . . . St. Catherine of Sienna, speaking to our Saviour, said much more: "That rather than behold again such a frightful infernal form, she would choose [to?] walk in a road all of fire to the day of judgment." According (16) to this, one of those monsters alone would be enough to make a hell of the place he is in. . . . But what will it be when reproaches and scorn are added to the sight of them? . . . Fool . . . who couldst so easily have saved thyself by restoring those ill-gotten goods, by breaking off that lewd practice, by one hearty sorrow, and thou wouldst not do it[:] why dost thou now complain? Thou wert thyself the occasion of thy misfortune. (17)

[Fourth Consideration: The Pain of Loss.] "I am cast away from the sight of thine eyes." Psalm xxx. 22 [sic]. . . . [10]

those whose eyes tempted and allured them from the path of virtue. . . .

—Last of all consider the frightful torment to those damned souls, tempters and tempted alike, of the company of the devils. These devils will afflict the damned in two ways, by their presence and by their reproaches. . . . Saint Catherine of Siena once saw a devil and she has written that, rather than look again for one single instant on such a frightful monster, she would prefer to walk until the end of her life along a track of red coals. These devils . . . have become as hideous and ugly as they once were beautiful. They mock and jeer at the lost souls whom they dragged down to ruin. . . . Why did you sin? . . . Why did you not give up that lewd habit, that impure habit? (377) You would not . . . restore those illgotten goods. . . . (378) Why did you not . . . repent of your evil ways and turn to God who only waited for your repentance to absolve you of your sins? (377) [NOTE.—Matt. 25:41 ("Depart from me, ye cursed . . ."), with which Father Arnall concludes his Friday-morning sermon, is quoted by Pinamonti on p. 22.]

—I am cast away from the sight of Thine eyes: words taken, my dear little brothers in Christ, from the Book of Psalms, thirtieth chapter, twenty-third[10] verse. (381)

Hell Opened to Christians	*A Portrait of the Artist*
For in sin there is a double malice: the first is the turning one's back on the uncreated good . . . ; the other is the fixing one's eyes on a created good as the chief object . . . of one's happiness. . . . Now the divine justice prepares a punishment in hell suitable to both these disorders, in punishing the conversion to the creature . . . with the pain of sense . . . and . . . the aversion from God, with the pain (22) of loss. . . . (23) This pain [of loss] in substance is a hell of itself greater than all the rest; for, says St. Thomas, "The worst damnation consists in this, that the understanding of man be totally deprived of divine light, and his affection obstinately turned from the goodness of God." This pain, therefore, is infinite . . . if all the other pleasures of heaven were multiplied a thousand times over and over, they could never equal the joy the blessed have in beholding God face to face (20, 21). . . . Though in this life we have but a very obscure knowledge of the infinite happiness which consists in enjoying God; yet in hell the damned, for their greater torment, will have a most lively comprehension of so great a good; and [know] that it is through their fault they have lost it. . . . (21)	—Sin, remember, is a twofold enormity. It is a base consent to . . . the lower instincts, to that which is gross and beastlike; and it is also a turning away from the counsel of our higher nature . . . from the Holy God Himself. For this reason mortal sin is punished in hell by two different forms of punishment, physical and spiritual. (382)
	Now of all these spiritual pains by far the greatest is the pain of loss, so great, in fact, that in itself it is a torment greater than all the others. Saint Thomas . . . says that the worst damnation consists in this that the understanding of man is totally deprived of divine light and his affection obstinately turned away from the goodness of God. God . . . is a being infinitely good and therefore the loss of such a being must be . . . infinitely painful.
	In this life we have not a very clear idea of what such a loss must be but the damned in hell, for their greater torment, have a full understanding of that which they have lost and understand that they have lost it through their own sins and have lost it for ever. At the very instant of death the bonds
In this life, the soul . . . continues in [the body] as a fire under ashes, but breaking loose from the body is in a violent state, like fire lighted in [illegible] . . . so is a soul in endeavouring	of the flesh are broken asunder and the soul at once flies towards God as towards
to get to her centre, which is God. (21–22)	the centre of her existence. . . . (382)

Hell Opened to Christians	*A Portrait of the Artist*

... It has sometimes happened that a mother led into captivity and parting from her son ... [has] fallen down dead ... merely by the excess of grief; what death will a soul feel then in parting with God for ever? (22) ... God [is] ... the centre of happiness to a rational mind ... [and] to be violently separated from this object, and that for ever, must be a torment without its equal. ... (22)

And if it be pain for a mother to be parted from her child. ... O think what pain ... it must be for the poor soul to be spurned from the presence of the supremely good and loving Creator. ... This, then, to be separated for ever from its greatest good, from God, and to feel the anguish of that separation, knowing full well that it is unchangeable, this is the greatest torment which the created soul is capable of bearing. ...

[Fifth Consideration: The Sting of Conscience.] Consider, that as in dead bodies worms are engendered from putrefaction, so in the damned there arises a perpetual remorse from the corruption of sin, which is called the sting of conscience. ... (25)

The second pain which will afflict the souls of the damned in hell is the pain of conscience. Just as in dead bodies worms are engendered by putrefaction so in the souls of the lost there arises a perpetual remorse from the putrefaction of sin, the sting of conscience, the worm, as Pope Innocent the Third calls it, of the triple sting.

This worm, more cruel than any asp, will make three wounds in the heart of every damned soul, which may be further illustrated to us by the word of Innocent III, in his book of the Contempt of the World:—"The memory will afflict, late repentance will trouble, and want of time [i.e., neglect of good occasions] will torment."

Hell Opened to Christians	*A Portrait of the Artist*
. . . First of all then, the memory will afflict. It is a great torment to [the?] miserable wretch to remember his past happiness. . . . (26) He who once gave himself over to all sorts of pleasure; whose palate was filled with the greatest dainties; whose flesh had all the ease imaginable, and wallowed in all kinds of impurity, is now delivered up to everlasting lamentations, suffering, and despair. . . . (26) Judge what a misfortune it will be, after a great number of years, to remember a forbidden pleasure, a momentary delight (26) vanished like a shadow, changed into an eternal torment. (27)	The first sting inflicted by this cruel worm will be the memory of past pleasures. O what a dreadful memory will that be! . . . he who delighted in the pleasures of the table [will remember] his gorgeous feasts, his dishes prepared with such delicacy . . . (383) . . . the impure and adulterous the unspeakable and filthy pleasures in which they delighted. . . . [They are] condemned to suffer in hell-fire for ages and ages. How they will rage and fume to think that they have lost the bliss of heaven for the dross of earth . . . for bodily comforts, for a tingling of the nerves.
Consider, the second wound of this devouring worm will be a late and fruitless sorrow for sins committed. (27) . . . divine justice will fix the understanding of those miserable wretches, continually to think on the sin they have committed. . . . (27) St. Augustine . . . says moreover, that they will behold their abominations as they are in themselves, because God will impart to them his own knowledge of sin, so that it will appear to them as it does to God, that is, an abyss of deformity and malice. . . . And though they shall deplore their sins for ever, yet they shall never come to any composition with God. . . . (28)	. . . the second sting of the worm of conscience [will be] a late and fruitless sorrow for sins committed. Divine justice insists that the understanding of those miserable wretches be fixed continually on the sins of which they were guilty and moreover, as Saint Augustine points out, God will impart to them His own knowledge of sin so that sin will appear to them in all its hideous malice as it appears to the eyes of God Himself. They will behold their sins in all their foulness and repent but it will be too late
Consider, the third wound which this sting of conscience causes in the damned. It is an infinite grief for having neglected so many fair occasions of saving themselves. . . . (28) [This] will be the most cruel viper which will gnaw our hearts. . . . (29) Was I not told of it by my	and then they will bewail the good occasions which they neglected. This is the last and deepest and most cruel sting of the worm of conscience.

Hell Opened to Christians	*A Portrait of the Artist*

ghostly fathers? . . . Was I not assured by faith, that the end of sin was damnation? And I . . . would not open my eyes to my own good. . . . There was a time when God invited me by so many inspirations, entreated me by so many voices, allured me by so many promises, deterred me by so many threats. . . . Now . . . after having shed a sea of tears, I shall never compass what formerly I might have obtained with one only tear. . . . (29) [The thought of this] will make those unfortunate souls, with an hellish fury, to curse sometimes God, whom they hate, as their enemy: sometimes the devils, whom they abhor as traitors: sometimes their companions who entice them to sin; and sometimes their ownselves, for having been so mad. . . . God, who was once so compassionate of my miseries . . . will now become inexorable. (29)

The conscience will say: . . . You had the sacraments and graces and indulgences of the church to aid you. You had the minister of God to preach to you . . . if only you had . . . repented. No. You would not. . . . God appealed to you, threatened you, entreated you to return to Him. (384) . . . And now, though you were to flood all hell with your tears . . . all that sea of repentance would not gain for you what a single tear of true repentance shed during your mortal life would have gained for you. . . . [F]illed with hellish fury they curse themselves for their folly and curse the evil companions who have brought them to such ruin and curse the devils who tempted them in life and now mock them in eternity and even revile and curse the Supreme Being Whose goodness and patience they scorned . . . but Whose justice and power they cannot evade.

[Sixth Consideration: Despair on account of the extension of the pains of hell.] Consider, that man in this life, though he be capable of many evils, he is not capable of them all at once; because here one evil corrects the other, and one poison oftentimes drives out another, but in hell it will be quite otherwise; for pains there will lend each other a fresh sting. . . . (31)

—The next spiritual pain to which the damned are subjected is the pain of extension. Man, in this earthly life, though he be capable of many evils, is not capable of them all at once inasmuch as one evil corrects and counteracts another, just as one poison frequently corrects another. In hell, on the contrary, one torment instead of counteracting another, lends it still greater force:

Hell Opened to Christians	*A Portrait of the Artist*
Moreover, what has been hitherto considered, was in relation to the external senses: but as the internal powers are more perfect, so they are more capable of pain, and therefore, will be the more tormented. . . . [As the damned] had made an ill use of all their senses and powers, to sin, so they deserved in every one of their senses and powers, to be punished with so many pains. . . . (32) The fancy will always be afflicted with frightful imaginations. . . . The sensitive appetite will, like the ebbing and flowing of the sea, be continually swelling and falling . . . into rage and anguish. . . . Their	and, moreover, as the internal faculties are more perfect than the external senses, so are they more capable of suffering. Just as every sense is afflicted with a fitting torment so is every spiritual faculty;
understanding will be filled with interior darkness, more terrible than the exterior, which fills their prison. . . . (32)	the fancy with horrible images, the sensitive faculty with alternate longing and rage,
There [sic] will be obstinate in malice, without being able, during the whole space of eternal years, to have the least inclination to good, but continually adding malice to malice. . . . (32)	the mind and understanding with an interior darkness more terrible even than the exterior darkness which reigns in that dreadful prison. The malice, impotent though it be, which possesses these demon souls is an evil of boundless extension, of limitless duration. . . . (385–86)
. . . [Hell] is the centre of all evils: and as all things are found to be much stronger in their centre than elsewhere . . . so the evils that are in hell will not only be many without number, but intense without comparison, and pure, without mixture. Pains in this place will have no contraries to temper and soften them. . . .	. . . Hell is the centre of evils and, as you know, things are more intense at their centres than at their remotest points. There are no contraries or admixtures of any kind to temper or soften in the least the pains of hell.

Hell Opened to Christians	*A Portrait of the Artist*
(33) Moreover, things that are otherwise good in themselves, in this place become bad. Company, which elsewhere is a comfort to the afflicted, will here be their greatest trouble; the light which in other places is so much coveted, will be hated here, more than darkness itself; knowledge, which in this world does so much delight (33), will be there more tormenting than ignorance. . . . In this present life our sorrows are either not long or not great, because nature either overcomes them by habits, or puts an end to them by falling herself under the weight . . . [b]ut in hell the rules are quite contrary, for the pains there will always continue in the same state; intolerable as to intenseness, and endless as to duration: . . . As there is nothing moderate in the torments, so there is no rest in the tormented, who are continually kept, not barely alive, but in their full senses, to have greater feeling of their misery. . . . It is what the divine Majesty, injured by sinners, requires: it is what the blood of Christ, that is trampled upon, demands: it is what heaven itself, despised and postponed to filth and corruption, insists on. (34)	Nay, things which are good in themselves become evil in hell. Company, elsewhere a source of comfort to the afflicted, will be there a continual torment: knowledge, so much longed for as the chief good of the intellect, will there be hated worse than ignorance: light, so much coveted by all creatures . . . will be loathed intensely. In this life our sorrows are either not very long or not very great because nature either overcomes them by habits or puts an end to them by sinking under their weight. But in hell the torments cannot be overcome by habit, for while they are of terrible intensity they are at the same time of continual variety. . . . Nor can nature escape from these . . . tortures by succumbing to them for the soul is sustained and maintained in evil so that its suffering may be the greater. . . . . . . this is what the divine majesty, so outraged by sinners, demands, this is what the holiness of heaven, slighted and set aside for the lustful and low pleasures of the corrupt flesh, requires, this is what the blood of the innocent Lamb of God . . . trampled upon by the vilest of the vile, insists upon. (386)

Hell Opened to Christians	*A Portrait of the Artist*
[Seventh Consideration: The Eternity of Pain.] ... O eternity, then, O eternity! (39) Consider, that were the pains of hell less racking, yet, being never to have an end, they would become infinite. What then will it be, they being both intolerable as to sharpness, and endless as to duration? (38) ... were it proposed to the damned to suffer either by the sting of a bee in their eye for a whole eternity,	... Eternity! O, dread and dire word. Eternity! (387) Even though the pains of hell were not so terrible as they are yet they would become infinite as they are destined to last for ever. But while they are everlasting they are at the same time ... intolerably intense, unbearably extensive.
or to undergo all the torments of hell for as many ages as there are (38) stars in heaven, they would ... choose to be thus miserable for so many ages, and then to see an end of their misery than to endure a pain so much less, that was to have no end. (39) ... Let us go on, and imagine ... a mountain of this small sand [as in an hourglass], so high as would reach from earth to heaven. ... Let us then imagine this great mountain to be multiplied as often as there are sands in the sea, leaves on trees, feathers on birds, scales on fish, hairs on beasts, atoms in the air, drops of water that have rained or will rain to the day of judgment ... [a]nd yet ... we are assured by faith ... that all these years shall pass, and when over, none of our pains will be lessened, nor so much	To bear even the sting of an insect for all eternity would be a dreadful torment. What must it be, then, to bear the manifold tortures of hell for ever? ... You have often seen the sand on the seashore. ... Now imagine a mountain of that sand, a million miles high, reaching from the earth to the farthest heavens ... and imagine such an enormous mass of countless particles of sand multiplied as often as there are leaves in the forest, drops of water in the mighty ocean, feathers on birds, scales on fish, hairs on animals, atoms in the vast expanse of the air: ... Yet at the end of that immense stretch of time not even one instant of eternity could be said to have ended. (387)
as one instant taken from eternity. (39) ... eternity expects thee in a place of torment, always the same, with the same pains. (40) ... So that we may say, that eternity not only every moment tortures the damned, but that to the damned every moment is turned into so many eternities. (41)	... An eternity of endless agony ... without one ray of hope, without one moment of cessation ... (388) ... an eternity, every instant of which is itself an eternity of woe. (389)

Hell Opened to Christians	*A Portrait of the Artist*
Consider, that men reasoning always as men, are astonished that God, for so short a pleasure of a sinner, should have decreed an everlasting punishment in the fire of hell. . . . But ought not we rather to wonder at the astonishment of worldlings, grounded on the ignorance of spiritual things [?] "The sensual man perceiveth not the things that are of the spirit of God. . . ."—I Cor. ii. 14. If sinners did but comprehend the malice of their sin, they would soon change their wonder. . . . (41)	. . . Men, reasoning always as men, are astonished that God should mete out an everlasting and infinite punishment in the fires of hell for a single grievous sin. They reason thus because, blinded by the gross illusion of the flesh and the darkness of human understanding they are unable to comprehend the hideous malice of mortal sin. . . .
Consider . . . that every mortal sin is either a tacit or express contempt of the divine will, and an injury to God . . . in a manner infinite. . . . (41–42) . . . if the pain due to the offenders of God were to end, both the judge and the sentence would be condemned . . . the malice of sin is so exorbitant as not to be atoned and satisfied for, by the good works of all creatures; and, therefore, to pay this debt, it was necessary the Son of God should take from his veins, as a just price, the treasures of his divine blood. (42)	. . . sin . . . is a transgression of His law and God would not be God if He did not punish the transgressor.

. . . To retrieve the consequences of that sin [Adam's and Eve's] the Only Begotten Son of God . . . lived and suffered and died a most painful death. . . . (389) |

This extensive listing of passages has seemed necessary in order to make it clear that when I call *Hell Opened to Christians* the primary source of Joyce's sermon on hell I am not basing my judgment on mere analogies, random parallels, or echoes but on actual correspondences, following in the same sequence and often expressed in the same words, and so conspicuous as to be undeniable. I do not mean that Joyce simply parroted Pinamonti, even in the most similar passages. But the fact remains that much of the famous sermon on hell (recently elevated to textbook rank) was cribbed.

Three questions should now be considered: the relation of both works to their parent tradition; Joyce's adaptation of his source; and the theological milieu through which Pinamonti's tract probably came to Joyce's attention.

Discussion of the first of these will reveal another and important reason why an unmistakable relationship between the two works can be demonstrated only through side-by-side comparison. The melodramatic impressiveness of both inclines a reader to ascribe more originality and singularity to them than either author would have claimed. The truth is that much of their content has indeed been "the common possession of devotional writers for hundreds of years," and far more so than has been pointed out.[11] For instance, in Consideration 26 of the manual *Preparation for Death,* St. Alphonsus Liguori, founder of the Redemptorists and author of the "old neglected book" of Stephen's devotions, writes that the smoke of the "utterly dark" fire of hell will form "a storm of darkness" to torment the damned; that, according to St. Bonaventure, the stench of one of their bodies would kill all on earth; that the pain of earthly fire, "created for our use," cannot be compared with that of hellfire, "made . . . purposely to torment the damned," each of whom "shall be in himself a furnace of fire"—the blood in the veins, even the marrow of the bones. Yet these are as nothing beside the infinite pain of losing "God, who is an infinite good." Unaided human reason may question the justice of punishing a moment's sin with an eternity of pain; but sin's infinite offense merits no less. And, since the creature "is not capable of suffering pain infinite in . . . intensity, God inflicts punishment infinite in extension."[12] These and many other passages echo Arnall's words so closely that anyone unacquainted with *Hell Opened to Christians* could plausibly suggest this section of *Preparation for Death* as their source. And Liguori is but one of many who have written of hell in a similar vein over a period spanning centuries.

Professor Rogers holds that, Gibbon and popular opinion notwithstanding, detailed pictures of hell torments are at most a minor element in Christian writings of the early centuries; and E. B. Pusey's catena of patristic opinion, although part of a book designed to prove the universality of belief in everlasting punishment, on the whole supports this view.[13] Luridly detailed portrayals of horrors, though stemming from earlier apocryphal writings, are the work of monks and friars of the later Middle Ages.[14] Still, although the church has never pronounced on the matter, from earliest times writers have located hell within the earth as the place farthest from God and fittest to sustain heat and the darkness that, as Aquinas says, the thick cloudy fire and the massed bodies of the damned will produce.[15] Agreeing that mortal sin merits no less than an eternity of torment, ancients and moderns, Protestants as well as Catholics, have drawn vividly the pains of the fire that burns corporeally forever without consuming. Tertullian's overly familiar passage imagines the proud kings, poets, and tragedians dissolving in the lake of brimstone; Gregory the Great warns readers that a certain dissolute monk's vision of the faggots prepared to burn him was but a type of hellfire's torments, adapted to our limited understandings; one Drithelm, according to Bede, saw the souls of the damned in globes of black fire, rising and sinking like sparks; Jonathan Edwards exhorts those hardened in sin to imagine passing even a quarter-hour in a glowing furnace.[16] And yet, as in Arnall or Pinamonti, such pains "are nothing in comparison with the loss of God."[17] The lost, says the seventeenth-century Jesuit Lessius (Leys), feel this infinite loss eternally without the slightest mitigation; Aquinas holds that they can will only evil, envying the blessed and hating God himself for their pangs.[18]

Even a cursory account like the foregoing will demonstrate that, even if Pinamonti had never written, the sermon on hell still could not have sprung spontaneously from Joyce's brain. A glance over the more immediate ancestry of both works will make this still clearer. Sullivan holds that the similar images in passages of the sermon and of the *Sodality Manual* indicate a "more than incidental connection" between them. Yet identical images occur in many writers, especially in the Jesuit scholars and preachers of seventeenth-century Europe. In a widely imitated section of his *De perfectionibus moribusque divinis* (1620) the gifted Flemish Jesuit Leonard Lessius holds, like Liguori, that, in the lake of brimstone twenty thousand feet wide, fires will rage within the body, bowels, and bones of the damned.[19] *Contemplations of the State of Man* (1684), an English work once attributed to Jeremy Taylor, frequently urges the torment of bearing forever even a slight pain (the scorching of a finger, an insect's sting, a pinprick), let alone those of hell, as in Arnall's sermon, the *Manual,* and a score of other works.[20] The probable source of the *Contemplations* is the treatise *On the Difference between the Temporal and the Eternal (ca.* 1640). Here the Spanish Jesuit J. E. Nieremberg describes the stench of the damned (one of the eight pains of hell) in terms markedly similar to Pinamonti's and Joyce's, even to citing the authority of St. Bonaventure.[21] "The Egyptians," says the esteemed Catholic scholar, Bishop Challoner, "were in a sad condition when, for three days, the whole kingdom was covered with a dreadful darkness"; yet, unlike them, the damned in hell shall never see morning but shall ever endure "the intolerable stench of those half-putrified carcases which are broiling there."[22]

Another of Father Arnall's hyperboles that appears in the *Manual* seeks to convey the vastness of eternity by means of a mountain of fine sand, carried away by a bird at the rate of a grain every million years, and then successively rising and falling as often as there are stars in heaven, leaves on trees, etc.—at the end of which inconceivable period, eternity will not even have begun. Striking though this image is, its inclusion in any Catholic book of devotion proves nothing at all: it is virtually a literary convention in such works. Who, asks Farrar in 1877, has not heard sermons "to the effect that if every leaf of the forest trees, and every grain of the ocean sands stood for billions of years, and all these billions were exhausted, you would still be no nearer even to the beginning of eternity than at the first . . ."?[23] Farrar does not stay for an answer; however, Father G. B. Manni, still another Jesuit of the seventeenth century, writes that so many ages "as there are stars in heaven, drops of water in the sea, and motes in the air, and particles of dust in the earth" would not make up eternity. Let all the space between earth and heaven, he continues, be filled with fine sand, and every one hundred thousand million [*sic*] ages let an angel carry away a single grain. Could the damned believe that after this their torments would end, they would rejoice.[24] Liguori agrees, however, that this cannot be, even after so many ages as there are grains of sand in the sea or leaves on the trees, and Nieremberg conveys this stern denial in almost identical terms: "cuantas hojas hay en los campos, cuantos granos de arena hay en la tierra," etc.[25] Along with the familiar mountain of sand (angelically reduced at the relatively rapid pace of a grain a year), Jeremias Drexel, S.J., imagines a strip of parchment girdling the earth, closely inscribed with small figure 9's. "And yet this [figure] is nothing to *Eternity*."[26] The bird that carries off grains of sand in Father Arnall's illustration may be found in Heinrich Suso (or Seuse), the saintly Dominican mystic of the fourteenth century: if there were a millstone thick as earth and broad as all heaven, and "if there came a little bird every hundred thousand years, and took from the stone as much as the tenth part of a grain of millet," the lost would wish nothing more than that their torments might end with the stone—and yet this cannot be.[27]

There is no need of more examples to prove that, although Joyce is specifically indebted to Pinamonti, his model is in turn part of a literary and religious tradition so extensive and widely diffused that no distinct indebtedness on Pinamonti's side (save to his fellow Jesuit preachers) seems demonstrable. For the same reasons it seems equally clear that any effort to specify the *Portrait* sermon's sources on the basis of isolated resemblances in expression or imagery will fail through the very abundance of such parallels. Only a work whose organization, scale, and proportion also clearly correspond to Joyce's can even be considered as a primary source, and to my knowledge all of these requirements are met conclusively only by *Hell Opened to Christians*.

Since not only the themes of the *Portrait* sermon but even its modes of expression occur so frequently in Catholic devotional writing, especially in the work of Jesuits, it is hard fully to understand Father Noon's objection that the "purely negative and harrowing sermon . . . is neither Catholic nor Ignatian."[28] It is true, of course, that, unlike the writings of Suso or Liguori, Arnall's sermon and Pinamonti's tract do not lead the reader beyond threats of punishment to considerations of the divine love and mercy; their sole purpose is, in the latter's words, "to fright us into our duty" (*Hell Opened,* p. 35). But can their teaching be called not "characteristic" solely because it is partial, incomplete? Before the great Dominican Luis de Granada, surely an unexceptionable authority, goes on to speak of hell as "a dark and obscure lake under the earth, . . . in which is heard only the groaning . . . of the tormentors and the tormented," he points out that meditations on hell are profitable in moving us to do penance and in making us fear God and hate sin.[29] That is, fear of the Lord in itself is not wisdom, but it is the indispensable prelude to wisdom. And the literature of religious fear is by no means confined to the Middle Ages or the Counter-Reformation. As will be shown further on, at least one picture of hellfire as lurid as Arnall's or Pinamonti's, written by a Redemptorist father and printed *permissu superiorum,* was widely circulated in the late nineteenth century, arousing the indignation of liberals, the annoyance of some Catholics, and—perhaps—the interest of James Joyce.

Pinamonti, of course, could not have dreamed of claiming uniqueness for his book, and to recognize Joyce's dependence on a source is not to deny the originality of the retreat episode. Arnall's explanation of the word "retreat" (*Portrait,* pp. 361–63) has no counterpart in the Italian's book, nor has the synopsis of the next day's sermon on death and judgment (pp. 364–68) or the exposition of the scheme of redemption that precedes the sermon on hell and the exhortations that conclude each half. Anyone looking for parallel descriptions of death and burial or of the souls thronging to judgment will find them readily enough, but this is a pointless labor in the case of a writer educated by priests.[30] And, for the most part, what Joyce has taken from his model he has made his own. The close punctuation, the inept, sometimes obscure syntax of the original become clear and swift; archaic or technical terms beyond schoolboys' range are dropped or substituted; even an ambiguous pronoun reference (in St. Augustine's opinion that the lost will behold sin as God does) is corrected. Participial constructions and excessive periodicity are replaced by full predication and more colloquial sentence structure, yet at the same time the sermonistic parallelism, balance, and suspensions of the original are made more telling. And Joyce does not always copy his model's order, scale, and emphasis in detail, even in the morning sermon. His taunting devils are far more explicit and display a moral fastidiousness unknown to Pinamonti's. His elaboration upon the reek of the "jellylike mass of liquid corruption" is matched or surpassed elsewhere, but not in his model's relatively squeamish analysis of hell's stench. The lack of any mitigating reference to heaven and the divine love by Arnall is not truly Ignatian. But when Father Arnall warns against yielding to the promptings of corrupt nature in place of "fixing one's eyes on a created good," and when he greatly simplifies Pinamonti's logical demonstration that infinite punishment is justified by the infinite enormity of sin, his practice accords with the Ignatian precept that devotions should be adapted to the condition of the exercitant. For the same reason he gives carnal sins added emphasis before his adolescent hearers and presents the lost souls' reviling of God as the culmination of malice (*Portrait,* p. 385) instead of merely ranking it with other expressions of their rage. Obviously, the third point of Pinamonti's sixth consideration—the despair of the damned on comparing

their lot with that of the saints—is so unsuited to Joyce's dramatic purpose that it becomes the only point omitted altogether. It bluntly asserts
the ancient and widely held belief that "God and his saints rejoice" at the
pangs of the damned as a sign of divine justice fulfilled. Since even Aquinas experienced difficulties in justifying this idea, it would be absurd to
have Arnall expound it before boys insufficiently steeled in the school of
double-think to reconcile it with their preacher's concluding words on the
divine love.[31]

Considered as a whole, Joyce's version emerges less as an abridgment
than as a synopsis or précis, tersely setting forth under seven points what
Pinamonti develops leisurely under twenty-one with more-than-ample
exempla, analogies, cited authorities, synonymous repetitions, and over-
whelming questions. Joyce keeps all these devices, especially repetition,
but his judiciously sparing use of them invariably heightens the desired
effect rather than diffusing it by excess. To convey the vastness of hellfire,
Pinamonti employs a (relatively) tame picture of sinners burning from
within and a story (told by St. Caesarius) concerning the devil's admission
to a certain soldier, both buttressed by the analogy of an unvented oven
and the authorities of Chrysostom, Isaiah, Job, and the Second (*sic* for
A.V. Eighty-third) Psalm. Joyce, by repeating and particularizing words
and images, tautens the passage into the epitome of fiery terror, tempered
just enough by the bathos of the devil's fusible mountain, and prunes away
all else. Conversely, Arnall's reiteration that God cannot let pass one venial
sin, even if doing so would end all the world's misery, seems to be the development of what Pinamonti only adumbrates (*Hell Opened*, pp. 41–42),
although it is probably reinforced by memories of an 1897 Lenten retreat
sermon by a Father Jeffcoat which, says his brother, aroused in Joyce a
"brain-storm of terror and remorse."[32] But, if we cannot always see the
rationale of Joyce's selections from his source, it is at least clear why many
exempla are omitted. By the principle of anticipation the boys might feel
the hellishness of living with a scolding wife (Company of the Damned,
Hell Opened, pp. 15, 17), but probably not the sense for the apposite gesture
that prompted a deceived husband to lock up his wife with the decaying
corpse of her lover (Sorrow for Sins Committed, pp. 27–28). It would be
tactless of Arnall to take for granted his hearers' familiarity with a losing
gambler's rages, as Pinamonti does (Company of the Devils, p. 17). And
theatregoers too restless to endure a play without comic entr'actes (Un-
changeableness of Pain, p. 40) would be as far beyond the college boys'

experience as the "noble lord," perhaps of contemporary Italy, who tosses on his bed of down, foaming and cursing, when pinched with the colic (Intenseness of the Pains of Hell, p. 34).

There remains the interesting question of how Joyce came by Pina-monti's obscure tract. Any answer to this will necessarily be conjectural in part, but clues in Joyce's second novel, seen in relation to the movement in nineteenth-century religious thought to which they allude, provide a larger factual basis than those underlying several current articles of faith about Joyce. Joyce may, of course, have found his copy during rambles like those of Stephen Daedalus among the Dublin bookstalls "which offered old directories and volumes of sermons and unheard-of treatises . . . at . . . a penny each or three for twopence" (*Stephen Hero*, p. 145; cf. *Ulysses*, p. 239). It is now known that when he arrived at Zurich in October, 1904, Joyce was at work on the eleventh chapter of *Stephen Hero*, set at Belve-dere College, and that he had completed the preceding ten chapters, not merely the lone first chapter and notes which Gorman mentions, well be-fore his departure from Dublin earlier that year. Since it is therefore likely that the retreat episode alluded to in the surviving portion (*Stephen Hero*, pp. 56–57) was already written, there is no need to conjecture how Joyce managed to acquire *Hell Opened* while he was abroad. But to assume that he simply came across Pinamonti's tract in some Josh Strong's bookshop is to beg the important question of why and how he singled out this work, so perfectly suited to his needs, from the scores of similar books, tracts, and sermons that crowded Dublin bookstalls. It is unlikely that J. F. Byrne, who remembers *Hell Opened*, read the tract or called Joyce's attention to it; had he done either, he would at least have pointed out the indebtedness. It is far more probable that Joyce deliberately sought out the tract because he knew he could put it to use and that he knew this because he was ac-quainted, even familiar, with the discussion of doctrines concerning hell carried on in England and Europe during the later nineteenth century. As I will show, it would have been as hard for a serious undergraduate of the 1880's to remain ignorant of the eternal punishment question, of the larger hope that many devout persons wished to trust less faintly, as it would have been for an Oxford student of the 1840's not to hear of the apostolic claims of the Church of England. And in the Wandering Rocks episode of *Ulysses*, probably written early in 1919, there are clear indications that Joyce had heard of it. "That book by the Belgian Jesuit, *Le Nombre des Élus*" (*Ulysses*, p. 220), on which Father Conmee muses approvingly, is *Le*

Rigorisme, la doctrine du salut et la question du nombre des élus (Brussels, 1899) by the distinguished Louvain professor, Auguste Castelein, S.J. It argues, like other books published closer to Joyce's home, against the belief prevalent during the Middle Ages and sustained well into the modern era by Cornelius à Lapide (*Portrait,* p. 503), Massillon, and others that the damned incalculably outnumber the saved or even those in purgatory.[33] It does not matter whether Joyce read this scarce book, which found much Catholic approval despite a scathing attack on its liberalism by the Redemptorist F. X. Godts. What matters is that only one more than casually acquainted with the question of eternal punishment and its ancillary issues could have known of the work's existence or of its message's dramatic appropriateness to the thoughts of Conmee, at his ease in both worlds. And when in the same episode Haines confidently imputes to Stephen an *idée fixe* related to eternal punishment, it may be more than the piece of aesthetic-tea chatter it appears. As will be seen, Stephen's reported perplexity on finding "no trace of hell in ancient Irish [Hebrew?] myth" can be taken, and may have been designed, as an irreverent capsule parody of the exegeses by, say, F. W. Farrar or E. H. Plumptre. I believe, in fact, that Buck Mulligan's diagnosis of Stephen ("they drove his wits astray . . . by visions of hell") contains more substance than one expects from this spirit that denies. The *Portrait* Stephen's half-formed vision of a priestly vocation dissolves before the threatened loss of his freedom—a consideration weakened by its anticlimactic juxtaposition with his sudden awareness of overtones of effeminacy in the priesthood and of his dislike of early rising. And the sight of hell vanishes, leaving not a rack behind. But the earlier Stephen-in-revolt exclaimed as strongly as John Stuart Mill against "obscene, stinking hells" and a millennium of "fried atheists" (*Stephen Hero,* p. 232), and the creator of both Stephens reverted mockingly to the topic in one of his few epistolary references to Dedalus, over a decade later.[34] I do not propose to add another shelf of books to the Alexandrian library that Joyce is already alleged to have assimilated in some twenty years, but I believe that there are enough clear indications in his works to warrant an examination of certain phases of the eternal punishment question that may have led him to *Hell Opened to Christians* and to larger considerations as well.

The movement in Protestant theology toward subjectivity and humanism during the later nineteenth century was primarily a sympathetic response to the increasing dominance of humanitarian secularism and scientific—especially evolutionary—modes of thought, despite the unquestionable importance of Schleiermacher, Coleridge, and F. D. Maurice. It is impossible even to outline that movement here (much less Catholic reaction to it); but, during its course, such liberal and philanthropic Anglicans as A. P. Stanley and Charles Kingsley, like the freethinkers and rationalists they opposed, increasingly found it as repugnant to believe in an afterlife of eternal physical and spiritual torment for a huge majority of the human race as to accept a purely substitutionary theory of the Atonement or Moses' authorship of the Pentateuch.[35] Those who attacked eternal punishment did not form a concerted movement, and no one of them is entirely typical. Their opponents, Catholics especially, lumped them all as Universalists, although Anglicans like Farrar and Plumptre repudiated this eschatology stemming from Origen. But learned and articulate Universalists like Andrew Jukes played a strong part in the movement, and Farrar's position especially is often difficult to discriminate from theirs. All these writers affirm the punishment of sin, although they find it to consist primarily in the pain of loss rather than that of sense; but they deny that such punishment is purely retributive, as Pinamonti represents it. (Joyce's Stephen found no sense of retribution beyond the grave in "Irish myth" [*Ulysses*, p. 245].) Instead, they affirm on the basis of Scripture and inner conviction that the majority of souls—not all—enter the future with the same capacities for repentance, growth, and education that they had in life.[36] On philological grounds they reject the mistranslations and accreted meanings of "hell," "damnation," and "eternal."

Such attacks increased noticeably in the years following *Essays and Reviews*, a volume pervaded with similar ideas on continuing spiritual growth in the lives of men and nations. An adequate account would deal with F. W. Robertson, Erskine of Linlathen, A. R. Symonds, and others as well; but in terms of popular impact the names of F. D. Maurice and F. W. Farrar lead all the rest. In his *Theological Essays* of 1853, which cost him his professorship, Maurice held that the punishment of evil, though retributive, may also be reformatory, and he denounced all dogmatic playing with Scripture texts. To know the infinite love of God as manifested in Christ is eternal life, while eternal punishment is the being without this knowledge.[37] A direct and influential (again, upon the general public) consequence of this book involved the career of John William Colenso, future pentateuchal critic. The Low Church *Record's* noisy opposition to his consecration as missionary bishop of Natal, following his dedicating a volume of sermons to Maurice, did not succeed.[38] However, Colenso's continuing reflections on the doctrine of eternal punishment led him to reprehend it in 1855 from the viewpoint of a working missionary (in vigorous terms that Father Conmee's comfortable musings travesty) and to renounce it altogether, on exegetical grounds, five years later.[39] Hence, after the appearance of *The Pentateuch and Book of Joshua Critically Examined* (1862 ff.) and Colenso's testimony at his subsequent trial, several reviewers found a relation between the later book's enormities and the Bishop's earlier doctrinal unsoundness.[40] If Colenso's and H. B. Wilson's (of *Essays and Reviews*) trials for heresy were indirect consequences of Maurice's teaching, their acquittals in turn were a major influence on the closing of ranks that took place among religionists in the following years. In its decision reversing the 1862 verdict of the Court of Arches condemning Wilson and another essayist, the Judicial Committee of the Privy Council had decided that the expression of a hope that the punishment of sinners might be terminable did not contradict the teaching of the Church of England. Protestants of several factions and—to some extent—Anglo- and Roman Catholics as well were now almost under the necessity of committing themselves for or against the new ideas. Most conservatives aligned themselves against all "neologisms," even forming at times an uneasy united front. For instance, in 1864, while memories of Wilson's and Colenso's acquittals were still fresh, the scholarly Tractarian leader E. B. Pusey in an Oxford sermon described the company of the damned in terms that echo the murky early jeremiads of C. H. Spurgeon, the popular evangelist—between whose ilk and Pusey's, relations were ordinarily on a Sweeney-Eliot footing: "fierce, fiery eyes of hate ever fixed on thee . . . sleepless in their horrible gaze; hear those yells of blaspheming concentrated hate, as they echo along the lurid vault of hell."[41] Maurice had held the essence of eternal punishment to consist in the pain of loss, which Pusey stresses in this sermon, giving only a phrase to the torments of sense. Yet even these excerpts show plainly how little mitigation was afforded by the substitution of spiritual pains for corporeal ones. Despite Lecky's claim that pictures of torment had nearly vanished from theological writing by the 1860's, orthodox representations of infernal tortures in various forms persisted well into Joyce's college years.[42]

Dean Farrar's once-famous sermons on *Eternal Hope*, preached late in 1877 in Westminster Abbey, added little doctrinally to the positions taken by Maurice (and, it may be added, Tennyson) and developed by others;

their importance to us lies in the astonishingly wide public interest that they and Pusey's reply to them created. This holds true of Catholic writers as well, as is shown by the number of articles on Farrar's subjects that appeared in Romanist periodicals in the next two decades. Such writers could make no concessions to Universalism, but at the same time many showed that they were not indifferent to the tensions produced by medieval conceptions of hell in a scientific and humanitarian age. In words that might have come from *Eternal Hope*, an article of 1882 urged that heaven and hell be regarded as not primarily "*places*" but *states*"—of eternal union with God or of lasting hostility toward him.[43] During Joyce's second year in college, an Irish Jesuit published a book, possibly modeled after Father Castelein's, with the object of proving that the saved outnumber the lost, contrary to the upholders of "severe opinions."[44] (This is not to imply that anything like a wave of liberal sentiment swept over British Catholicism but only to indicate that concern with the question was not confined to Protestants.) Although thoughtful Catholics might find ironical amusement in the near-approaches of some trusters in the larger hope to the reprobated Romish doctrine of purgatory, they also recognized that the bandying-about of unsanctioned teaching by popular preachers and in books like Pinamonti's had imposed needless strains on belief and furnished their most militant opponents with a whole arsenal. Instead of reaching for "the extreme limit of human imagination," warned the *Catholic World* in 1893, let the preacher remember that, since the chief pains of hell are spiritual, analogies between the *poena sensus* and earthly fire are irrelevant at best. For terror to have effect, its reality must be believed in, and such belief is waning.[45] Although this writer clearly speaks only for himself, his feelings were not unique. Not long before, the Catholic convert and distinguished biologist, St. George Mivart, had avowed that the breed of the "repulsive and widely known book entitled *Hell Opened to Christians*" was a lion in the path of many Catholics, professing and would-be, and that "hundreds of lecturers" were gaining aid and comfort from such gratuitous additions to what the church had defined.[46] Mivart did nothing for the cogency of his argument by defending the repulsive book's methods as the only means by which the preacher can convey the *relative* superiority of heaven; and the authorities were unsympathetic toward his contention that Catholics may believe, like Universalists, in a gradual amelioration of the lot of the damned. In the notoriety they achieved among Catholics, however, Mivart's articles are comparable with the *Eternal Hope* sermons—so much so that his unspecified lecturers may have gained additional aid and comfort from, say, Achilles Daunt's rebuttal of his ideas (*Tablet*, December 17, 1892), containing a detailed exposition of the pains of sense according to Liguori, whose similarities to Pinamonti we have already seen.

Mivart calls *Hell Opened* "widely known," and there are indications that it was, if chiefly *sub rosa*; yet the bad fame he ascribes to it properly belongs to one of its lineal nineteenth-century descendants. Over ten years before, the influential *Dublin Review*, in an important article directed against the followers of Maurice, had considered the problem that was to vex Mivart and had anticipated at least part of his verdict. After explaining what is of Catholic faith concerning hell, the *Review* admitted that many books and preachers have spoken of physical torments in language "far from philosophically correct" and added the important corollary that, since no Catholic need give credence to such details offered them "in the nature of illustration," the question of hellfire sermons is to be tried chiefly on pragmatic and aesthetic grounds. And, in the *Review's* estimation, "grotesque horrors such as the late saintly Father Furness [*sic*] used to describe in his retreats, are bad in art and ineffective in result."[47]

The "saintly Father Furness" was the Reverend John Joseph Furniss, C.SS.R. (1809–65), and the "grotesque horrors" are displayed in his thirteen penny "Books for Children, and Young Persons," first printed by James Duffy probably between 1856 and 1863—displayed most of all in Book X, *The Sight of Hell.* It was this tract of thirty-two pages that sustained most of the assaults of which Mivart speaks. Many of these denunciations were never printed, but, in those that were, *The Sight of Hell* stands out as Exhibit A in so many cases against everlasting punishment that it is not exaggeration to call it a principal cause of all such litigation.

Born of a Catholic family, Father Furniss in 1850 joined the Redemptorists, only recently come to England, moved by his lifelong admiration of St. Alphonsus Liguori. During the next thirteen years he took part in over a hundred retreats in England and Ireland, many of them among the potato-famine poor. After 1855, however, he concentrated upon separate children's missions, for which he evolved an approach all his own. "Children," he declared, "cannot reason, you must make them understand through their feelings and imagination."[48] And, like Pinamonti, whose tract he appears to have known and used, Furniss was nothing if not concrete: at least two of his hearers remembered the sermon on hell as "very terrible" after thirty-five years.

Hell, exactly four thousand miles distant, is filled with torrents and fogs of fire so hot that one spark would dry up all the water of earth; yet it burns without giving light, cloaked in rolling sulphurous clouds of smoke. The shrieks of "millions and millions of tormented creatures mad with the fury of Hell" assail the ears; the stench of countless corpses, one of which, says St. Bonaventure, would infect all the earth, tortures the smell; a river of tears shed by the damned, who weep for the pain and "because they have lost the beautiful heaven," flows forever. Each soul has a "striking devil" (see Job 2: 7) to ulcerate its body and a "mocking devil" to torment it with thoughts of good occasions lost, while every nerve, bone, and muscle "quivers" with fire that rages in the skull, shooting out of eyes and ears. Enduring one insect's sting for a lifetime, or beholding at midnight the ghost of one long dead, would only foreshadow the pain and terror of hell's venomous creeping worms and sights and sounds dreadful beyond description. And yet these, in turn, are nothing compared with the pain of having lost the heavenly joy which the damned, for their greater torment, are allowed to glimpse at Judgment.[49]

Morbid as this is, we have met its like before (although not in rivalry with *The Water Babies*), and by itself it might have attracted no more lasting attention than Furniss' penny-dreadful word-paintings of phosphorescent charnel-house horrors or the drunkard's vile life and death.[50] During their guided tour of the inferno, however, the children behold a series of dungeons along the flaming walls. In the first stands a girl who thought only of vanities:

> What a terrible dress she has on—her dress is made of fire. On her head she wears a bonnet of fire. It is pressed down close all over her head; it . . . burns into the skin; it scorches the bone of the skull and makes it smoke. The red hot fiery heat burns into the brain and melts it. . . . Think what a headache that girl must have.

But most occupants are children:

> But listen! there is a sound just like that of a kettle boiling. Is it really a kettle which is boiling? No; then what is it? . . . The blood

is boiling in the scalded veins of that boy. The brain is boiling and bubbling in his head. The marrow is boiling in his bones!

In the fifth dungeon:

> See! it is a pitiful sight. The little child [from another tract, *The Terrible Judgment*] is in this red hot oven. Hear how it screams to come out. See how it turns and twists . . . in the fire. It beats its head against the roof of the oven. It stamps its little feet on the floor of the oven. You can see on the face of this little child what you see on the faces of all in Hell—despair, desperate and horrible! . . . God was very good to this child. Very likely God saw that this child would . . . never repent, and so it would have to be punished much more in Hell. So God in His mercy called it out of the world in its early childhood.[51]

The curious logic of party spirit lets the author's memorialist assure us that only "vague and unsound" Protestant elements took up arms against Furniss, while at the same time, it seems, his loving circumstantiality should not be read with too much literal-mindedness—even, presumably, by Catholics. (We also learn, however, that in his last illness Father Furniss often repeated the opinion of Blosius that anyone dying in a perfect act of resignation will escape hell and purgatory.)[52] Conjectures aside, these three passages in which horrific eschatology is set forth in the tone of a children's primer, together with the *permissu superiorum* on its title page, brought the tract an astonishing celebrity. As late as 1895 its Dublin publisher estimated total sales of the "Books for Children" at over four million, adding that they still sold "very extensively . . . especially No. X [*The Sight of Hell*] and some others, owing to the attacks made upon them on public platforms and in the press by enemies of the Church." Father Furniss often distributed his tracts to the children at retreats, where they are said to have circulated at the rate of a thousand a month "with great effect."[53] The effect may have been greater on adults than on children, who often manage to keep a saner perspective than philanthropic liberals or "the great army of free-thinkers . . . besieging the venerable superstitions of the past"[54] who held up *The Sight* as the epitome of iniquitous priestcraft. In his *History of European Morals* (1869) W. E. H. Lecky viewed it in a lengthy note as the continuation of medieval efforts to infuse young minds with "a spirit of blind and abject credulity" and quoted substantially

from three dungeon-sights in order to alert Englishmen, referring interested readers to an unnamed "book on *Hell*, translated from the Italian of
Pinamonti."[55] Lecky's famous book by itself would have been enough to
make both priests' works widely known. It may have led the prominent
Unitarian minister, William Rathbone Greg, best remembered for *The
Creed of Christendom*, to procure the copy of *The Sight of Hell* from which
he quoted in 1872 to show that "material conceptions of the place of punishment" had by no means been discarded in the enlightened present.[56]
In such extravagant eschatology as the striking devil, the dress of fire, and
the child in the oven, Greg found, like the *Dublin Review*, an explanation
of the average Christian's professed belief in hell and practical disregard of
it. A master-in-chancery, one Gerald Fitzgibbon, acknowledged the same
year in *Roman Catholic Priests and National Schools* that Lecky's book
led him to Furniss and Pinamonti, whose iniquities enabled him to see
the national education issue as a struggle between a Church of England
Ormazd and a Romish Ahriman.[57] Like Greg and Fitzgibbon, Mrs. Annie
Besant emphasized that *The Sight* represented "Roman Catholic *authorized* teaching" and scornfully examined excerpts from the passages given
in Greg to support her attack on the illogicality of eternal punishment.[58]
And the lasting effects of the imagery of Furniss, as well as its continuing diffusion, are suggested by a report of nearly twenty years later that
Mrs. Besant's denunciations of "the frightful immorality of . . . doctrines
about Hell have been hailed with enthusiastic plaudits from a large London audience."[59]

Neither Mrs. Besant nor Greg mentioned Pinamonti. However, Dean
Farrar did, both in the immensely popular *Eternal Hope* sermons, in their
twentieth printing by 1904, and in their longer sequel, *Mercy and Judgment* (1882), written in answer to Pusey's *What Is of Faith as to Everlasting
Punishment?* (1880) and still of value. In the former, as instances of the
"utterly untenable forcing of . . . metaphoric language" by popular hellfire
preachers, Farrar adduced an otherwise unidentified pamphlet of extracts
"from Pinamonti and Father Furniss (permissu superiorum) containing
passages too unutterably revolting, illustrated by woodcuts of such ab-
horrent atrocity, that even to look at them seemed to involve guilt." In
the latter book he reverted twice in the strongest terms to the "frightful
woodcuts of Pinamonti" and again warned the reader that it is *permissu
superiorum* ("two sad and startling words") that the "coarse ravings of a
vulgar imagination" in such "dreadful" tracts as *The Sight of Hell* are given

to the public.[60] One final reference from the 1880's is of particular interest, not as a critical assessment of *The Sight* ("this farrago of abominable and blasphemous trash") or as yet another anthologizing of the boiling boy and the red-hot oven, but for the arresting statement that *Hell Opened to Christians* by "the Jesuit Pinamonti" was "translated or adapted" by Furniss as *The Sight of Hell.* The Reverend Sir George W. Cox is partly in error here; *The Sight,* though clearly indebted to its predecessor, is based primarily on St. Frances of Rome's vision of the three levels of hell, and Furniss was not "also a member of the Society of Jesus."[61] Still, this faulty information would have been of interest to anyone whose curiosity had already been piqued by *The Sight.*

No further witnesses need be called upon to prove the conspicuousness of this work during the late Victorian debate over the scriptural basis for belief in a terminable and remedial punishment after death, the alleged paucity of the saved, and related issues. What is equally clear is that any-one acquainted—even indirectly—with the written or unwritten literature of these questions not only must have been introduced to Furniss' tract but must also have garnered an impression of it somewhat as follows: *The Sight of Hell* is the *ne plus ultra* among those crudely materialistic repre-sentations of tortures that are designed to terrify into obedience; its teach-ing is sanctioned by the Catholic church;[62] and behind it—perhaps even as its source—is a sinister work by an Italian Jesuit which, as we have seen, enjoyed an unsavory repute in Joyce's schooldays. From the references in *Ulysses,* it is plain that Joyce had heard of the eternal-punishment issues at least before the date of the Wandering Rocks; and, since it is difficult to imagine Father Castelein's *Le Rigorisme* cropping up in Zurich conversa-tions some twenty years after the book's publication, it is reasonable to infer that Joyce's knowledge of the question dates from a much earlier time (probably from his college years) and that his knowledge was more than superficial. And, if it was, then Father Furniss' *Sight of Hell* almost certainly formed part of it. True, Joyce might have been introduced to famous painters of hellfire by means of the sermons that were plentiful during his youth: "Just imagine a Mission," wrote a Catholic layman in sympathy with Mivart, "without a good orthodox sermon on Hell!"[63] Yet for all their "material fire of the most terrible description" that, according to this writer, formed the ordinary teaching of hell among Catholics, such sermons would hardly have dwelt upon the failure of modern critics to find everlasting damnation of the sinful or the unbaptized taught in the

Bible—which, after all, was the root principle of the entire liberal movement under discussion here and which Haines seems to allude to in *Ulysses*. It is interesting, however, that Father J. A. Cullen, S.J., spiritual father
at Belvedere and the probable original of Father Arnall, was noted for a
"lurid" style of sermon.[64] I know of no evidence that he ever employed
either of the two tracts in describing the punishment of sin, but it is told
that an 1849 mission conducted by two Jesuits who "dealt generously in
death and Hell-fire" had an immense effect on him and that Cullen himself remembered a presumably similar Redemptorist mission five years
later as the decisive event of his youth.[65] It would have been theatrically
appropriate had Father Furniss taken part in this second mission, as he
might have; but he did not. Most of his books, however, received their
imprimatur the following year, and their contents may have been known
to Furniss' associates who preached there. In any event, although actual
sermons heard by Joyce undoubtedly contributed much to the retreat episode, this does not rule out the likelihood of Joyce's firsthand knowledge
of writers on the larger hope. The indignation displayed in *Stephen Hero*
over "obscene, stinking hells" strongly resembles the tone of the more
outspoken denunciations of Furniss that have been reviewed. And this
feeling is surely the author's own, not that of a persona; its absence from
the *Portrait* is a measure of the increased distance between the later work's
protagonist and his creator and not a sign that the earlier attitude was a
Heroic pose or that the subject had faded from Joyce's mind.[66]

Joyce could have made little use of *The Sight*; its episodic lack of coherence and childish tone are equally unsuited to Joyce's preacher and to his
hearers. Its chief importance (if, as I think, he knew of it) lay in calling
his attention to Pinamonti's rigorous and vigorous analyses, whose effi-
ciency, force, and scientific precision have been noted by Father Merton.[67]
However, the problem of just how *Hell Opened to Christians* came into
Joyce's hands is ultimately of the same order as the question of whether
the retreat sermon of the *Portrait* corresponds to a particular event in the
author's life. Even if the latter question could be answered affirmatively,
this would not alter the fact that the correspondence between Joyce's and
Dedalus' lives is primarily an inward one. Joyce in the *Portrait* seeks a
local habitation (seldom a name) for stages in the self-realization of a
personality—one that he had largely left behind him by the time of writing. He is concerned with psychological and metaphorical appositeness of

event to thought and feeling rather than with literal accuracy in recording circumstances. Searching as he was for external correlatives of inward experience, he would and must have echoed George Moore's "Je prends mon bien où je le trouve"—from contemporary theological literature, from obscure Dublin bookstalls, even from hearsay. It is his "inspired cribbing," his gift for transforming such unwieldy material as *Hell Opened to Christians* into one of the most dramatic and effective portions of the novel, that makes examination of Joyce's sources worthwhile.[68]

Notes

1. Editions of Joyce's works cited in the text are: *A Portrait*, in *The Portable James Joyce*, ed. Harry Levin (New York: Viking, 1947); *Stephen Hero*, ed. Theodore Spencer (New York: New Directions, 1944); and *Ulysses* (New York: Modern Library, 1934). Permission of the publishers to quote from these editions is gratefully acknowledged.

2. James T. Farrell, *The League of Frightened Philistines* (New York, [1945]), pp. 51–52; Marvin Magalaner (with R. M. Kain), *Joyce: The Man, the Work, the Reputation* (New York, 1956), pp. 25, 114; W. Y. Tindall, *James Joyce* (New York and London, 1950), p. 9; Hugh Kenner, *Dublin's Joyce* (London, 1955), pp. 127, 128; W. T. Noon, S.J., "James Joyce and Catholicism," *James Joyce Review*, I (December, 1957), 13. With this last cf. *Catholic World*, CV (June, 1917), 395–97.

3. *Joyce among the Jesuits* (New York, 1958), pp. 36–37, 128–30, 138, 141–42. (Quoted by permission of Columbia University Press.)

4. *Silent Years* (New York, 1953), pp. 18–19; cf. *ibid.*, p. 152.

5. Percy Dearmer, *The Legend of Hell* (London, 1929), pp. 46–47.

6. Text in *Opere del padre Gio: Pietro Pinamonti della Compagnia di Gesù, con un breve Ragguaglio della sua vita. . . .* (Parma, 1706), pp. 295–311.

7. Frederic W. Farrar, *Eternal Hope* (New York, 1880), p. liii; cf. Dearmer, *Legend of Hell*, p. 11.

8. As Father Arnall explains, mortal sin has two aspects. Since the malice of the first consists in seeking forbidden satisfaction through the senses, it is punished through the senses. The pain of sense, strictly speaking, is fire; the other torments in Pinamonti and writers in this tradition are called "accidental." The far greater malice of sin's second aspect lies in the soul's abandoning of God, and this is punished with the far greater torment of the *poena damni* or eternal separation from God. This is the "core" of eternal punishment, and, although the fire is real, not metaphorical, no one can specify the exact nature of its action, as St. Augustine declared *(City of God* xx. 16).—Joseph Hontheim in *Catholic Encyclopedia* (1910), *s.v.* "Hell."

9. The corresponding sections are as follows. Pinamonti, Consideration I: *Portrait*, pp. 373–74, par. 1; II: p. 374, par. 2–p. 376, par. 1; III: p. 376, par. 2–p. 377, par. 2 *passim*; IV: p. 382, par. 2–p. 383, par. 1; V: p. 383, par. 2–p. 385, par. 2; VI: p. 385, par. 3–p. 386; VII: pp. 387–90 *passim*.

10. Arnall's reference to Ecclesiastes 7: 40 at the opening of the retreat (*Portrait,* p. 360) should be, of course, to Ecclesiasticus; and it might be inferred, assuming Joyce took these biblical references from *Hell Opened,* that here on page 381 he intended once more to satirize his preacher's learning, this time by changing the verse number given in Pinamonti. If so, he inadvertently achieved just the opposite effect. Both errors may have been mere slips of the pen. Yet in the first, oddly, Arnall's "Remember only thy last things" is almost the same as the translation of the verse in *Hell Opened* and quite different from "In all thy works remember thy last end, and thou shalt never sin" in the Douay Version, even though Joyce must have had to look up Pinamonti's incomplete reference (p. 4) to "Eccl. vii" in order to find the verse. And, if he did so, then both the "free" translation and the blunder of the first were probably deliberate on Joyce's part.

11. Sullivan, *Joyce among the Jesuits,* p. 141.

12. *Preparation for Death,* trans. Anonymous (Louisville, n.d.), pp. 224–27, 229, 237. Cf. *Portrait,* pp. 373–75, 382, 385.

13. Clement F. Rogers, *The Fear of Hell as an Instrument of Conversion* (London, 1939), esp. chaps. iv and v; E. B. Pusey, *What Is of Faith as to Everlasting Punishment?* (3d ed.; Oxford and London, 1881), pp. 172 ff.

14. G. G. Coulton, *Five Centuries of Religion,* I (Cambridge, 1923), esp. 29, 61, 70–73, 89, and Appendix II.

15. Tertullian *Apologeticus* xlvii; St. Gregory *Dialogues* xlii; *Summa Theol.,* Part III, Suppl., Q97, arts. iv and vii.

16. Tertullian, "Of Public Shows" xxx (cf. *Apologeticus* xlviii); St. Gregory *Dialogues* xxxi (cf. xxix–xxx, xxxvi, and *Moralia* xv); Bede *Ecclesiastical History* xii; Edwards, *Works* (New York, 1881), IV, 260–61. See also Augustine *City of God* xxi. 2–4; *Summa Theol.,* Part III, Suppl., Q97, arts. i, v, and vi; or even Robert Pollok, *The Course of Time* (Edinburgh, 1827), Book I, ll. 250–69.

17. St. Alphonsus Liguori, *Reflections on Spiritual Subjects,* trans. Anonymous (Boston, 1851), p. 114.

18. Lessius, *The Names of God . . .* [selections from *De perfectionibus*], trans. T. J. Campbell (New York, 1912), pp. 221–22; *Summa Theol.,* Part III, Suppl., Q98, arts. i, iv, and v.

19. Lib. xiii, cap. xxiv, xxix (text of *Opuscula* [Paris, 1881], I, 463, 509).

20. Taylor, *Works* (London, 1853), II, 390–93. Robert Gathorne-Hardy discusses this work's origins in *The Golden Grove,* ed. L. P. Smith (Oxford, 1930), p. 328.

21. *Obras escogidas,* ed. D. E. Zepeda-Henriquez (Madrid, 1957), II, 210, 214–15. *La Diferencia* was translated into Latin, Italian, and English.

22. *Think Well On't: or, Reflections on the Great Truths of the Christian Religion* (Derby, 1843), pp. 45–46. (First published in 1728.)

23. *Eternal Hope,* p. 67.

24. *Four [Considerations] on Eternity* [with works by Pinamonti and La Nuza], trans. Anonymous (London, 1877), p. 94. Manni's *La Prigione eterna dell' inferno* (1669), which I have not seen, is said to be similar to *Hell Opened to Christians* (St. George Mivart, *Nineteenth Century,* XXXII [December, 1892], 902).

25. *Preparation for Death,* p. 238; *Obras escogidas,* II, 24.

26. *Considerations of Drexelius upon Eternity,* trans. Ralph Winterton (London, 1689), p. 92. Cf. Nieremberg, *loc. cit.*

27. *Little Book of Eternal Wisdom,* trans. Anonymous (London, [1910]), p. 68. Coulton, Wright, Lecky, and others deal thoroughly with medieval ideas of future punishment; for recent times the best chart is Ezra Abbot's valuable bibliography appended to W. R. Alger's *Critical History of the Doctrine of a Future Life* (Philadelphia, 1864)—historically important, but often more exhortative than critical. Dearmer's important *Legend of Hell* is primarily a study of the scriptural basis of the belief.

28. "James Joyce and Catholicism," p. 13.

29. *Summa of the Christian Life,* trans. and ed. Jordan Aumaun (St. Louis and London, 1957), III, 347, 349.

30. E.g., the accounts of death and judgment in Pinamonti, *Opere,* pp. 151–52, 156–58, 262–63; Liguori, *Preparation for Death,* pp. 215–22; St. Francis of Sales, *Philothea or an Introduction to the Devout Life* (New York and London, [1923]), pp. 30, 32–33.

31. *Summa Theol.,* Part III, Suppl., Q94, art. iii.

32. Stanislaus Joyce, *My Brother's Keeper,* ed. Richard Ellmann (New York, 1958), pp. 80–82. See also *Stephen Hero,* p. 57, and Sullivan, *Joyce among the Jesuits,* pp. 36–37.

33. Coulton, *Five Centuries,* I, 445–49; Dearmer, *Legend of Hell,* pp. 59–61. Coulton's confusion of Castelein's book with F. X. Godts's (*op. cit.,* II, 665) is repeated by Dearmer (*op. cit.,* p. 59 n.).

34. "He throve on the smell / Of a horrible hell / That a Hottentot wouldn't believe in" (*Letters,* ed. Stuart Gilbert [New York, 1957], p. 102).

35. Writing in a friendly spirit, Lecky in 1865 described the main characteristic of modern Christianity as a "boundless philanthropy," even to the point of "effeminate sentimentality" (*History of the Rise and Influence of the Spirit of Rationalism in Europe* [rev. ed.; New York and London, 1925], I, 347–48). Cf. Charles Haddon Spurgeon, *Sermons* (New York, 1893–94), II, 264 (*ca.* 1857).

36. As in E. H. Plumptre, *The Spirits in Prison . . .* (New York, 1885), pp. 21–23.

37. *Theological Essays* (2d ed.; New York, 1854), p. 341.

38. G. W. Cox, *Life of John William Colenso* (London, 1888), I, 47–48, 149.

39. *Ten Weeks in Natal* (Cambridge, 1855), pp. 252–53; *St. Paul's Epistle to the Romans . . .* (New York, 1863), pp. 164–85, 198.

40. E.g., *Christian Observer,* LXII (1862), 940.

41. *Everlasting Punishment* (Oxford and London, 1864), p. 15. Cf. Spurgeon, *Sermons,* I, 313; II, 275–76.

42. Lecky, *Rationalism,* I, 338.

43. [Richard J.(?) Clarke], "Eternal Punishment and Eternal Love," *The Month,* XLIV (January, 1882), 15.

44. Nicholas Walsh, S.J., *The Comparative Number of the Saved and the Lost* (Dublin, 1899), p. 106.

45. Augustine F. Hewitt, "Ignis aeternus," *Catholic World,* LVII (1893), 19, 24.

46. "Happiness in Hell," *Nineteenth Century,* XXXII (December, 1892), 902, 916–18;

"Last Words on the Happiness in Hell: A Rejoinder," *ibid.*, XXXIII (April, 1893), 646–48. Mivart's dissatisfactions led finally to his break with ecclesiastical authority and subsequent excommunication.

47. "Everlasting Punishment," *Dublin Review*, V (3d ser., 1881), 137–38.

48. T[homas] Livius, C.SS.R., *Father Furniss and His Work for Children* (London, etc., 1896), p. 58.

49. *The Sight of Hell* (Dublin and London, n.d.), pp. 3–4, 6–9, 13–17.

50. *God and His Creatures* (the collected edition of the *Books* [London, 1864]), pp. 162–64, 323–27.

51. *Sight of Hell*, pp. 17–18, 20–21. Furniss also wrote *God Loves Little Children*.

52. Livius, *Father Furniss*, pp. 114, 139, 168.

53. *Ibid.*, pp. 101, 116, 171.

54. Annie Besant, *On Eternal Torture* (London, [1874]), p. 3.

55. *History of European Morals from Augustus to Charlemagne* (5th ed.; London, 1882), II, 223–24, n. 2. Lecky appears to have modified his opinion of 1865. See above, n. 42.

56. *Enigmas of Life* (Boston, 1875), pp. 267–69 n.

57. Fitzgibbon's overstatements and inaccuracies drew a singularly inept reply from T. E. Bridgett, C.SS.R., reprinted in his *Blunders and Forgeries* (London, 1890), pp. 114–56.

58. *On Eternal Torture*, pp. 7–8.

59. Mivart, "Last Words on the Happiness in Hell," p. 646.

60. *Eternal Hope*, p. liii; *Mercy and Judgment* (2d ed.; London, 1882), pp. 106–7, 136.

61. *Life of John William Colenso*, I, 158–59.

62. Cf. *Stephen Hero*, p. 232: "they believe in the infallibility of the Pope and in all his obscene, stinking hells."

63. H. McCann, in *The Tablet*, LXXXI (February 18, 1893), 258.

64. Sullivan, *Joyce among the Jesuits*, 128–29.

65. Lambert McKenna, S.J., *Life and Work of Rev. James Aloysius Cullen* (London, 1924), pp. 13–14, 34, 97.

66. One final point suggests that Joyce knew *The Sight of Hell*. We have seen that the bird carrying away the sandhill of eternity a grain at a time is a stock image. Father Arnall makes an extended use of it; Pinamonti, however, ignores it. But the bird appears in one of Furniss' hyperboles as part of a strikingly ill-reasoned illustration: "Think of a great solid iron ball, larger than the Heavens and the earth. A bird comes once in a hundred millions of years and just touches the great iron ball with a feather of its wing. Think that you have to burn in a fire till the bird has worn the great iron ball away with its feather. Is this Eternity? No" (p. 24).

67. *The Seven Storey Mountain* (New York, 1948), p. 211.

68. Richard Ellmann, Introduction to *My Brother's Keeper* by Stanislaus Joyce, p. xv.

5

Joyce and the Artist's Fingernails

S. L. GOLDBERG

One of the best-known passages in *A Portrait of the Artist as a Young Man* is that in which Stephen Dedalus brings his aesthetic theory to a resounding conclusion. Having expounded his views on Beauty and Art, he turns to what he calls the natural aesthetic 'forms': the lyrical, the epical, and the dramatic. The first is directly personal, emotional and unselfconscious; in the epical the personality of the artist expresses itself in a narrative that flows around his characters and action.

The dramatic form is reached when the vitality which has flowed and eddied round each person fills every person with such vital force that he or she assumes a proper and intangible aesthetic life. The personality of the artist, at first a cry or a cadence or a mood and then a fluid and lambent narrative, finally refines itself out of existence, impersonalizes itself, so to speak. The aesthetic image in the dramatic form is life purified in and reprojected from the human imagination. The mystery of aesthetic, like that of material creation, is accomplished. The artist, like the God of creation, remains within or behind or beyond or above his handiwork, invisible, refined out of existence, indifferent, paring his fingernails.[1]

All kinds of critical sermons have been preached on this text, from denunciations of Ireland to denunciations of I. A. Richards, but even in the more humdrum context of Joyce's own work it has a special interest—if only because, being so obviously a pointer to his artistic direction and so unobtrusively ambiguous, what the reader makes of it is usually an index of what he makes of Joyce's art itself. And in fact it is impossible to grasp what Joyce meant by impersonal, dramatic art without also understanding what it means in his actual practice, and especially in his central achievement, *Ulysses*.

*   *   *

S. L. Goldberg, "Joyce and the Artist's Fingernails," *Review of English Literature* 2 (1961): 59–73. All efforts to find current rights holder have been unsuccessful.

Leaving aside Joyce's more pious readers who are evidently so overcome by the image of a non-existent God indifferently paring his fingernails that they cannot follow what Stephen says, there are three very popular misconceptions of his meaning.

The simplest is that of the plain, blunt technician, to whom the most important fact about Joyce is his use of the stream of consciousness, and to whom the novel is impersonal and dramatic when it manages to dispense with the 'omniscient narrator' in favor of direct representation by dialogue, narration by a character, the stream of consciousness, and so on. As he sees it, Stephen is foreshadowing Joyce's technical achievement in *Ulysses* and *Finnegans Wake*, where he tells his story without appearing to tell it at all; the novelist paring his fingernails is really boasting, 'Look! no hands!'

A more common interpretation is that Joyce is advocating such a complete impartiality or neutrality of moral attitude as amounts to indifference—a sort of super-Flaubertian Realism. The impersonal novelist is he who portrays life with the implacable objectivity of a recording angel; apart from that, he simply shrugs his shoulders or pares his nails. To express opinions about morality, to make judgments, is not his business. And was it not Joyce who replied, when his brother wanted to discuss Fascism, 'Don't talk to me about politics. I'm only interested in style'?[2] Many readers find this same attitude, seasoned with a mistrustful distaste of mankind, typical of all his work. To some it is a matter for rather naive approval, to others for indignant rejection; but in either case they see Joyce, intent on his fingernails, coldly withdrawn from the dust and heat of ordinary mortality.

A third group of critics (mainly American by birth and Roman Catholic by persuasion) offer a more subtle and in some ways more plausible view. Joyce is a Realist, they agree, but one whose apparent indifference is only ironic, a tactic by which to parody and expose the absence of values in the world he so aloofly portrays. And Stephen is part of that world. When he maintains that the artist must avoid moral judgments, he only betrays his crippling self-conceit, his futile Aestheticism, for Joyce, his creator, saw that the most realistic and impersonal picture of modern life is that which demonstrates its infinite distance at every point from a real, impersonal spiritual order and a real, impersonal moral code. What makes him a great artist, indeed, is that while he looks as if he is paring his fingernails, he is really wielding a spiritual scalpel.

Each of these views obviously has something to recommend it, for each of them does point to some aspect of Joyce's work. On the other hand, each one of them in its own way also provokes the same uneasy doubt: if that is all Joyce means theoretically, if that is all his work means imaginatively, is that the kind of moral intelligence of which vital and significant novels are made? Is not his work perhaps richer, dramatically and morally, than some of his admirers think?

Joyce certainly made no bones about moral and social judgments in his first book, *Dubliners*, for all its naturalistic Realism. It was not his fault, he wrote to Grant Richards, that 'the odour of ashpits and old weeds and offal hangs round my stories. I seriously believe that [by suppressing the book] you will retard the course of civilization in Ireland by preventing the Irish people from having a good look at themselves in my nicely polished looking-glass.'³ *Dubliners*, in fact, is the book that really does fit the parodic-Realism view of his work; and it is quite apparent from *Stephen Hero* (which is probably more accurate *historically* than its final 'version' as the *Portrait*) that the young Joyce did start off with just such a conception of his art in mind. He would dissociate himself from the joyless, priest-ridden materialism of Ireland; he would 'vivisect' its decay; he would reveal it as an Inferno that parodied Dante's; and in some way, he felt, by expressing his own nature freely and fully, he would 'bring to the world the spiritual renewal which the poet brings to it.'⁴ The young man clearly took his moral purposes as an artist very seriously indeed; equally clearly, however, he was much more definite—and excited—about what he rejected than about his proposed 'spiritual renewal.' For all his proclamations about the moral force of art, a work like *Stephen Hero*, or any work conceived in the same purely critical and negative spirit, could hardly embody a vital and positive vision of life. Realism of that kind represented a dead-end. And it is Joyce's dawning realization of this, I believe, that lies behind Stephen's theory of 'dramatic' art in the *Portrait*.

Not all the confusion about his meaning is the critics.' In the course of his discussion Stephen himself seems to shift between three different, though related, ideas. The first is the simple difference between different literary *genres*: lyric, narrative, and drama. The second is the difference between progressively complex attitudes to life and the art-forms they require for expression. Certain *modes* of art—the drama and novel most notably—ideally express, not pure subjective emotion or even personal judgments *about* life, but rather a vision *of* life, which is objective in the sense that we cannot separate the artist's 'attitudes' from our sense of his work as a reflection (though not necessarily a naturalistic reflection, of course) of life as it 'really is.' This impersonal mode of art is only possible, Stephen implies, when the artist's 'attitude' embodied in the work has grown so complex, so self-aware, so mature that it demands a specific and searching image of reality for its expression, which it shapes and orders as a pervasively informing presence. He calls this kind of art 'dramatic' only by analogy, however. Drama is the *genre* in which the author must express his meaning in and through a projected image of a common reality, but the particular conventions of the *genre* are not necessary to Stephen's mode. Thus a work in any form might fit his description: a lyric like 'O Western Wind' hardly answers, but what of such impersonally mature 'lyrics' as 'Dejection: An Ode' or 'Sailing to Byzantium'? Nevertheless, Stephen also implies that 'dramatic' art is the best, so that in addition to these descriptive distinctions he also entangles a third—a normative one. Only in the 'dramatic' mode, apparently, do the characters and action assume 'a proper and intangible aesthetic life.' This now suggests that 'epical' art is only an imperfect version of 'dramatic,' and imperfect because not self-subsistent, integral, self-explanatory, impersonally meaningful without necessary reference outside it to the peculiar situation and characteristics of its maker. In general, therefore, Stephen is speaking only of the artist as artist, and suggesting that the artist's 'attitudes' or values are what project and at the same time inform his image of life, that it is ultimately *their* meaningful rhythm, *their* enactment, not the artist's ordinary personality or that of an assumed narrator, that is like a divine Providence moving behind yet within his work. All this has nothing whatever to do with naively naturalistic objections to the 'omniscient narrator' in the novel; omniscience is implicit in the very convention of third-person narration, and the demand for 'dramatic' realization of values in the novel is based on an analogy with the drama deeper than the merely technical. In the end, this aspect of Stephen's theory is really the invocation of a principle that applies to all art: that style and technique be organically related to the 'subject,' so that all together make one total and impersonal articulation. This was the lesson that Joyce, like Henry James, was one of the first novelists to learn from Flaubert. Nor, we might notice, is there any suggestion in Stephen's theory that narrative 'point of view' (or any other device for that matter) is anything but a conventional medium for moral point of view. When we examine Joyce's use of it in *Ulysses*, for example, we find that the stream of consciousness marks no essential difference from say, James's use of it. Both novelists make us participate in their characters' point of view, and when they need to supplement it or qualify it or endorse it, they both abandon it for 'omniscient' narration. In the matter of technique, just as Stephen merely reaffirms the basic principles of the craft of fiction, so Joyce the novelist, for all his virtuosity, punctiliously observes them.

Nothing illustrates Stephen's theory in all its aspects better than a comparison between *Stephen Hero* (which Joyce abandoned about 1906) and *Ulysses* (written between 1914 and 1921). There are a number of passages in the early book that Joyce obviously reworked for the later one—the account of the citizen who later became the central figure of the 'Cyclops' episode, for example, and Stephen's critical attitude to the Irreconcilables which later became the dramatic form and substance of the whole episode. An even more interesting case, however, is the funeral of Stephen's young sister, some of the very phrases of which were later incorporated in the 'Hades' episode of *Ulysses*. Here is part of the early account:

At the mortuary chapel Mr. Dedalus and his friends had to wait until the poor mourners had first been served. In a few minutes the service was over and Isabel's coffin was carried up and laid on the bier. The mourners scattered in the seats and knelt timidly on their handkerchiefs. A priest with a great toad-like belly balanced to one side came out of the sacristy, followed by an altar boy. He read the service rapidly in a croaking voice and shook the aspergill drowsily over the coffin, the boy piping responses at intervals. When he had read the service he closed the book, crossed himself, and made back for the sacristy at a swinging gait. Labourers came in and bore out the coffin to a barrow and pushed it along the gravel-path. The superintendent of the cemetery shook hands with Mr. Dedalus at the door of the chapel and followed the funeral slowly. The coffin slid evenly into the grave and the grave-diggers began to shovel in the earth. At the sound of the first clods Mr. Dedalus began to sob and one of his friends came to his side and held his arm . . .

[When the returning funeral stops at a pub, the drivers of the carriages are called in to share the second drink.] They all chose pints and indeed their own bodily tenements were not unlike hardly used pewter measures. The mourners drank small specials for the most part. Stephen, when asked what he would drink, answered at once:

—A pint—

His father ceased talking and began to regard him with great attention, but Stephen, feeling too cold-hearted to be abashed, received
his pint very seriously and drank it off in a long draught. While his
head was beneath the tankard he was conscious of his startled father
and felt the savour of the bitter clay of the graveyard sharp in his
throat.

The inexpressively mean way in which his sister had been buried
inclined Stephen to consider rather seriously the claims of water and
fire to be the last homes of dead bodies. The entire apparatus of the
State seemed to him at fault from its first to its last operation. No
young man can contemplate the fact of death with extreme satisfaction and no young man, specialized by fate or her step-sister chance
for an organ of sensitiveness and intellectiveness, can contemplate
the network of falsities and trivialities which make up the funeral of
a dead burgher without extreme disgust.[5]

Although the observation, as always in *Stephen Hero*, is as engagingly
direct as the animosity, it is all too obvious why Joyce abandoned a novel
in this vein. For example, the painstakingly 'objective' description of the
funeral and the hero's moral judgment on it fall so promptly apart that
Stephen's reflections, when they arrive, come like an unexpected slap on
the ear: nothing about the funeral itself seems to warrant so violent a
reaction to it. Even more embarrassing, however, is the judgment on Stephen himself: again, nothing about his 'rather serious' reflections seems
to require the conclusion that he is a specialized organ of sensitivity and
intelligence. The apparent difference between the author's sense of his
hero and ours only causes us to wonder if Joyce is not being ironical at
Stephen's expense, to search for a possible subtlety. Unfortunately, nothing in *Stephen Hero* resolves the doubt; the tone is almost uniformly flat-
tering to Stephen. (It is perhaps significant that Joyce is able, within the
space of two pages, to speak of his hero's 'complex radiance of thought'
and his 'ingenuous arrogance,' to present him as a 'wholehearted young
egoist' but not an 'inhuman theorist,' although in no case does the judgment seem unquestionably apt.[6]) We are inevitably driven outside the
book to try to discover how seriously Joyce meant us to take him. Exactly
the same difficulty arises with another of his works, the play, *Exiles*. It has

recently become fashionable to discover profound ironies in his treatment of its hero, Richard Rowan, and subtle metaphysical meanings in
what the somewhat stiff, factitious dialogue and action do *not* express.
The only alternative to supposing such unlikely—or at least undemon-
strable—meanings in the work is that the author has failed to make us
share his valuation of his hero, that, while he could criticize Rowan for
some of his faults, he could not see those his creature most intimately
shared with his creator. It is perhaps significant that in both *Stephen Hero*
and *Exiles* the hero's intellectual genius is an essential—and totally unac-
ceptable—premise of the work; in both cases, the work itself seems to be
precisely the kind that his own hero would write. In other words, though
one is a narrative and the other a play, Stephen's account of 'epical' art fits
them like a glove: in both the author's personality merely flows round
the action; the characters in both fail to achieve a proper and intangible
aesthetic life of their own. The shaping values, which ought to stand in
the maturity of self-examination, of a full sense of the complexities of life,
patently do not.

The case is very different with the *Portrait of the Artist*, of course, but to
see Joyce's art at its most richly 'dramatic' we must turn to *Ulysses*, and the
'Hades' episode offers a characteristic, though not exhaustive, example.

In the first place, Paddy Dignam's funeral is dramatically rendered and
evaluated not through the consciousness of an incredibly super-sensitive
young man, but through that of an ordinarily sensitive and intelligent burgher. We, as readers, participate in Leopold Bloom's view of the funeral,
not simply learning of 'objective' details through his registration of them,
but also perceiving the significance of those details in the context of the
other experiences he brings to bear upon them. The second difference
from the art of *Stephen Hero*, however, is that we also see *through* Bloom's
consciousness as well. At various points in the chapter the narrative 'point
of view' shifts so as to reveal Bloom as himself one of the 'objective' elements of the situation, with a significance in it that, ironically, only we can
appreciate. The observer is himself 'placed.' Nevertheless, there is no sharp
discontinuity between his sense of the funeral and ours. The actual effect
of our shifting viewpoint is less to satirize Bloom than to qualify him
and, finally, to *endorse* his moral consciousness, limited though it is, as a
fit vehicle for our own. Indeed, the structure of the 'Hades' chapter—like
that of the book itself—could be said to be the dramatic affirmation of

Bloom and the essential human virtues he embodies. Two little episodes, the very beginning and the very end of the chapter, mark the progress in his position. On both occasions he is snubbed. He is the last invited into the funeral carriage before it sets off; he is obviously the outsider:

> Martin Cunningham, first, poked his silkhatted head into the creaking carriage and, entering deftly, seated himself. Mr. Power stepped in after him, curving his height with care.
> —Come on, Simon.
> —After you, Mr. Bloom said.
> Mr. Dedalus covered himself quickly and got in, saying:
> —Yes, yes.
> —Are we all here now? Martin Cunningham asked. Come along Bloom.[7]

At the end he is snubbed more violently. He notices that the pompously respectable lawyer, Mr. Menton, whose attitude to himself he pithily describes as 'hate at first sight', has dented his hat:

> Got a dinge in the side of his hat. Carriage probably.
> —Excuse me, sir, Mr. Bloom said beside them.
> They stopped.
> —Your hat is a little crushed, Mr. Bloom said, pointing.
> John Henry Menton stared at him for an instant without moving.
> —There, Martin Cunningham helped, pointing also.
> John Henry Menton took off his hat, bulged out the dinge and smoothed the nap with care on his coatsleeve. He clapped the hat on his head again.
> —It's all right now, Martin Cunningham said.
> John Henry Menton jerked his head down in acknowledgement.
> —Thank you, he said shortly.
> They walked on towards the gates. Mr. Bloom, chapfallen, drew behind a few paces so as not to overhear. Martin laying down the law. Martin could wind a sappyhead like that round his little finger without his seeing it.
> Oyster eyes. Never mind. Be sorry after perhaps when it dawns on him. Get the pull over him that way.
> Thank you. How grand we are this morning.[8]

The similarity of the two situations only underlines the difference: the devastating finality with which Bloom's silent comment places Menton and all he represents. Against the backdrop of eternity, it is Bloom whose dignity is genuine and inviolable, who has, and deserves to have, the last word. This is a moral authority he has accumulated over the course of the chapter; and it may suggest, perhaps, how the structure of Joyce's art, far from a static pattern of 'symbols' and 'leitmotifs' as it is commonly supposed, is actually a poetic action, a development of moral awareness—Bloom's in the first instance, ours in the last—in which characters, events, setting, symbols, and techniques are all finally absorbed.

By focusing the various themes enacted in the chapter as whole, Bloom's thoughts constitute the setting in which Dignam's funeral is judged. He notes an old woman peering through a curtain at the funeral ('glad to see us go we give them so much trouble coming'), or Dedalus senior, ageing, 'full of his son,' and remembers his own children; he observes the deadness of a passing street, a house where a murder was committed, the lack of vitality in people and places; and as he does so, both Dignam's death and his own unfolding attitudes towards it gradually assume a richer significance in the contexts his observations project: the continual cycle of life and death, the creeping paralysis of age and decay, the paralysis of Ireland, and the ineluctable isolation of the individual in life as in death.

For about the first half of the chapter Bloom is himself rather more the object of our attention than what he observes or thinks. In part he seems the representative of the universal condition of his society: as each of his fellow mourners is cut off from the others by his private troubles, and cut off, too, from real family life, so Bloom is still further isolated from the rest by his race, his notorious cuckoldry, and his father's suicide. All through *Ulysses* Bloom is qualified by the pathos of his spiritual isolation, placed by our compassion as Dignam is by his. Yet part of his integrity lies in his utter lack of either self-importance or self-pity, and this is subtly played off against the attitude of his companions and his society. When old Dedalus, for example, rages in egotistical violence against his son, Bloom silently judges him, accurately but with sympathy: 'noisy selfwilled man. Full of his son. He is right . . . '[9] Or again, when the others exchange conventionalities about suicide, it is Bloom who realizes what it really involves of loneliness and pain. As the funeral progresses, Bloom's compassion for his companions, for children, for people down on their luck, for animals, and for Dignam and Dignam's family plays with increasing force against empty-hearted conventionality and the feeble heart of the city through which he passes. In short, it is he who registers the decay all round him, and realizes—in the sense that includes *exhibits*—at least something of the vitality it lacks.

This is especially so in the second half of the chapter. Once the funeral reaches the cemetery, Bloom's consciousness unmistakably becomes both the central arena of the action and the agent bringing diverse experience together and infusing it with form and value. The texture of his monologue grows denser, subtler, ranging more freely as it develops the implications of the earlier section. His thoughts continually turn from death to life, always perceiving one in relation to the other, and sharply antiseptic to the excesses of self-indulgent grief. The meaning of Dignam's burial emerges from his somber meditations—upon the constant renewal of life, for instance, as he ponders the graveyard-keeper's sexual vigor; or upon the widowed Queen Victoria at last abandoning grief for her Consort: 'her son was the substance. Something new to hope for not like the past she wanted back, waiting. It never comes. One must go first: alone under the ground: and lie no more in her warm bed.' At the open grave he suddenly thinks, 'If we were all suddenly somebody else.' Among the insidiously sentimental 'stone hopes' of the graveyard, 'old Ireland's hearts and hands' paralyzed in eternal and useless grief, he perceives the waste; garlands of bronzefoil, as he observes, mean less than real flowers that live and die.[10]

Towards the religious aspects of the funeral (including the same toad's-belly priest as appeared in *Stephen Hero*, incidentally), Bloom's attitude is completely skeptical, but it is not quite the same as Stephen's was. Bloom is a pagan, no doubt, but neither stupid nor superficial. His naturalism permits him to recognize that, however conventional the gestures of the priest and congregation, 'he has to say something'; death requires more than 'shovelling them under doublequick.' Yet 'once you are dead you are dead'—the heart, 'seat of affections,' is truly broken, and we must live as best we can even by the 'love that kills.'[11]

The climax of the whole chapter is preceded by Bloom's sight of a well-fed rat among the graves, the main significance of which is precisely the unnerving horror he does *not* feel (and which some of his theologically sounder critics think he should). For Bloom to 'accept life' on the conditions he does, he must also accept the rat: it has a final, demonstrative necessity. By looking it in the face without panic, he assumes a qualified but genuine authority:

> The gates glimmered in front: still open. Back to the world again. Enough of this place. Brings you a bit nearer every time. Last time I was here was Mrs. Sinico's funeral. Poor papa too. The love that kills. And even scraping up the earth at night with a lantern like that case I read of to get at fresh buried females or even putrefied with running gravesores. Give you the creeps after a bit. I will appear to you after death. You will see my ghost after death. My ghost will haunt you after death. There is another world after death named hell. I do not like that other world she wrote. No more do I. Plenty to see and hear and feel yet. Feel live warm beings near you. Let them sleep in their maggoty beds. They are not going to get me this innings. Warm beds: warm fullblooded life.[12]

Though there are obvious ironies in Bloom's failure to achieve that warm full-blooded life, he is never mean, never hostile to life.

After this passage, the narrative point of view once again leaves Bloom's for the more 'objective' rendering of the Menton episode. Bloom's attitudes have been established, related to those of others, commented on by silent juxtapositions, explored and placed; we have increasingly participated in his sense of the funeral. Now, at the end, we see him again in relation to others, and the shift is the means by which our response is crystallized: the 'omniscient' view swings behind Bloom's so that we cannot distinguish one from the other. The moral values of character and artist—with all qualifications granted—here converge. The art speaks impersonally, but only the more subtly and eloquently for that.

*   *   *

Obviously, Stephen's description of 'dramatic' art posits an artistic detachment of some kind or other. As I have suggested, many critics would define it as that characteristic of *Finnegans Wake*, taking the *Portrait* and *Ulysses* as its 'lyrical' and 'epical' forebears. A moment's reflection might suggest the improbability of so programmatic an interpretation, but only a critical reading of Joyce's work can reveal its falsity. Apart from anything else, drama depends on the artist's maintaining a middle position towards his material, a mixture of involvement and detachment. With too close an involvement, his work becomes lyrical (or at most 'epical'); with too great a detachment, he begins to seek an impossible holism, to try—whether in the belief that whatever is is right or whatever is is wrong—to portray everything that is simply because it is. And in a work of art where *everything* can be included, as in *Finnegans Wake*, drama gives way to an abstract, substantially unreal dialectic. Properly speaking, both the *Portrait* and *Ulysses*, although in different ways, are Joyce's dramatic works.

Like other heroes of dramatic art, Bloom serves his author's meaning both as dramatic agent and dramatic image. In 'Cyclops,' for instance, his blundering but very relevant stand for Love against hatred and violence, just because it is founded in his very person and actions, measures the citizen's attitudes, and does so far more effectively than the denunciations of *Stephen Hero*, even though the debasement of the language of politics— which is also the language Bloom must use—can be rendered only by the gigantic parodies that envelop the scene. Those critics who suppose that Joyce is simply parodying the whole of modern life will have it, nevertheless, that Bloom's 'sentimentality' fares no better than the citizen's *realpolitik*; both, in their view, are ruthlessly parodied, just as sexiness is parodied in 'Nausicaa' or the clichés of communication in 'Eumaeus' and the mechanized chaos of modern society in the book as a whole. Similarly, with 'Hades,' they see Joyce savagely exposing Bloom's complete unconsciousness of any Christian significance in the death and burial of Paddy Dignam, and the spiritual barrenness of the society his unconsciousness represents. To them, the world of *Ulysses* is a static Inferno inhabited by lost souls incapable of real moral action. Certainly that it is one way of looking at modern life. In all its essentials—its spiritual absolutism, its transcendental disgust, and its fundamental incapacity for *dramatic* expression—it is the way the protagonist of *Stephen Hero* looks at it. Yet *Ulysses*, however subtle its symbolism, however elaborate its parodies, and however much spiritual implication may be found in them, is as a whole surely more compassionate, and more vitally dramatic, than a vast symbolic machine motivated only by a consuming hostility to all the emptiness and misery of mass industrial society. Its hero and its ironies are rather more complex than that.

Even as a political image, Bloom never becomes merely a stock-figure of intellectual debate. Joyce was not the man to subscribe to any particular creed or platform, of course; when he turned his hand to journalism in Trieste, he still viewed politics as a moralist, deeply skeptical, despite his intense patriotism, of 'those big words that make us so unhappy.' All through *Ulysses* (and especially in 'Circe') he steers his hero between the twin temptations of social complacency and bourgeois idealism, between the blind passions of self-interest and self-immolation, quietly vindicating the small words in which sanity and moral freedom are to be found. Their incarnation is the unlikely figure of Bloom, humble, confused, yet within his limits critical and integrate. Clearly, no one knew better than Joyce that a society of Blooms would not be the New Jerusalem, but, as Bloom says to the citizen, he is not talking about the New Jerusalem, he is talking about injustice. The structure of 'Hades' is typical of *Ulysses* as a whole: the dramatic tension derives from the interplay of what Bloom makes of his world and what Joyce—and we—make of Bloom, yet the fact that it is an interplay, not a simple contradiction, is what generates the deepest and most complex irony in Joyce's vision of life: although as a dramatic image Bloom is the hapless victim of his society, as a dramatic agent he also remains outside it—partly because he is excluded by it, but partly because he possesses the moral vitality fairly to judge it.

The effect of his freedom is to add a necessary dimension to his world. He represents both the general condition and the irreducible surd, the complicating factor; to explore him fully Joyce needed both the resources of a sophisticated, analytic realism and the deeper, affirmative images of myth. Joyce's achievement, in fact, was to portray and place him, deeply compromised as he is, without degrading him into a Bovary, or a Babbitt, or a Kipps, or a sentimental, Chaplinesque 'little man.' It hardly needs saying that such understanding and respect were beyond the artist as a young man. Yet although Joyce's concern with 'dramatic' art is sometimes interpreted as a retreat from life, it was on the contrary part of his attempt to come more closely and more profoundly to grips with reality—a reality that included himself. Where his early 'objectivity' and 'realism,' harboring a bitter but unexamined hostility, could express only the ambiguity of his personal attitudes, we might say of *Ulysses* what he himself said of Ibsen's work: to the torment of its critics, it reflects the obscurity of life like a mirror.

*   *   *

We are indebted to the following for permission to reproduce material from the works of James Joyce: Jonathan Cape Ltd. for *A Portrait of the Artist as a Young Man* and *Stephen Hero* and The Bodley Head Ltd. for *Ulysses*.

Notes

1. *A Portrait of the Artist as a Young Man*, 1942, pp. 244–5.

2. Quoted by Richard Ellmann in his introduction to Stanislaus Joyce, *My Brother's Keeper*, 1958, p. 23.

3. *Letters of James Joyce*, ed. Stuart Gilbert, 1957, pp. 63–64.

4. *Stephen Hero*, 1944, pp. 25, 129–30, 141, 165, 171; and *passim*.

5. *Ibid*, pp. 149–50.

6. *Ibid*, pp. 109–10.

7. *Ulysses*, 1937, p. 79.

8. *Ibid*, p. 107.

9. *Ibid*, p. 107.

10. *Ibid*, pp. 99–101, 94, 102, 105.

11. *Ibid*, pp. 96, 107.

12. *Ibid*, pp. 106–7.

6

The Meditative Structure of Joyce's *Portrait*

THOMAS F. VAN LAAN

Students of James Joyce's *A Portrait of the Artist as a Young Man* owe a great debt to James R. Thrane and Elizabeth F. Boyd, whose independent studies have shown quite conclusively that the hell-fire sermons in Chapter Three result from inspired cribbing of Giovanni Pietro Pinamonti's *L'Inferno aperto*, called *Hell Opened to Christians* in its nineteenth-century English translation.[1] The parallel passages and the analyses of Joyce's changes provide valuable insights to his artistic procedure. Equally important, however, is the concrete demonstration of Joyce's thorough familiarity with the tradition of meditation derived from Ignatius Loyola's *Spiritual Exercises,* for it is the Ignatian system which gives form to Pinamonti's work as well as to Stephen's "old neglected book written by Saint Alphonsus Liguori" and numerous other tracts which, as these articles show, Joyce apparently knew.[2] Since Joyce, as a member of the Catholic Church under the charge of Jesuit priests, undoubtedly practiced the Ignatian system of meditation until it was deeply ingrained upon his consciousness, and since in writing the *Portrait* he made deliberate use of works based on this system, it seems evident that a full consideration of the nature of the Jesuit spiritual exercise might shed even further light on the novel and on Joyce's artistry in general.

The Ignatian spiritual exercises provide a coherent system of meditation for approximately one month of extremely intensive internal analysis.[3] Ignatius arranges the exercises in four "weeks": (1) meditations on sin designed "to reform what has been deformed by sin"; (2) meditations on the life of Christ up to Palm Sunday designed "to make what is thus reformed conform to the Divine model, Jesus"; (3) meditations on the

Thomas F. Van Laan, "The Meditative Structure of Joyce's *Portrait*," *James Joyce Quarterly* 1 (Spring 1964): 3–13. Reprinted with permission from *James Joyce Quarterly*. Copyright 1964.

Passion designed "to strengthen what thus conforms"; and (4) meditations on the Resurrection and Ascension designed "to transform by love the already strengthened resolutions."[4] The one recurrent feature of these meditations is the pattern of the individual exercise.[5] This pattern, consisting of some preparatory material, the meditation proper, and a colloquy, can be most readily explained by using Joyce's borrowed passages as illustrative material, even though these passages represent public sermon rather than private meditation. Father Arnall's preliminary talk (pp. 108–111) explains the purpose of the retreat, but its basic intention lies in such words as these: "I will ask you therefore, my dear boys, to put away from your minds during these few days all worldly thoughts, whether of study or pleasure or ambition, and to give all your attention to the state of your souls" (p. 110). His request corresponds to the opening prayer of the Ignatian exercise, in which the exerciser seeks grace for the proper performance of his meditation. Following this prayer comes the first prelude, or composition of place, in which the exerciser must imagine himself as concretely situated in the very spot where the event of his meditation occurred, or if the exercise is devoted to a particular sin, he must establish in his consciousness a vividly realized setting appropriate to the sin under consideration. The almost excessively vivid and concrete sermons on Judgment Day and hell precisely fulfill this requirement, and the priest later explicitly refers to the second of these as a "composition of place" (p. 127). In the second prelude, the exerciser asks God to grant him a desire in keeping with the subject matter of the meditation, so that, for example, if the subject is a particular sin, he will feel shame for having committed that sin. An appropriate request concludes the sermon on hell: "I pray fervently to God that not a single soul of those who are in this chapel today may be found among those miserable beings whom the Great Judge shall command to depart for ever from His sight. . . ." (p. 124). Then follows the meditation proper, in which the exerciser thoroughly examines the nature of his subject in an attempt to reach full understanding, a step which Joyce fulfills in the evening sermon with its intention to "consider for a few moments the nature of the spiritual torments of hell" (p. 127). In the Ignatian system the meditation proper is usually divided into three or five points, which explains Father Arnall's division of the spiritual torments into the pains of loss, conscience, extension, intensity, and eternity. The last significant step in the regular exercise is the colloquy, in which the exerciser speaks directly to God, to Christ, to the Virgin, or to all three in turn, "exactly as one friend speaks to another, or as a servant speaks to a master, now asking him for a favor, now blaming himself for some misdeed, now making known his affairs to him, and seeking advice in them."[6] In Joyce this colloquy is fulfilled by the priest and the boys repeating the act of contrition in versicle and response. The full exercise then concludes with a *Pater Noster*, but Joyce omits it from his sequence.

Louis Martz and Helen Gardner have shown the capacity of this pattern to influence secular literature, especially the work of John Donne and other poets who belong to what Martz has called the meditative tradition;[7] it would therefore not be unusual to find the Ignatian system exerting an influence on the *Portrait* even beyond that already indicated by source study. Nor should one expect to find, in tracing such influence, a rigorous imitation of the exercise. Although Joyce's borrowed passages conform to the original pattern, variation would be highly likely because the practiced exerciser was expected to follow the lead of his individual affections.[8] Consequently, it is necessary to isolate the essential features of the pattern. Primary among these is the introspection which Martz sees as the key to the meditative tradition and which certainly characterizes Joyce's presentation of Stephen.[9] Equally significant is the special development in terms of three different faculties of the mind. In Ignatius' pattern the first prelude, which collects and reconstructs images, belongs to memory; the meditation proper, which thoroughly analyzes the subject matter, belongs to understanding; and the colloquy, which gives full play to the deeply roused emotions, represents the work of will. Despite any variation, then, the exercise, or its offshoots, will undoubtedly project this pattern of memory, understanding, and will, or as Martz suggests, "composition, analysis, and colloquy."[10] Finally, a special feature of the pattern is the interrelated organization through which a portion of the exercise acts as a microcosm of the whole: the individual points of the meditation proper must also be examined in turn by memory, understanding, and will, so that the structure of each point thus repeats the basic structure of the entire exercise.

Examination of the *Portrait* in terms of this pattern shows that the relationship between the Ignatian system and Joyce's novel does not end with the borrowed sermons. The sequel to the evening sermon illustrates how Joyce has adapted the meditative pattern to the purposes of drama. Immediately after dinner Stephen goes to his room "in order to be alone with his soul" (p. 135). The preaching has had the desired effect because he now fears "intensely in spirit and in flesh" (p. 136). Behind the closed door which gives his room the atmosphere of a retreat, he kneels to pray. But his thoughts are confused and uncontrollable:

> Why was he kneeling there like a child saying his evening prayers? To be alone with his soul, to examine his conscience, to meet his sins face to face, to recall their times and manners and circumstances, to weep over them. He could not weep. He could not summon them to his memory. He felt only an ache of soul and body, his whole being, memory, will, understanding, flesh, benumbed and weary. (p. 136)

Through the language of this passage Joyce indicates explicitly Stephen's abortive desire to perform a typical spiritual exercise, in which he would indeed be "alone with his soul." "Examination of conscience" is a term which Ignatius uses to refer to the exercises of the first week, the meditations on sin (pars. 24–43). To meet one's sins "face to face" is the special function of the first prelude; and the "memory, will, understanding" of the final sentence expresses, of course, the over-all divisions of the individual exercise.

Stephen fails to perform the necessary meditation; overwhelmed by his weakness, he crawls timidly into bed. But it is then, so intensely does he realize his fallen state, that the exercise takes place without the collaboration of his as yet unaroused will. As he lies in bed, "the leprous company of his sins closed about him, breathing upon him, bending over him from all sides" (p. 137). He tries to escape them by squeezing tight his eyelids, "but the senses of his soul would not be bound and, though his eyes were shut fast, *he saw* the places where he had sinned and, though his ears were tightly covered, *he heard*."[11] Joyce completes this clearly defined composition of place through the hideous field which Stephen experiences in his dream, the goatish creatures of which readily fulfill Ignatius' demand that the sinner imagine his "whole composite being as an exile here on earth, cast out to live among brute beasts" (par. 47). This composition of place does not introduce a formal meditation, but it does lead to understanding. When Stephen awakes in his fear, he realizes that "that was his hell. God had allowed him to see the hell reserved for his sins: stinking, bestial, malignant, a hell of lecherous goatish fiends. For him! For him!" (p. 138). The result is the vomiting which symbolically purges his sins and the consequent capacity to put his will, which he had previously used only to fight off his vision, to the use for which it is intended in the exercise, a colloquy, addressed in this case to the Virgin (pp. 138–139). The exercise completed, his newly-oriented and aroused will can direct him to confession, the act which has been his desire and purpose throughout the chapter.

This carefully constructed passage offers ample evidence of Joyce's use of the Ignatian pattern to dramatize an alteration in Stephen's relationship to the world around him. At the same time, the dream and its aftermath form but one stage in the conversion process which is the substance of Chapter Three. Here the intricate structure of the Ignatian system becomes significant, for just as the individual point of the meditation proper parallels the entire exercise, the structure of this episode repeats the structure of its chapter, which also follows the pattern of a meditation on sin. The early pages of Chapter Three (pp. 102–108), which render Stephen's preoccupation with his numerous sins, focus upon the past by summarizing his experience since the end of Chapter Two; memory predominates. Joyce achieves the effect of a composition of place through several devices. He locates Stephen temporally and spatially in the school room while the sins appear to him in meditation. Evocative images suggest the real presence of gluttony (Stephen's belly anticipates stuffing itself with the thick, starchy stew), lechery (Stephen pictures "the squalid quarter of the brothels" and its denizens), and pride (he scrawls a design which "began to spread out a widening tail, eyed and starred like a peacock's"). The necessary concrete vividness is established by details of taste ("thick peppered flourfattened sauce"), smell and touch ("their soft perfumed flesh"), and sight and sound:

> as he prowled in quest of that call, his senses, stultified only by his desire, would note keenly all that wounded or shamed them; his eyes, a ring of porter froth on a clothless table or a photograph of two soldiers standing to attention on a gaudy playbill; his ears, the drawling jargon of greeting.

The succeeding section of the chapter (set apart by asterisks in the text) includes Father Arnall's explanation of the retreat, the sermon on Judgment Day, the description of hell, and the examination of spiritual torments. It constitutes an elaborate development of the Church's understanding of the nature and wages of sin and thus corresponds to the meditation proper of the Ignatian pattern. Since the reader experiences the sermons through Stephen's consciousness, Stephen tends to fulfill the role of exerciser. Joyce indicates that the understanding gained indeed becomes Stephen's own individual acquisition, for it is during this section that the food of the opening paragraph gets transformed into a nightmare of grease (p. 111), woman becomes a symbol of shame and then loses her sensuality altogether in the vision of the Virgin and the purified Emma (pp. 115–116), and the schoolmates whom Stephen in his pride had detested (p. 104) now lull his aching soul and touch his heart in his new "quietude of humility and contrition" (p. 126). It is the function of the Ignatian meditation proper to arouse the will for its exalted association with God in the colloquy, and it is precisely as a result of the understanding gained through the retreat that Stephen, whose will had been stifled, can carry out his confession and penance, his only significant act of will in this chapter. The last section of Chapter Three corresponds, then, to the colloquy of the Ignatian exercise; here Stephen's aroused will speaks out, not to God, Christ, or the Virgin, but to the priest who hears his confession. Joyce's substitution has thematic propriety because it illustrates that the change in Stephen's relationship to his surroundings is one which places him squarely within the framework of the Church, where the individual speaks to God through His intermediary.

Ignatius saw the spiritual exercises as a method of "preparing and disposing the soul to rid itself of all inordinate attachments, and, after their removal, of seeking and finding the will of God in the disposition of our life for the salvation of our soul" (par. 1). Joyce shows, at the end of the chapter, that Stephen has at least temporarily achieved this desired result. The greasy, starchy, earthy food of gluttony has been replaced by the simpler and predominantly white "pudding and eggs and sausages and cups of tea" (p. 145). The craving, indicative of sin, has turned to calm expectancy, while the dull day and gathering darkness of the chapter's beginning yield to the tender shade and the implicit dawning of this conversion breakfast. Chapter Three closes with Stephen partaking of the communion which symbolizes salvation as he surrenders himself freely to "another life! A life of grace and virtue and happiness!" (p. 146). The achievement of the chapter is noteworthy: in order to give coherent form to a fictional episode depicting the return of a sinner to the arms of the Church, Joyce skillfully adapts a pattern already employed by the Church to help effect that return under actual circumstances.

Additional consideration reveals achievements even more remarkable, for Joyce further transforms the Ignatian pattern into a device of art by using it to organize material lacking the religious appropriateness of Stephen's return to the Church. The structure of Chapter Three is far from unique; each of the other chapters duplicates its particular movement from memory through understanding to will. Each chapter begins, for example, with a passage focusing upon the past and summarizing an existence extended over a long period of time. This technique reaches its fullest development in Chapter Five, where the typical review of his progress since the end of the preceding chapter is supplemented by a series of scenes which re-dramatizes his rejection of home, of school, of Ireland, and of the priesthood, and thus establishes to memory the entire past which impinges upon his dedication to art. In each chapter these opening sequences emphasize the factual in the manner of the composition of place: Uncle Charles' daily visit to his "arbour," Stephen's comically heroic devotional program, and the mundane pawn tickets which follow so bathetically the hawklike man's mystical experience:

1 Pair Buskins.
1 D. Coat.
3 Articles and White.
1 Man's Pants.

The opening of Chapter One is now notorious for its evocation of all five senses, but this necessary requisite of the composition of place animates the beginning of every chapter in the novel, as has already been suggested in the analysis of Chapter Three and can be further seen by these details from the first two pages of Chapter Two: the smell and taste of Uncle Charles' tobacco, the sight of his hatbrim and pipebowl projecting beyond the door of the outhouse, the sound of his humming, the feel of the grapes and sawdust in Stephen's hands.

The function of the Ignatian composition of place is to lay down a combined setting and subject matter which the rest of the exercise then elaborates. In the same fashion Joyce's introductory sequences establish a theme which succeeding passages develop until Stephen has before him all the impressions necessary to lead him to some relevant conclusion. The first two pages of Chapter One emphasize, among other things, Stephen's deeply felt individuality ("That was his song") and the contrasting power of external authority (the eagle), which here resides in the Church (it is Dante who threatens him). The section on his early school experiences defines Stephen's increasing awareness of self, as he turns from the chaos of everyday experience to the more individual and more secure realms of daydream, dream, and illness. The Christmas quarrel introduces him to the possibility that the Church's authority, which he already acknowledges only through superstitious fear, may be open to question; the quarrel also provides him, in his father and Mr. Casey, living examples of individuals who indeed question it, at least in word. Once back in school, the conflict becomes intensely personal. Through the medium of Father Dolan the eagle strikes, and Stephen finds it impossible to go on accepting an authority of sadistic injustice, one which, moreover, violates his sacred individuality ("It was his own name that he should have made fun of if he wanted to make fun," p. 56). As a result of these incidents, Stephen realizes that somehow he must oppose external authority if he is to preserve his personal integrity.

The pattern emerges in the other chapters as well. In the beginning of Chapter Two, acute awareness of the material environment of Ireland evokes in Stephen a counter yearning for the ideal in the figure of Mercedes. The subsequent action teaches him that his surroundings will not allow this dream to materialize, for the "real" Mercedes fails him after the fleeting victory of the play, and amid such surroundings, his dreams necessarily congeal into the lust symbolized for him by the letters carved in the desk at Cork. Chapter Four's initial conflict between piety and the worldliness with which Stephen pursues it develops into a close examination of the pious life when Stephen is asked to search his soul for signs of a vocation, and he realizes the impossibility of pursuing a career which excludes (as he thinks) not only worldliness but also beauty, truth, and art. The central portions of Chapter Five contrast Stephen's cold and aloof artistic intellectualism with the homely lore of the priest, Davin's nationalism, McCann's political belligerence, Lynch's animality, Temple's empty humanism, and Cranly's emotionalism; Stephen's observation of his fellows convinces him once and for all of his complete incompatibility with his surroundings. Each of these central portions consists of a thorough analysis of the chapter's thematic components; each stresses the gaining of understanding, which is glimpsed through Stephen's emerging consciousness as if through the accumulating realization of an exerciser performing a meditation.

In keeping with the final major section of the Ignatian pattern, which emphasizes the will, each chapter of the *Portrait* ends with an act of will performed by Stephen as a direct result of the understanding he has gained through his experience. His realization of the impossible situation imposed upon him by authority prompts his first rebellion, and Joyce emphasizes the part played by will: "Yes, he would do what the fellows had told him. He would go up and tell the rector that he had been wrongly punished" (p. 54). At the end of Chapter Two, when he seeks the prostitute, Joyce presents the decision as the sexual ravishing of his soul by some power very much like a newly-roused and unrestrainable will: "He felt some dark presence moving irresistibly upon him from the darkness, a presence subtle and murmurous as a flood filling him wholly with itself" (p. 100). What here seems external is in fact the result of Stephen's understanding within the chapter, for he turns to the prostitute seeking directly in Dublin's sordid reality the ideal which had previously eluded him, and in her arms he gains the strength, fearlessness, and certainty (p. 101) which he knew he would find when he met "in the real world the unsubstantial image which his soul so constantly beheld" (p. 65). The desire for a vocation which can give him everything lacking in the priesthood ultimately produces the central act of will in the whole novel, his assumption of the mythological significance of his name in his dedication to art. Finally, the fully realized incompatibility of Chapter Five leads to his avowal of *non serviam* and his acceptance of the necessity of exile.

The similarity which these endings have to the final section of the Ignatian pattern is not limited to the dominance of will, for each contains some kind of colloquy as thematically appropriate as that which concludes Chapter Three. In Chapter One, where Stephen restricts his rebellion to the limits permitted by authority, his outpourings are directed to the rector, who like some benevolent God is expected to right all wrongs. In Chapter Two, Stephen serves another God, one more fittingly addressed by "the cry that he had strangled for so long in his throat": "It broke from him like a wail of despair from a hell of sufferers and died in a wail of furious entreaty, a cry for an iniquitous abandonment, a cry which was but the echo of an obscene scrawl which he had read on the oozing wall of a urinal" (p. 100).

The colloquy of Chapter Four is spoken to the bird girl who serves as icon for the new divinity of art to which Stephen now responds: "—Heavenly God! cried Stephen's soul, in an outburst of profane joy" (p. 171). Chapter Five has a double colloquy. Stephen addresses his *non serviam* to Cranly, who as unfrocked priest and intimate friend is the obvious recipient of this specifically secular and human confession. But the real colloquy of the chapter comes when Stephen, with even this last connection between himself and his surroundings severed, speaks out through six pages of diary entries to the one true God: a combination of his own individual soul, life, and the "old artificer" whose act he shall one day imitate.

Stephen's final colloquy represents a goal toward which he has progressed throughout the entire novel. Just as the ending of each chapter follows logically from the established premises, Chapter Five achieves, if not a full resolution, at least a result and a recapitulation of all the forces which have exerted their influence on Stephen's developing personality. Inevitably, the novel as a whole repeats the pattern of the individual chapters. It falls naturally into three coherent parts, which roughly correspond to the divisions of memory, understanding, and will. This division can be seen in part through Joyce's treatment of "place." The school and home of Chapter One, which admittedly evoke symbolic overtones, are predominantly naturalistic, defined through the accumulated images of memory. The next three chapters reverse this relationship. Naturalistic details abound, but they are overshadowed by the understanding which arises from their confluence into such major symbols as the filth of Ireland, the hell of the Church's damnation, and the charnel house of priesthood. In Chapter Five, where the will is the dominant faculty, setting becomes immaterial in both senses of the word; Joyce presents Stephen in motion before a sparsely realized background, and at the very end of the novel, in the writing of the diary, will and setting merge into one essence.

But the division manifests itself most clearly in the differing functions of the chapters. It has long been recognized that the first two pages of the *Portrait* epitomize all the themes which Joyce later develops in detail. Actually, the entire opening chapter serves to bring into focus the major theme which incorporates all the varied motifs: Stephen's search for an authority or standard or myth which would be compatible with his individual desires and encompass his personal truths. The second section, consisting of Chapters Two, Three, and Four, presents Stephen's search for this myth. He learns that he must reject two possibilities—the transitory, perhaps degrading, unspiritual rule of flesh and the external, unworldly, fleshless rule of spirit—and in his ultimate choice acknowledges the necessity of electing only a fusion of both flesh and spirit. Chapter Five forms yet a new division; in each of the preceding chapters Stephen had moved from one allegiance to another; in Five, by clinging to the decision with which he begins, he achieves an element of that stasis which characterizes his definition of art. This sense of definiteness itself suggests the resolved will, and Joyce emphasizes the impression by focusing throughout the chapter on an additional sign, Stephen's irrepressible arrogance. Chapter Five, which differs from its predecessors in featuring two colloquies, may, in fact, be regarded as a series of colloquies in which Stephen, through conversation and composition, pontificates his firmly determined convictions.

The structure of the *Portrait* thus follows the pattern of the Ignatian spiritual exercise even to the extent of its microcosmic interrelation of parts, so that while each chapter achieves the pattern and purpose of the separate points of the meditation proper, the whole novel effects a kind of secularized spiritual exercise carrying its central figure through the progressive stages of memory, understanding, and will. Ignatius directed that the meditator should always end his exercise with a *Pater Noster*. Significantly, in the final sentence of the *Portrait*—"Old father, old artificer, stand me now and ever in good stead"—Joyce creates a parody of the *Pater Noster* which, with its substitute deity and unhumble familiarity, sums up the entire progress of Stephen Dedalus.

The intricate structure of the *Portrait* has always been admired. The remarkably analogous correspondences between the novel and the spiritual exercises make it extremely likely that the intricacy results from Joyce's conscious employment of the Ignatian pattern of meditation. The reason for this employment is not far to seek. In *Stephen Hero* he had a work which was amorphously naturalistic and "social" in focus, to use Harry Levin's term.[12] In coming to revise it he faced the task of imposing upon it a greater formal coherence while at the same time translating it into the psychological analysis more in keeping with his altered understanding of Stephen's adventures. His own experience presented him with the Ignatian spiritual exercise, a ready-made system already containing the introspective focus in a pattern which gives shape to miscellaneous units and organizes them into a highly integrated and meaningful whole. If Joyce adopted this pattern only for its formal characteristics, his action nevertheless produced important thematic consequences. It will be remembered that the purpose of the Ignatian exercise is the "preparing and disposing of the soul to rid itself of all inordinate attachments, and, after their removal, of seeking and finding the will of God in the disposition of our life for the salvation of our soul." Except for the difference involved in what is meant by the will of God, this statement neatly characterizes Stephen's purpose throughout the novel, and if cast into an infinitive phrase, it would summarize Stephen's *action,* in the sense that Francis Fergusson has given the term. By making use of the Ignatian system, then, Joyce has erected a structure equivalent to the meaning which it shapes. Similarly, the technical fusion of religious pattern with aesthetic discipline that went into the novel's ordering of random experience parallels Stephen's own fusion of Aquinas and Aristotle in his theory of art. Because of this parallel the structure helps to define the double source of Stephen's maturity and to re-affirm the religious basis of his ultimate dedication. An awareness of the meditative structure of *A Portrait of the Artist as a Young Man* thus serves the reader by giving him a key to not only the particular arrangement Joyce has given Stephen's progress but also the meaning which that arrangement defines.

Notes

1. "Joyce's Sermon on Hell: Its Source and Its Backgrounds, "*Modern Philology,* LVII (1960), 172–198; "Joyce's Hell-Fire Sermons," *Modern Language Notes,* LXXV (1960), 561–571.

2. James Joyce, *A Portrait of the Artist as a Young Man* (New York: The Viking Press, 1956), p. 152. All subsequent citations to the novel are to this edition.

3. The material in this paragraph is based primarily on *The Spiritual Exercises of St. Ignatius,* trans. Louis J. Puhl (Westminster, Maryland, 1954).

4. See *Spiritual Exercises,* par. 4. The quoted material is from Paul Debuchy, "Spiritual Exercises of Saint Ignatius," *The Catholic Encyclopedia* (New York, 1912), XIV, 227.

5. See *Spiritual Exercises,* pars. 45–72.

6. *Spiritual Exercises,* par. 54.

7. *The Poetry of Meditation* (New Haven, 1954); "Introduction" to *John Donne: The Divine Poems* (Oxford: Clarendon Press, 1952).

8. Martz, p. 46.

9. "Donne and the Meditative Tradition," *Thought,* XXIV (1959), 269–278.

10. *The Poetry of Meditation,* p. 38.

11. Italics added.

12. *James Joyce: A Critical Introduction* (Norfolk, Conn., 1941), p. 48.

III

The Text and Textuality
of *Ulysses*

Identifying foundational essays for *Ulysses* poses a formidable challenge. The sheer volume of criticism written on this work vastly outpaces the number of interpretations for the rest of Joyce's canon. The reasons are both apparent and potentially misleading. *Ulysses* stands out as the most powerful rendering of combined modernist and postmodernist sensibilities in the twentieth-century canon. Its stylistic and thematic multiplicity invites responses from a range of diverse readers, and its combination of grittiness and sophistication insures that none of them will lack fertile grounds for investigation.

However, a reader's bias toward the concept of linear development can provoke a distorted perception of the novel's place in the canon. The cognitive assumption of an evolutionary progress makes it easy to see *Ulysses* as the product of Joyce's mature artistic period that, in contrast to *Finnegans Wake*, remains relatively accessible to most readers. This view has the result of unfairly categorizing the stories in *Dubliners* as apprentice pieces, of seeing the narrative of *A Portrait of the Artist as a Young Man* as a demonstration of the author's movement toward creative maturity, and of dismissing *Finnegans Wake* as the esoteric exercise of an aging impresario. More significantly, such an assumption muffles creative echoes in other areas of Joyce's canon that could provide illuminating examples of long-term artistic commitments.

While any work of literature has features that can be subjected to simplistic or faulty interpretations, misprision of elements in *Ulysses* can have sweeping consequences. Whatever one's point of view on aspects of the narrative, the broad and ongoing impact of *Ulysses* remains an indisputable condition of contemporary literary studies. The ways we have learned to read *Ulysses* set the pattern for how we read all the fiction published since its appearance.

Nonetheless, no study of the length of this project can hope to do more than sketch the framework of the novel's critical heritage. Consequently, what follows is a view of the analytical tradition surrounding *Ulysses* that is even more selective than those that have appeared in the introductions to the previous sections. That being said, one can still discern certain clear patterns from even a discriminating representation of previous scholarly studies.

Paradoxically, it is the complexity of *Ulysses* that contributes to its accessibility. Because of the encyclopedic quality of its narrative, *Ulysses* exercises interpretive dispensations for readers not found in many other works. Its diversity liberates one from the conventional imperative to generate interpretations that reconcile all apparent disunities, and instead its narrative encourages readers to feel free to concentrate on mastery of very specific concepts as points of entry into Joyce's discourse. Criticism of the novel over the past few decades attests to the popularity and the validity of such tightly focused, and in some cases discursive, approaches to understanding narrative subtleties, but these recent examinations rest upon the rich critical heritage of broader conceptualizations no longer familiar to many. The more we recover, the greater will be our sense of what we understand in the novel.

This task is more challenging than it is for those approaching the interpretive heritage of *Dubliners* or *A Portrait of the Artist as a Young Man*. The criticism that surrounds *Ulysses* generally appeared much earlier than did analyses of Joyce's previous works. In part this related directly to the concurrence of Joyce's growing notoriety as a writer with the book's initial appearance and to the eagerness of prominent members of the literary world to discuss his work publicly.

In part the early development of a robust critical commentary on *Ulysses* also reflected the pragmatic awareness that Joyce and his supporters had acquired since he first began writing. When serialized portions of the novel appeared in the *Little Review* and the *Egoist* and readers in the United States and in Europe for various reasons questioned the value of the work, Joyce and those around him who believed in his work saw the need to address, often preemptively, perplexing interpretive, economic and legal issues that adhered to his writing.[1] With this in mind, Joyce encouraged Valery Larbaud, the French man of letters, to deliver a public lecture on the novel in December of 1921, several months before the actual appearance of *Ulysses,* and to have the talk printed five months later in *Nouvelle Revue Française.*[2]

After *Ulysses* came out in February of 1922, Joyce's friends continued to offer increasingly sophisticated critical interpretations. The following year T. S. Eliot published an important overview in the *Dial.*[3] Four years later a Los Angeles journalist, Paul Jordan Smith, brought out a concise but thoughtful summary that gave an informed sketch of Joyce's biography and the cultural context from which he emerged and then went on to provide a chapter-by-chapter breakdown of the narrative.[4] Smith also offered a useful corrective to Joseph Collins's earlier assessment of Joyce.[5]

Over the next few years, Joyce took an increasingly active hand (as he would later with the promotion of *Finnegans Wake*) in the production of criticism of *Ulysses.* In 1930 Stuart Gilbert, who with Valery Larbaud and Augustine Morel had worked on the first French translation of *Ulysses,* brought out under Joyce's guidance a book-length study that particularly stressed Homeric allusions in the text and the importance of source material.[6] Four years later Frank Budgen drew upon his friendship with Joyce and his recollections of the time they spent in Zurich while Joyce was composing much of the first draft of *Ulysses* to provide a straightforward firsthand introduction to the novel.[7]

Up to this point, most critics were simply struggling to find fundamental strategies for reading Joyce's novel. As with early criticism of Joyce's other works, the net effect of these pioneering efforts was to make manageable dauntingly diverse material by emphasizing a single point of view. From this template, as more and more individuals experienced *Ulysses,* critics introduced increasingly diverse modes of analysis.

Both Edmund Wilson's 1931 study and Harry Levin's 1941 introduction to Joyce introduced independent scholarly assessments.[8] However, a major development in studies of *Ulysses* occurred later in the 1940s when Richard M. Kain published *Fabulous Voyager: James Joyce's "Ulysses."*[9] Although Kain's interpretive approach may now seem obvious and even quaint, at the time of the book's publication Kain did what no previous reader had thought to do. He offered a detailed study of the Dublin locale that served as a setting for the novel, and in the process he gave readers a more vivid account than previously conceived of the world that Bloom, Stephen, and Molly inhabited.

Kain's work, and that of Robert Martin Adams a decade and a half later, paved the way for the more overtly referential studies that followed.[10] In the late 1960s Weldon Thornton produced an invaluable gloss of the cultural context of Joyce's narrative giving detailed information about the social, historic, religious, typographic, biographic, and miscellaneous Irish folklore to which Joyce's narrative frequently alluded.[11] Six years later, Don Gifford incorporated and expanded Thornton's findings into an annotated guide of his own.[12]

One can trace the demand for the work of Adams and the reference guides of Thornton and Gifford to seminal essays like Edmund Epstein's "Cruxes in *Ulysses*: Notes toward an Edition and Annotation." Looking at the intratextual connections that Epstein made in his work, that statement might initially seem like a large claim for contemporary readers to accept, yet the work of scholars like Epstein did more than clarify specific cruxes, it also established our sense that Joyce's allusiveness is too encyclopedic to permit glossing every reference.

Studies like his that not only pointed out the significance of Irish references but went on to comment on how they shaped one's interpretive experience domesticated the unfamiliar. They signaled a paradigmatic shift privileging diversity and multiplicity and removing the burden of the presumptive need to move toward closure. This essay in particular presented insightful comments that dispelled the ambiguities of passages steeped in local color while allowing us to sustain the creative indeterminacies that Joyce inculcated into his discourse. Most noteworthy, Epstein paved the way for guidelines for understanding the text—foregrounding pluralism and celebrating subjectivity—that have become critical commonplaces but were arresting assertions when he first made them. Overall, Epstein's sense of the flexibility of Joyce's narrative, his outlining of what is available for glossing and what demands explication or analysis, gave subsequent readers the idea that interpretations and scholarship could find an equilibrium that enhanced rather than occluded comprehension.

Coincidentally with Epstein's work on content, A. Walton Litz was conducting extremely important research on the evolution of the form of Joyce's novel. Though much is now made of the composition process that shaped *Ulysses* and critics now move with ease through discussions of Joyce's diverse creative stages, it was Litz, working in the mid-1950s with materials held by the British Museum, who first drew readers to an awareness of its complexity and who offered marvelous insights into the impact of these methods of writing on the final version of the novel.[13]

In the essay reprinted here, "Early Vestiges of Joyce's *Ulysses*," Litz called attention to the development of the creative process that played such a key role in imbuing the imaginative dexterity and narrative suppleness into Joyce's works. Litz's careful comparison of passages in *A Portrait of the Artist as a Young Man*, *Stephen Hero*, and *Ulysses* gave students of Joyce's canon their first extended exposure to the author's complex approach to composition that produced *Ulysses*, making important links between textual, biographical, and exegetical criticism.

Most directly, Litz's work laid the foundation for decades of textual criticism, some quite sophisticated and all deeply indebted to these pioneering efforts. The first, and arguably most generally accessible, contribution derived from Litz's work came from Miles Hanley's realization that a firm understanding of where words occurred in Joyce's novel gave readers a profoundly developed sense of its direction.[14] Phillip Herring, seeing what Litz was able to do with Joyce's draft material, saw that placing prepublication work, or at least facsimiles of it, before other readers would greatly enhance their abilities to connect diverse elements in the text and to extend Litz's findings.[15]

Litz's achievement, however, went well beyond establishing patterns for textual criticism, although it certainly did that. His analysis made clear for subsequent critics the imaginative patterns informing Joyce's writing. The immediate result was a series of books that offered close attention to the development of the narrative through an implicit understanding of the creative approach that Litz had highlighted.[16] Clive Driver extended these resources further with the reproduction of the manuscript version of *Ulysses*.[17] And Michael Groden, a student of Litz's at Princeton, brought the work of the fifties to its logical conclusion with a synthesis and extension of Litz's discoveries.[18] (Of course, it also goes without saying that both the multivolume collection *The James Joyce Archive* and the Hans Walter Gabler synoptic edition of *Ulysses* took their emphasis from Litz's achievements and indeed moved forward with Litz's enthusiastic support.)[19]

Engaging interpretive cruxes and recognizing compositional structure stand as key features in any attempt to understand *Ulysses*. However, the element most evident to the majority of readers, particularly those approaching the work for the first time, remains the encyclopedic quality of its discourse. The apparent wanton discursiveness of the narrative would be a daunting feature were it not for the work of early critics like Marvin Magalaner whose views offer reasoned guidelines for responding to specific referentiality in *Ulysses*.

Magalaner's essay from the early 1950s, "The Anti-Semitic Limerick Incidents and Joyce's 'Bloomsday,'" gave a very detailed account of the extratextuality informing the expressions of ethnic prejudice found in the pages of *Ulysses*. It not only addressed mob violence against Jews in Limerick in the spring of 1904. It detailed the subtle and at times not so subtle reactions to this thuggery printed in Standish O'Grady's respected journal the *All Ireland Review*. With deft skill Magalaner showed not simply the ugly side of overt hostility to Jews in Ireland but also the more insidious racism that ran through the consciousnesses of those who would see themselves as right-thinking individuals.

Most directly, this essay gave contemporary readers a sense of the nonchalant anti-Semitism that permeated Irish (and indeed European and American) society before the horrors of the Holocaust made such overt expressions intolerable. The careless disparagement of Bloom in particular and of Jews in general by Deasy, Haines, Mulligan, and others throughout the text does more than reflect intolerance. It underscores an obliviousness to this rancor within Irish society that most modern readers would not comprehend.

Magalaner's study introduced a topic that subsequently became the subject of additional detailed and sophisticated examinations. Numerous essays appeared exploring this issue from a range of perspectives and with diverse conclusions. This in turn stimulated larger studies, and in 1989 Ira Nadel produced a wide-ranging scholarly work in the first book-length examination of the topic.[20] Seven years later Neil R. Davidson offered a more narrowly focused view of the issue, looking at *Ulysses* and at its reflections of cultural contexts.[21] And three years after Davidson's book appeared, Marilyn Reizbaum published her long-awaited examination of Joyce and Judaism, neatly complementing the books that had preceded hers.[22] While it would be unfair to any of these authors to read their studies as simple expansions of Magalaner's work, it remains clear that his assessment of contexts showed the rich area of interpretive possibilities derived from extratextual study of Judaism.

Even beyond that achievement, by highlighting the interpretive value derived from a fuller understanding of particular cultural aspects of the novel, Magalaner's work allowed other critics to offer guides making *Ulysses* accessible to general readers without feeling the need to touch on more specialized topics. A very obvious beneficiary of this phenomenon was Harry Blamires, whose workmanlike account of the structure of *Ulysses* made Joyce's book less formidable to countless first-time readers.[23]

One finds an even more significant interpretive achievement, and a work that elaborates upon the approach adumbrated by Magalaner, in David Hayman's seemingly innocuous general introduction.[24] *"Ulysses": The Mechanics of Meaning* in fact stands out as a tour de force. It demonstrates how much a sophisticated and sensitive critic can convey with plain language and incisive interpretive skills. Hayman, himself an esteemed Joycean by the time *The Mechanics of Meaning* appeared, knew well the work of Litz, Epstein, Magalaner, and other pioneers, and he could integrate and extend their discoveries in a marvelous and above all lucid understanding of the novel.

Simple language and direct expression, however, were not incorporated into the template for subsequent work. Indeed, theoretical diversity, with its incumbent highly refined vocabularies, began to reconfigure all aspects of Joyce studies in the 1970s. Mark Shechner's book-length psychoanalytic examination of the novel prefigured the work that Sheldon Brivic and others would continue in the closing decades of the century.[25] In the early 1980s, Karen Lawrence's study of the stylistic variations within *Ulysses* both recalled the monumental achievements of Litz's criticism and brought new epistemologies to bear upon those findings.[26] Subsequent writers like Patrick McGee, Zack Bowen, Robert H. Bell, Bernard Benstock, Enda Duffy, and Kimberly Devlin would show the range of insights that the new approaches privileged.[27]

Ulysses criticism shows no signs of abating, and the growing diverse response attests to the way its complexity repays a range of perspectives of the work. In addition to evolving approaches to familiar epistemologies, hybrids of common methodologies—gender studies, postcolonial approaches—highlight the subtle critical insights still available to determined readers.[28] At the same time, as one sees from looking at the essays reprinted in this section, the profound impact of the early critics of the novel upon the way we continue to understand it cannot be overestimated. Their questions now define the way we see the novel, their insights have become received wisdom, and their assumptions are now taken as obvious facts.

Notes

1. For a good account of this, see Joseph Kelly's *Our Joyce: From Outcast to Icon* (Austin: University of Texas Press, 1998), esp. 15–131. See also *The United States of America v. One Book Entitled "Ulysses" by James Joyce: Documents and Commentary: A 50-Year Retrospective*, ed. Michael Moscato and Leslie LeBlanc (Frederick, Md.: University Publications of America, 1984).

2. Valery Larbaud, "James Joyce," *Nouvelle Revue Française* 18 (April 1922): 385–409.

3. T. S. Eliot, "*Ulysses*, Order, and Myth," *Dial* 75 (November 1923): 480–483.

4. Paul Jordan Smith, *A Key to the "Ulysses" of James Joyce* (Chicago: Covici, 1927).

5. Joseph Collins, *The Doctor Looks at Literature: Psychological Studies of Life and Letters* (New York: George H. Doran, 1923).

6. Stuart Gilbert, *James Joyce's "Ulysses": A Study* (London: Faber and Faber, 1930).

7. Frank Budgen, *James Joyce and the Making of "Ulysses"* (London: Grayson, 1934).

8. Edmund Wilson, "James Joyce," in *Axel's Castle: A Study of the Imaginative Literature of 1870–1930* (New York: Scribner's, 1931), 91–236; Harry Levin, *James Joyce: A Critical Introduction* (Norfolk, Conn.: New Directions, 1941).

9. Richard M. Kain, *Fabulous Voyager: James Joyce's "Ulysses"* (Chicago: University of Chicago Press, 1947).

10. Robert Martin Adams elaborated upon that approach with his book *Surface and Symbol: The Consistency of James Joyce's "Ulysses"* (New York: Oxford University Press, 1962).

11. Weldon Thornton, *Allusions in "Ulysses": An Annotated List* (Chapel Hill: University of North Carolina Press, 1968).

12. Don Gifford, with Robert J. Seidman, *Notes for Joyce: An Annotation of James Joyce's "Ulysses"* (New York: Dutton, 1974).

13. Within a few years of the appearance of the essay reprinted here, Litz produced a study of Joyce's approach to writing that remains the starting point for serious textual critics and close readers of both *Ulysses* and *Finnegans Wake*: A. Walton Litz, *The Art of James Joyce: Method and Design in "Ulysses" and "Finnegans Wake"* (London: Oxford University Press, 1961).

14. Miles Hanley, comp., *Word Index to James Joyce's "Ulysses"* (Madison: University of Wisconsin Press, 1937). The *Ulysses* that Hanley indexes is the 1934 Random House edition.

15. Phillip F. Herring, *Joyce's "Ulysses" Notesheets in the British Museum* (Charlottesville: University Press of Virginia, 1972) and *Joyce's Notes and Early Drafts for "Ulysses": Selections from the Buffalo Collections* (Charlottesville: University Press of Virginia, 1977). Herring, a student of David Hayman, was no doubt also influenced by Hayman's textual studies of *Finnegans Wake*, which will be discussed in the next section.

16. Two obvious examples of this are S. L. Goldberg, *The Classical Temper: A Study of James Joyce's "Ulysses"* (London: Chatto and Windus, 1961), and Stanley Sultan, *The Argument of "Ulysses"* (Columbus: Ohio State University Press, 1964). However, a close examination of essays on *Ulysses* that appeared over the next few decades would show the strength, both implicitly and explicitly, of Litz's findings.

17. Clive Driver, ed. *"Ulysses": A Facsimile of the Manuscript,* 3 vols. (New York: Octagon, 1975).

18. Michael Groden, *"Ulysses" in Progress* (Princeton, N.J.: Princeton University Press, 1977).

19. *The James Joyce Archive,* ed. Michael Groden et al., 63 vols. (New York: Garland, 1977–79); James Joyce, *Ulysses,* ed. Hans Walter Gabler et al. (New York: Garland, 1984).

20. Ira B. Nadel, *Joyce and the Jews: Culture and Texts* (Iowa City: University of Iowa Press, 1989).

21. Neil R. Davidson, *James Joyce, "Ulysses," and the Construction of Jewish Identity* (Cambridge: Cambridge University Press, 1996).

22. Marilyn Reizbaum, *James Joyce's Judaic Other* (Palo Alto, Calif.: Stanford University Press, 1999).

23. Harry Blamires, *The Bloomsday Book: A Guide Through Joyce's "Ulysses"* (London: Methuen, 1966).

24. David Hayman, *"Ulysses": The Mechanics of Meaning* (Englewood Cliffs, N.J.: Prentice-Hall, 1970).

25. Mark Shechner, *Joyce in Nighttown: A Psychoanalytic Inquiry into "Ulysses"* (Berkeley and Los Angeles: University of California Press, 1974).

26. Karen Lawrence, *The Odyssey of Style in "Ulysses"* (Princeton, N.J.: Princeton University Press, 1981).

27. Patrick McGee, *Paperspace: Style as Ideology in Joyce's "Ulysses"* (Lincoln: University of Nebraska Press, 1988); Zack Bowen, *"Ulysses" as a Comic Novel* (Syracuse, N.Y.: Syracuse University Press, 1989); Robert H. Bell, *Jocoserious Joyce: The Fate of Folly in "Ulysses"* (Ithaca, N.Y.: Cornell University Press, 1991); Bernard Benstock, *Narrative Con/ Texts in "Ulysses"* (Urbana: University of Illinois Press, 1991); Enda Duffy, *The Subaltern "Ulysses"* (Minneapolis: University of Minnesota Press, 1994); Kimberly J. Devlin, *James Joyce's Fraudstuff* (Gainesville: University Press of Florida, 2002).

28. See, for example, Michael and Paula Gillespie's summary of the significant trends of interpretation through the last quarter of the twentieth century, *Recent Criticism of James Joyce's "Ulysses"* (Rochester, N.Y.: Boydell and Brewer, 2000).

7

Early Vestiges of Joyce's *Ulysses*

A. WALTON LITZ

No writer ever revised more carefully or used his rough notes and sketches more economically than Joyce. Each work grows out of its predecessor and prepares the way for a succeeding work already contemplated. *Ulysses* was first conceived as a short story for *Dubliners*, the *Portrait* is a prologue to *Ulysses*, and many of the themes and characters of *Finnegans Wake* are adumbrated in the earlier works.[1] Even *Chamber Music*, which appears to be unrelated to Joyce's great achievements, can be shown to foreshadow the action of *A Portrait* and to hold the key to many passages in *Ulysses* and the *Wake*.[2] There is a sense in which one can say that James Joyce wrote only one book, a continuous effort to endow his own life and the Dublin of his youth with a universal significance. T. S. Eliot has emphasized this continuity in his foreword to the catalogue of the 1949 Joyce exhibition in Paris: "Joyce's writings form a whole; we can neither reject the early work as stages, of no intrinsic interest, of his progress towards the latter, nor reject the later work as the outcome of decline. As with Shakespeare, his later work must be understood through the earlier, and the first through the last; it is the whole journey, not any one stage of it, that assures him his place among the great."[3]

The unity of Joyce's accomplishment is nowhere more evident than in the evolution of the texts of his major works. Phrases, characters, and long passages are deleted from one manuscript only to appear later in a different context. Thus many of the early unpublished *Epiphanies*, written in Paris during the winter and spring of 1902–3, eventually found their place in the texts of *Stephen Hero*, the *Portrait*, and *Ulysses*.[4] Joyce's economical methods of revision are clearly illustrated by five manuscript sheets

A. Walton Litz, "Early Vestiges of Joyce's *Ulysses*," *PMLA* 71 (March 1956): 51–60. Reprinted by permission of the Modern Language Association of America. Copyright 1957.

which were given to Harriet Weaver by Sylvia Beach in March of 1939. These sheets, fair copies in Joyce's hand of passages intended for his autobiographical novel, are evidence of the complex relationship that links *Stephen Hero* and the *Portrait* with *Ulysses*. Most important of all, they reveal his techniques of composition at the time when he began *Ulysses* and are the earliest extant manuscript fragments of that novel.

These sheets have never been described or discussed before and are not recorded in the recent Slocum and Cahoon *Bibliography*. I am deeply grateful to Miss Weaver for her permission to present them in this article. Each sheet is 8⁵⁄₁₆ by 6¹¹⁄₁₆ inches (21 by 17 cms.) in size. The left-hand edges are slightly ragged, suggesting that Joyce may have cut the pages from a notebook or from larger sheets; the wide left-hand margin of two inches was probably intended for corrections. The five pages comprise three distinct narrative units, which I have distinguished as Fragments *A*, *B*, and *C*. The left-hand column below is an exact transcript of the three fragments (deletions indicated in square brackets), arranged so that textual duplications and similarities in other works and MSS. are displayed in the parallel right-hand column.

FRAGMENT *A* (three sheets)

But the echo of his laughter had been the remembrance of Doherty, standing on the steps of his house the night before, saying:
—And on Sunday I consume the particle. Christine, *semel in die*. The mockery of it all! But it's for the sake of the poor aunt. God, we must be human first. Doherty meets his afflicted aunt. I am writing a mystery-play in half an act. Scene: Heaven. Enter two bouzes from Leitrim wearing blue spectacles. From Leitrim!
"What was it at all? Was it electric light or the *aurora borealis?*" "That was himself" "Glory be to God! It is the grandest thing I ever saw." I think that's a lovely touch. The
mockery of it! Ireland secretes priests: that's my new phrase. I must go. A

"Dr. Doherty and the Holy City" is one of Joyce's early (1904) notes for his autobiographical novel.[5] "—For this, O dearly beloved, is the genuine Christine . . ." Spoken by Buck Mulligan in Ulysses.[6]
"—The mockery of it . . ." Mulligan (*U* 5, 8). Buck Mulligan's aunt (*U* 6, 7, 8)

Compare Bloom's question in the *Circe* episode: "*Aurora borealis* or a steel foundry?" (*U* 427)

"—The mockery of it . . ." Mulligan (*U* 5, 8)

woman waits for me. God, the
humanity of Whitman! I contain all. I
embrace all. Farewell. Did you notice
Yeats's new touch with the hand up. It's
the Roman salute. *Salve!* Pip, pip!
O, a lovely mummer! Dedalus, we must
retire to the tower, you and I. Our lives
are precious. I'll try to touch the aunt.
We are the super-artists.
*Dedalus and Doherty have left Ireland
for the Omphalos—*

Compare the allusion to Whitman
on p. 18 of *Ulysses:* "Do I contradict
myself? Very well then, I contradict
myself." Doherty-Mulligan and
Whitman are linked in both contexts.
"—But a lovely mummer, he [Mulligan]
murmured to himself. Kinch, the
loveliest mummer of them all." (*U* 7)

This is the Martello tower, setting
for the first episode of *Ulysses.* Buck
Mulligan calls it "the *omphalos*"
(*U* 19). On p. 9 of *Ulysses* Stephen
thinks: "To ourselves . . . new
paganism . . . omphalos."

The rank smell of fried herrings
filled the kitchen and the bare table
was strewn with greasy plates [on]
to which [lay] glutinous fish-bones
and crusts were stuck by a congealing
white sauce. Clammy knives and forks
were abandoned here and there. A big
soot-coated kettle, [sat in] which had
been drained of the last dregs of shell
cocoa, sat in the midst of the disorder
beside a large jam-jar still half-full of
the oatmeal water which had served for
milk. Under the table the tortoiseshell
cat was chewing ravenously at a mess of
charred fish-[guts] heads and eggshells
heaped on a square of brown paper.

This description of the Dedalus kitchen
appears twice in abbreviated form
among the note-sheets for *Ulysses*
now in the possession of Miss Harriet
Weaver. First, with notes for the *Cyclops*
episode: "Dilly's Kitchen: oatmeal
water, cat devours charred fishheads
and eggshells heaped on square of
brown paper, shell cocoa in kettle,
sootcoated." And again among notes for
the *Eumaeus* episode: "Dilly's Kitchen:
oatmeal water, cat devours charred
fishheads & eggshells heaped on brown
paper, shell cocoa in sootcoated kettle"

The scene finally reached print in *Ulysses* as follows: " . . . Stephen's mind's eye being too busily engaged in repicturing his family hearth the last time he saw it, with his sister, Dilly, sitting by the ingle, her hair hanging down, waiting for some weak Trinidad shell cocoa that was in the sootcoated kettle to be done so that she and he could drink it with the oatmeal water for milk after the Friday herrings they had eaten at two a penny, with an egg apiece for Maggy, Boody and Katey, the cat meanwhile under the mangle devouring a mess of eggshells and charred fish heads and bones on a square of brown paper in accordance with the third precept of the church to fast and abstain on the days commanded, it being quarter tense or, if not, ember days or something like that." (*U* 604)

"Mrs Daedalus began to cry. Stephen, having eaten and drunk all within his province, rose and went towards the door:

—It's all the fault of those books and the company you keep. Out at all hours of the night instead of in your home, the proper place for you. I'll burn every one of them. I won't have them in the house to corrupt anyone else—

Stephen halted at the door and turned towards his mother who had now broken out into tears:

His mother, flushed and red-eyed sat by the range. Stephen, weary of the strife [lean] of tongues, leaned against the japanned wall of the fireplace. Noises and cries and laughter echoed in the narrow yard: and from time to time a nose was flattened against the window pane, fingers tapped mockingly and a young voice, faint and high in the dim evening, asked if the genius had finished his phrenology.—It is all over those books you read. I knew you would lose your faith. I'll burn everyone of them—

—If you had not lost [the] your faith— said Stephen—you would burn me along with the books—

—If you were a genuine Roman Catholic, mother, you would burn me as well as the books—"[7]

FRAGMENT *B* (one sheet)

shed his blood for all men they have no need of other aspersion.

Doherty's gibes flashed to and fro through the torpor of his mind and he thought without mirth of his friend's face, equine and pallid, and of his pallid hair, grained and hued like oak. He had tried to receive coldly these memories of his friend's boisterous humour, feeling that his coarseness of speech was not a blasphemy of the spirit but a coward's mask, but in the end the troop of swinish images broke down his reserve and went trampling through his memory, followed by his laughter:

I'm the queerest young fellow that
   ever you heard.
My mother's a jew, my father's a bird.
With Joseph the joiner I cannot
   agree
So here's to disciples and Calvary!

My methods are new and are causing
   surprise.
To make the blind see I throw dust
   in their eyes. . . .

"'If I told them there is no water in the font to symbolise that when Christ has washed us in blood we have no need of other aspersions.'"[8]

On page 5 of *Ulysses* Mulligan's face is described as "equine in its length." He has "light untonsured hair, grained and hued like pale oak." See also page 40 of *Ulysses*: "The oval equine faces. Temple, Buck Mulligan, Foxy Campbell."

Buck Mulligan chants this stanza of the Ballad of Joking Jesus, with two others, to Stephen in the first episode of *Ulysses* (*U* 20–21).

      "EDWARD THE SEVENTH
(*Levitates over heaps of slain in the garb
and with the halo of Joking Jesus, a
white jujube in his phosphorescent face.*)
My methods are new and are causing
   surprise.
To make the blind see I throw dust
   in their eyes." (*U* 576)

FRAGMENT *C* (one sheet)

rage:
—Devil out of hell! We won! We
crushed him to death!
  Fiend!—
  The door slammed behind her.
  Mr. Casey, freeing his arms from his
holders, suddenly
bowed his head on his hands with a sob
of pain.
—Poor Parnell!—he cried loudly—My
dead King!—
  He sobbed loudly and bitterly.
  Stephen, raising his terror-stricken
face, saw that his father's eyes were full
of tears.

With the exception of minor points of
punctuation, this passage is the same
as the conclusion of the dinner-table
scene in *A Portrait of the Artist as a
Young Man.*

These fragments are obviously from a late draft of Joyce's autobiographical novel. Internal evidence alone would be sufficient to establish this
fact. The finished style, the condensation of the scene between Stephen
and his mother, and the form "Dedalus" (instead of the earlier "Daedalus"
of *Stephen Hero)* point to a date of composition considerably after the
completion of the *Stephen Hero* manuscript in 1906.[9] The five sheets are
similar in size, quality of paper, and handwriting, and probably date from
the same period. Fragment *C* is practically identical with its counterpart
in the final version of the *Portrait,* and this fact, together with the *Ulysses*
adumbrations, suggests a late dating of the fragments. The terminal date
is obviously the end of 1913, since the *Portrait* began to appear serially in
the *Egoist* on 2 February 1914. The earlier limit is established by Joyce's
own account of the burning of the *Stephen Hero* manuscript, which I see
no reason to doubt even though it conflicts with the account given in Herbert Gorman's biography. "The 'original' original I tore up and threw into
the stove about eight years ago in a fit of rage on account of the trouble
over *Dubliners.* The charred remains of the MS were rescued by a family
fire brigade and tied up in an old sheet where they remained for some
months. I then sorted them out and pieced them together as best I could

and the present MS is the result."[10] Whatever one's final decision may be as to the burning of *Stephen Hero*, this letter indicates that Joyce dated the final phase of his work on the *Portrait* from 1911–12. There is confirmation of this in Gorman's biography, in a passage referring to late 1911 and early 1912: "Joyce was working again, when he had the time, on the third version of the novel (now definitely called *A Portrait of the Artist as a Young Man*) and he planned to make it much shorter than that behemoth of two thousand written pages he had envisaged under the title of *Stephen Hero*" (p. 208). The deletions in Fragment *A*, particularly of "sat in" and "lean," are such as would occur in a hasty copying from another manuscript; they appear to be the result of the eye outdistancing the hand, and suggest that at least one other version of the scene may lie between *Stephen Hero* and this text. These copying errors support a date for the fragments well along in the final (1911–13) period.

For the critic of *Ulysses*, Fragments *A* and *B* are of immense importance. Doherty is a prototype of Buck Mulligan, an intermediary between the Oliver St. John Gogarty of real life and the fictionalized Gogarty of *Ulysses*. His mocking attitude is the same as that of Mulligan, his features are described in the same words: "equine and pallid, . . . pallid hair, grained and hued like oak." There is also a suggestion of Cranly's condescension in his manner. In the opening chapter of *Ulysses* Mulligan links his arm in Stephen's, and Stephen thinks: "Cranly's arm. His arm"(*U* 9). "Cranly" and "Buck Mulligan" are both listed as characters for the *Telemachus* episode on one of the *Ulysses* note-sheets now in Miss Weaver's possession, an indication of the importance Joyce attached to Stephen's association of the two companions. Doherty is Mulligan as he was to have appeared in the *Portrait*, before Joyce decided to make these incidents the center of the first episode in *Ulysses*.

Fragments *A* and *B* both begin with the memory of Doherty-Mulligan's mocking laughter tormenting Stephen's mind. A probable context for Fragment *B* is established by the broken sentence which opens it, an echo from *Stephen Hero*. In the early novel Stephen attends a Good Friday service and watches two old women cross themselves with dry hands when leaving, not knowing why the font is empty. At the end of this scene Joyce penciled "If I told them there is no water in the font to symbolise that when Christ has washed us in blood we have no need of other aspersions" (p. 106). Joyce may have intended Stephen's recollection of Doherty's blasphemous gibes to come at the end of this scene. There is no trace of the incident in the final version of *A Portrait*.

Doherty's recitation of the Ballad of Joking Jesus is resented by Stephen in the manuscript fragment for the same reason it is resented in *Ulysses*: Stephen cannot believe because of the inconsistencies humorously emphasized in the Ballad, but he is revolted by Mulligan's light treatment of the blasphemy. Disbelief is as serious a matter to Stephen as belief. The first stanza of the Ballad is chanted by Mulligan in the *Telemachus* episode, along with two others, but the verses which close the fragment ("My methods are new and are causing surprise, / To make the blind see I throw dust in their eyes") do not appear until *Circe*, where they are spoken by the apparition of Edward the Seventh. Thus the "usurping" Mulligan and the "usurping" British government are placed in the same category; both are enemies of Ireland and of honest belief or disbelief, and Joyce the exiled Irish-Catholic judges them together.

Fragment *A* provides an insight into Joyce's method of composition. The paragraph referring to Doherty contains many "seeds" for the first episode of *Ulysses*. The Martello tower is already an ironic symbol of retreat. As "*the Omphalos*" it is an emblem of the human navel, the source of life, and of the stone in the temple of Apollo at Delphi that was supposed to mark the center of the earth. It represents a mystical center which can provide no refuge for Stephen; he is forced to give the key to Mulligan, and the tower has become the home of Haines (Fr. *haine* 'hate') and the Black Mass. One is reminded of Stephen's bitter reverie in the *Proteus* episode:

Will you be as gods? Gaze in your omphalos.
Hello. Kinch here. Put me on to Edenville. (*U* 39)

Doherty's contempt for the Mass is consistent with Buck Mulligan's parody of the sacrament in *Ulysses*. "*Semel in die*" prepares the way for Mulligan's daily mockery of the Mass while shaving, and in both contexts the ritual is treated as a magician's trick. Similarly, every element in the first paragraph of Fragment *A* is related to the *Telemachus* episode in some way. For instance, the reference to Whitman in the fragment differs from that in *Ulysses*, but the essential fact, the comparison between the blustering animalism of Doherty-Mulligan and Whitman, remains unchanged.

The paragraph in Fragment *A* describing the kitchen of Joyce's home has a fascinating career of revisions. It is reminiscent of many naturalistic descriptions of the sordid conditions of Stephen's home in *Stephen Hero*, and in the context it emphasizes the dreary background of Mrs. Dedalus' faith. The paragraph was not included in the *Portrait*, but it obviously epiphanized for Joyce the hopeless wretchedness of his home, since it persists in outline form through two of the note-sheets for *Ulysses*, and appears in an expanded version in the *Eumaeus* episode. During this development the context of the descriptive passage was altered: in *Eumaeus* it is Stephen's vivid memory of his home as he last saw it, some time after his mother's death, and in this connection it represents the spiritual and physical poverty of his family which Stephen fears will "drown" him.[11]

The evolution of this passage illustrates two important characteristics of Joyce's revisions. First, it demonstrates that his portrayals of his own life and home in the *Portrait* and *Ulysses* are faithful in spirit but not always historically accurate. Often scenes are shifted from one context to another, and substantially altered, during the course of revision. The rewritings of *Stephen Hero*, the *Portrait*, and *Ulysses* mirror Joyce's shifting attitude towards his early life: the movement is from the personal to the impersonal, from individual to general significance, from autobiography to biography. Joyce freely altered facts in his struggle towards a "dramatic" ideal.

Secondly, the changes in the passage illustrate the way in which a word or phrase is used by Joyce in his notes to suggest whole scenes or large segments of dialogue. The sequence of concrete images found on the *Ulysses* note-sheet ("oatmeal water, cat devours charred fishheads & eggshells heaped on brown paper, shell cocoa in sootcoated kettle") was used by Joyce to recall to his mind the entire scene. It is interesting to note that the images here are *visual*: later, in the notes for *Ulysses* and *Finnegans Wake*, rhythm and sound play an important part in effecting the recall. Having the broad outline of his work already in mind, Joyce used these abbreviated notations to remind himself of the material available for each stage of the composition. The analogy is with mosaic work, and the method reflects the static nature of his art.

Stephen's argument with his mother, a matter of one paragraph in Fragment A, covered five pages in *Stephen Hero* (pp. 115–119). In the *Portrait* it is simply alluded to in a conversation between Stephen and Cranly:

—Cranly, I had an unpleasant quarrel this evening.

—With your people? Cranly asked.

—With my mother.

—About religion?

—Yes, Stephen answered.[12]

In Fragment *A* all the descriptive details of the *Stephen Hero* account have been eliminated; the result is an increase of emotional intensity in the portrayal of his mother's grief and in Stephen's embittered reply. Diffuse personal arguments have been retired in favor of a single intense passage. But even this concentrated presentation seemed too personal, too much a figure of his own revolt, to be retained by Joyce in the *Portrait*.

Nothing from Fragments *A* and *B* was utilized in the published version of the *Portrait*. The section recounting the quarrel between Stephen and his mother was rejected for reasons of artistic economy. The remaining elements of the two fragments were later worked into the text of *Ulysses* in one form or another. Joyce first thought of *Ulysses* as a short story for *Dubliners*. While he was in Rome he wrote to his brother Stanislaus on 30 September 1906: "I have a new story for 'Dubliners' in my head. It deals with Mr. Hunter." Again, on 13 November: "I thought of beginning my story, 'Ulysses,' but I have too many cares at present." And once more, on 6 February 1907: "'Ulysses' never got any forrarder than the title."[13] Since it is known that Mr. Hunter of Dublin was one of the models for Leopold Bloom (Gorman, p. 176), one can assume that this contemplated story represents Joyce's first vision of Bloom's adventures. It is also known, from Joyce's conversation with Georges Borach, one of his Zürich language students, that at approximately the same time he "comprehended that 'Ulysses' could well furnish the sequel" to the *Portrait*, the first draft of which was then about half completed (Gorman, p. 224). One may surmise that Joyce decided to exclude "Ulysses" from *Dubliners* because he realized its potentialities as a novel-length successor to the *Portrait*.

The idea of Stephen's participation in a later work to be called *Ulysses* must have been well advanced by 1911–12, and the outline of the whole novel was probably visualized as well, since Gorman says that Joyce began to make "preliminary sketches for the final sections" of *Ulysses* early in 1914, immediately after finishing the *Portrait*. In the light of this information, it is almost certain that the scenes involving Doherty and Stephen were rejected during the final revision of the *Portrait* because Joyce was already planning the roles Stephen and Mulligan were to have in *Ulysses*. This confirms the *Portrait's* position as prologue and introduction to *Ulysses*, for Joyce made his last revisions of it with the characters, plot, and even some of the incidental scenes of the later work consciously in mind.

Fragments *A* and *B* reveal the characteristics of Joyce's technique at the time when he began *Ulysses*. The compression demanded by his theory of "epiphany" and the aloof tone resulting from his notion of "stasis" are everywhere evident.[14] Already apparent are the allusiveness and symbolic "thickening" (as in the "*Omphalos*" figure) that give his later works a dense texture comparable to that of poetry. The flow of Doherty's words through Stephen's mind has the quality of the "interior monologue" in *Ulysses*, and the treatment of time found in *Ulysses* and *Finnegans Wake* can be discovered in these fragments. Both of the scenes involving Doherty come to Stephen as memories prompted by his present situation, thus illustrating Joyce's desire to use memory as an agent for investing every moment with the richness of layer upon layer of associated experiences.

Notes

1. Herbert Gorman, *James Joyce*, New Ed. (New York, 1948), p. 176.

2. See W. Y. Tindall, "Joyce's Chambermade Music," *Poetry*, LXXX (May 1952), 105–116.

3. Bernard Gheerbrant, ed., *James Joyce: Sa Vie, Son Œuvre, Son Rayonnement* (Paris: La Hune, 1949).

4. The *Epiphanies* are now in the Lockwood Memorial Library, Univ. of Buffalo. See John J. Slocum and Herbert Cahoon, *A Bibliography of James Joyce, 1882–1941* (New Haven, 1953), p. 153, item a. x.

5. Gorman, *James Joyce*, p. 136.

6. *Ulysses*, Modern Library ed., p. 5. Throughout the remainder of this article page references to the Modern Library ed. of *Ulysses* will be inserted directly in the text, preceded by the letter "*U*" and enclosed in parentheses.

7. *Stephen Hero*, ed. Theodore Spencer (London, 1944), p. 119.

8. *Stephen Hero*, p. 106. Added in pencil at the end of Chapter xx of the MS.

9. For the dating of *Stephen Hero*, see Theodore Spencer's comments in his Introd. (*Stephen Hero*, pp. 5–6), and Joyce's letter to Grant Richards dated 13 March 1906 (Gorman, *James Joyce*, p. 148).

10. This passage, quoted on p. 137 of the Slocum and Cahoon *Bibliography*, is from a letter Joyce wrote to Harriet Weaver on 1 Jan. 1920. Herbert Gorman says that in 1908 Joyce "burned a portion of *Stephen Hero* in a fit of momentary despair and then started the novel anew in a more compressed form" (Gorman, *James Joyce*, p. 196). Gorman

may have mistaken the date, or he may, as Stanislaus Joyce suggests, have confused an attempt to burn *Dubliners* with the burning of *Stephen Hero*. We shall probably never know the exact details of this important event. The various accounts are summarized on pp. 136–137 of the Slocum and Cahoon *Bibliography*.

11. See *Ulysses*, p. 240.

12. *The Essential James Joyce*, ed. Harry Levin (London, 1948), p. 355.

13. Quoted by Gorman, *James Joyce*, p. 176.

14. For Joyce's remarks on the "epiphany" and "stasis," see p. 188 of *Stephen Hero*, and pp. 329–331 of *The Essential James Joyce*.

8

Cruxes in *Ulysses*

Notes toward an Edition and Annotation

EDMUND L. EPSTEIN

Ulysses constitutes a special case in modern literature. First of all, it is by an Irishman, and it is about Ireland, Dublin specifically, during a period that existed more than fifty years ago. If Joyce were less Irish, or if he had chosen to write a less Irish book, there would be as little need for scholarly attention to *Ulysses* as for any other large modern work. As it is, however, there exists a great need for work of some kind on the *places* of *Ulysses,* since Dublin is not a favorite city for literary attention. Readers who would be mentally at home in the Rue du Faubourg St. Honoré, beside the Serpentine, or even on the Nevsky Prospekt, find themselves adrift in a sea of Nelson Pillars, Sandycoves, Sandymounts, Eccles Streets, Kingstowns and Greens of all kinds, along with thousands of other Dublin and County Dublin places, many of which play an extremely important part in the story. This situation exists, of course, because until Joyce happened along Dublin lacked a Dickens, a Balzac or a Tolstoy to make its features famous and to impress the characteristic places and monuments of their cities on the mental retina of every literate man. But whatever the reason, the fact remains that an unprepared reader can be swamped by more detail of geography, a trap that Joyce certainly did not intend for his readers. Other sorts of details, such as speech mannerisms, slang terms, and the like appear constantly on every page of *Ulysses,* causing great hardship to those readers who realize that they are in foreign territory, and hopelessly confusing those readers who do not, who must often think that they are merely plowing through gibberish.

Edmund L. Epstein, "Cruxes in *Ulysses*: Notes toward an Edition and Annotation," *James Joyce Review* 1, no. 3 (1957) 25–36. Reprinted with permission from *James Joyce Review*. Copyright 1957.

Many of these traps are carefully hidden; so many slang terms seem to refer to something within the experience of the reader; but most of them are extremely deceptive and confusing. An example of this sort of confusion: at the end of the Wandering Rocks section, Simon Dedalus comes out of a "greenhouse" just in time to "bring his hat low" to salute the procession of the British rulers of Dublin (p. 249). Now the unlikeliness of the situation is evident; the scene takes place on Ormond Quay, which is a narrow street fronting on the Liffey, and there is not room for a greenhouse anywhere on the street. The "greenhouse" might be a green pub named after the fashion of the Scotch House, another pub; it might be, but it is not. A "greenhouse" in Dublin slang is a urinal, a fact that I discovered while reading the French translation of *Ulysses,* which kindly translates all of the slang terms in the book into non-slang French. Here is a point at which an extraordinary amount of confusion and "derailing" could occur. Some readers, in fact most readers, would have skipped over the reference and thus missed the point of Simon's gesture of obeisance to the gubernatorial procession, which gesture is less a mark of respect to British authority than a movement of the hat to conceal certain ineluctable adjustments of the garments necessary after trips to the greenhouse. Some readers would have tried to visualize the scene and failed, if they preferred the agricultural interpretation of the phrase, and others would have given way to the temptation to make every unknown noun in the book refer either to a beerhouse or to a brothel. (This last tendency is not confined to the common reader; editors of anthologies and critics of Joyce have made similar blunders. One editor, in fact, turned a highly respectable sporting-goods house still flourishing on O'Connell Street into a defunct brothel with a wave of his hand.) If the idealistic abstract plea for complete knowledge of a subject has no force, at least it is possible to imagine the *practical* havoc such minced references could work on the interpretation of the book by critics and by the common reader; unfortunately it is not necessary to strain your imagination on the subject.

Another example: Leopold Bloom lights a cone of incense in his bedroom in the penultimate chapter of *Ulysses;* why? Is he a mystic or a devil-worshipper; is he drunk with the soul of the mysterious East? After all, earlier in the day he did seem nostalgic for the countries of the East, if it is possible to be nostalgic towards a place you have never visited. The explanation is quite simple; the room smells from the activities of the day, and an age that knew not of air-conditioners had to make do with incense. As a matter of fact, cones of incense can still be bought in poorer neighborhoods even in New York, and for the same purpose. Yet if this is not realized, or pointed out, a great deal of confusion can result. A great deep in Bloom's personality seems to have opened before the eyes of the deceived reader; Bloom appears as a true mystic, a hidden and subtle romantic, and so on. There is a double (perhaps a triple) trap here: *one*, the reader will believe Bloom to be an open devil-worshipper; *two*, the reader will assume that here is a point at which the symbolic level of the story impinges grossly and clumsily on the realistic level, causing a rupture of the allegorical fabric; after all, people in real life do not make unprepared and unusual symbolic motions and perform ritual ceremonies unless they are complete prigs, or devotees of obscure cults, and Bloom is definitely neither. Joyce would be a clumsy literary craftsman if he would allow such an error of form to appear in his work. Realizing that there is a valid, necessary, compelling reason (on the realistic level) to burn incense (the room smells and is very stuffy), helps to restore the realistic level to unblemished unruptured perfection, and at the same time allows the symbolic meaning of the action, which *is* probably connected to the meaning that the East has for Bloom, to assume its proper emphasis in the allegorical framework of the story. Without a realistic reason the "raw" symbolism would be rather too much to take. The third trap that would be created by a gap in communication here is involved with the correspondence with the *Odyssey* that underlies the book. The burning of the incense corresponds to the purification of the house with burning sulfur by Odysseus after he has slain the suitors (Book 22). Assuming that Bloom is made to burn incense solely to correspond to an action of Odysseus in the *Odyssey* is to make both Bloom and Joyce ridiculous. One can see the implications of this, both for the actual passage itself and for the general conclusions on Joyce's method and, eventually, Joyce's literary stature. The common reader, with the assistance of J. Donald Adams and others, has been complaining of the vagaries of Joyce criticism for too long, but his criticisms are partly justified.

Other confusions are more innocent and do not lead to such complex misunderstandings; but they disturb the establishment of "composition of place," the heightened sense of physical and moral environment defined by St. Ignatius in the *Spiritual Exercises,* which I believe Joyce tried to achieve with his accounts of the realistic details of Dublin life in *Ulysses.* For example, John Henry Menton's hat acquires a dent (or "dinge") in the Cemetery scene and Bloom points it out to him, to do him a service, Bloom thinks. (He had done a similar service for the great Parnell, and got the same answer, "Thank you," but said in a warm tone of voice.) The act is difficult to justify if one imagines Menton wearing a fedora or a homburg. A dent in a soft hat is not such a dreadful thing; why should Bloom feel hurt when Menton answers with a cold "Thank you"? He must have been a fool to expect any more. Of course, the fact is that Menton, like most men of his day, wore either a derby, a bowler, a gentleman's hard hat, or a top hat, and a dent in a derby or a top hat looks very bad. Bloom deserved better for pointing it out. (By the way, it is rather startling to realize that *Ulysses* is swimming in derby hats. Practically all of the men except Stephen wear them; it certainly lowers the "epic" tone of the book quite a bit.)

The approach that illumines the physical and sartorial commonplaces of fifty years ago for the benefit of the common reader might with profit be applied to the fields of intellectual opinion and the trends of mental training of the post-Victorian period. It would certainly help if the reader knew what attitude to take toward Buck Mulligan's Hellenism to decide if Stephen's bitter description of Ireland as the "Faubourg Saint-Patrice" was justified, or if it was merely one more of those personal outbursts disguised as impersonal criticism that he has been indulging in all day. It might be interesting to do some research on Bloom's rather novel ideas for advertising layouts, which seem to be far ahead of their time. (By the way, it was probably never pointed out that *Ulysses* is the first book ever written with an advertising man as hero.) It might be of interest to observe how Bloom's humanitarianism is the fine old Victorian kind, and not the modern variety, which is based on Walt Disney's animals, not on abused carthorses. As for Bloom's interest in mnemotechnic, it would, I think, help the common reader to arrive at a just estimate of Bloom's character and talents if it could be determined whether there was an established and organized movement for memory training, or whether the introduction of this trait in Bloom depends solely on a metempsychotic polylingual pun: *mnemo*, the first element of the word, is pronounced in English in exactly the same way as the word *nemo*, the Latin word meaning "nobody," or more Homerically, "Noman," thus making mnemotechnic the art of being anonymous, or of being *Outis* as well as Odysseus. Both of these interpretations are probably valid; if you will recall Bloom is intensely interested in any system of self-improvement he comes across, such as the Sandow system for building a beautiful body ("On the hands down!"), which was probably wasted on him. It is, you see, my plan to account for everything on the realistic level that *can* be accounted for on that basis before looking for purely formal and symbolic structures. It seems to make the whole book more solid and more like the "epic of the city" as it has been, or should have been, called, and less like a vulgar paraphrase of the *Odyssey* or a shadowy symbolic paradigm of things.

The preceding suggested categories in the plan for adumbration of the time-concealed parts of *Ulysses* do not include many important things. The facts in the categories certainly help to get the "feel" of the period, and mere mistakes of fact can be avoided by consultation in the fields outlined above; but many, if not all, of the readers of *Ulysses* are already familiar with much of the material; the editor should make no claim of exclusive or secret knowledge of any kind. Nor will the inclusion of a list of the Dublin places mentioned in the book, with coordinates referring to an enclosed map of the region and notes on unavoidable suggestions of the places, be revealing more than many readers know already. Nevertheless, such a listing should be included, as well as a similar list containing the names of every character mentioned in *Ulysses,* whether or not he or she was a real person, and the important surrounding circumstances that determined Joyce in his decision to include them in the book. For example, "Boss Croker" is on one of the seals that dangle from the belt of the Cyclops character in one of the "gigantic" paragraphs of the Cyclops section. Croker was, as almost everybody knows, Richard Croker, the leader of Tammany Hall for many years, in the late nineteenth century. What is less well known is that Croker retired to Ireland after his labors in the municipal arenas and lived an expansive, philanthropic life as a country gentleman. He even raised horses, one of which won the English Derby. Joyce, with his rarefied sense of morality, as well as his exalted sense of irony, was almost morally bound to include the retired wardheeler among the great Irishmen of the ages, as a man of whom Ireland was proud, disregarding the sub rosa origin of his wealth, and regarding only the great air of respectability of his later life.

Other historical characters, like Wolfe Tone, may perhaps need less notice than Dubliners contemporary with the period of the book, but Irish history is not everyone's meat; there should, therefore, be notes on every historical character in the book, with extended discussion, if necessary, of special meanings and connotations suggested by Joyce. One such character will be Parnell, of course. Joyce's first published work dealt with the Parnell case, and he finally came to seem a great deal more than merely another betrayed Irish leader to Joyce. Parnell is perhaps the metempsychotic equivalent of Agamemnon in the *Odyssey*, and John Howard Parnell, his brother, might be Menelaus, for example. The note on the Parnells would include all of this reasoning, as well as general notes on the larger political and psychological meanings of the betrayal of Parnell that would suggest themselves to Joyce and influence his work.

There should be translations of every foreign phrase in *Ulysses*, with the usual notes on special contextual and semantic overtones where necessary. This category would eventually include more than five hundred notes on phrases in Latin, Greek, Hungarian, French, German, Italian, Irish, Elizabethan thieves' cant, pig latin, Hebrew and Yiddish.

There would also be definitions of every difficult or unusual word or expression, and every specimen of slang would be rendered into standard English. Of course, many definitions of words in *Ulysses* can be found in the OED or in the various volumes of Partridge on Unconventional Language and Slang; but which can be found in which? Determining the meaning of each difficult phrase or word is almost as difficult a task with these two great aids as it would be without them. And what of the slang words that are not included in the OED and in Partridge? There must be some. Besides these factors, there are, as in the category of the historical figures and geographical locations, overtones and special connotations and personal reasons for the specific phrases chosen by Joyce that should be noted. For example, in the Library Scene Stephen lets the word "nook-shotten" flash into his "subvocalic layer" as he realizes that his elaborate dialogue on Shakespeare has lost the interest of the unpleasant *littérateurs;* the word itself seems to mean "filled with coves and inlets." The meaning of the word would probably include the concept of "discontinuity" as well, expressing the derailing of the sense of composition of place that Stephen has built up so painfully and at such a cost of self-contempt; the "place" of course would be Elizabethan London. The most famous source of this uncommon word is Shakespeare ("the nook-shotten isle of Albion"), but beside the fact that the subject of Shakespeare is still hanging in the air there seem to be no connection of the word (an unusual word, to be sure) with anything else but itself. The context is not meaningful in Shakespeare to the events of *Ulysses.* However, the word "nook-shotten" *was* used in a famous gibe at one of Stephen's idols, Ibsen, with whom Stephen identifies quite closely. If Stephen *had* to be insulted, it would be some consolation to pick out an adjective that had been used on his hero. (Ibsen had been called "the nook-shotten Norwegian" by an unfriendly critic back in the first wild days of his invasion of England.) There are, after all, other influences of the personal character of Ibsen in *Ulysses.* Professor Goodwin wears a mirror in his hat, just as Ibsen did; but I fear that Goodwin's motives were not pure. If you will recall, he "used to bow Molly off the platform" after she had finished a concert "in the old-fashioned way" which was to bow low from the waist and stand behind the diva as she swept off the stage, with both arms extended out in front of you and slightly lowered at an angle of forty-five degrees to each other, with your hat in your right hand. The mirror in Professor Goodwin's hat might have provided more glimpses of the moon than Hamlet's father ever saw.

And you would probably be surprised to learn how many people miss the point of Buck Mulligan's description of George Moore as "lecturer on French letters to the youth of Ireland" (p. 212) because they do not know that "French letters" is a well-known British and Irish slang term for contraceptives. Besides the obvious joke, an important link in the sterility-fertility symbolic complex is lost for these readers.

Of course, sometimes Joyce uses long or unusual words for an effect of exaggerated dryness and scientific accuracy; and sometimes these words are difficult to define, even with the aid of a large dictionary, because Joyce seems to make them up out of Greek and (especially) Latin roots. Such words are "arenary" (sandy), "emunctory" (referring to wiping of the nose), and "imprevidibility" (unforeseeableness). These words also should be tracked down and defined, with the usual extra notice when necessary simply for the immediate convenience of the reader. Occasionally such a word will mislead even an experienced Joycean who is also a consummate classical scholar, like Stuart Gilbert, who slips up on the word "latration." The word occurs in the penultimate chapter (p. 710) where Joyce describes the various economic misfortunes from which Bloom is protected by his bank account and his insurance policy. One of the humiliations that a pauper would have to suffer is the "latration of illegitimate unlicenced vagabond dogs," which Gilbert defines as the "befouling" of Bloom. Actually the word is derived from "*latrare,* to bark (Lat.)," and, I believe, occurs nowhere else in modern English. Joyce can appear a great deal more innocent or a great deal more offensive than he actually is; he seems to like to play such tricks on his readers.

An extremely important part of the word-list would include all of the identifiable quotations in *Ulysses*, probably listed under their key words; where there is more than one key word, cross-references would have to be used. Stephen especially among the characters in the book seems to "think" in truncated quotations, a fact that he realizes and deplores because it suggests that he lacks originality and thus creativity. Some passages are almost completely impenetrable because of this habit of his and, to a lesser degree, of the other people of the book. Sometimes the quotation appears in full, with identification of source; such a one is the quotation from Augustine that flashes into Stephen's mind and gives him an instant of joy before he realizes ("Curse you!") that it is not his own creation (p. 140). Most of the time it happens that all of the quotation that we get is a fragment or even, sometimes, just a word. A particularly impressive example of the fragmented quotation occurs on p. 194. Stephen describes Shakespeare as a "lord of language." The original source of the phrase is Tennyson's "To Virgil," stanza II:

> "Landscape-lover, *lord of language* more than he that sang the
>   'Works and Days,'
> All the chosen coin of fancy flashing out from many a golden phrase
>   . . ."

but there is nothing in the context to suggest why Stephen should use this phrase of Shakespeare. Of course he may be quoting some critic or scholar who adapted Tennyson's phrase to Shakespeare; it certainly seems appropriate enough. But there is a much more relevant source than this. In Oscar Wilde's *De Profundis* (published in 1905, but Joyce committed other anachronisms in *Ulysses*) there occurs the following rather purple, but affecting passage:

> A week later, I am transferred here [Reading Gaol]. Three more months go over and my mother dies. No one knew better than you [Douglas] how deeply I loved and honoured her. Her death was terrible to me; but I, once a *lord of language*, have no words in which to express my anguish and my shame. Never even in the most perfect days of my development as an artist could I have found words fit to bear so august a burden; or to move with sufficient

stateliness of music through the purple pageant of my incommunicable woe . . . (*De Profundis*, Oscar Wilde, Philosophical Library, New York, n.d., p. 65).

Stephen's mind is superficially occupied with the intellectual drift of his argument and by the painful effort he is making to impress the snobs of Dublin with his critical powers; but underneath is still the terrible, obsessive sorrow and guilt for the death of his mother that he has been fighting off all day and that is corroding his morale and crowding in front of his mind in times like this. There is a whole clandestine anthology of matricide and unworthy paternity in *Ulysses*; it underlies much of the seemingly pointless choice of quotation and also much of the mannerism. Other topics beside the mother and the father complex influence the flow of the interior monologue. Sometimes the "censor" intervenes at a word that arouses painful associations in the "monologist"; this is true both of Stephen and of Bloom. For example, in the following quotation an important word is left out, and nothing in the context suggests what it could be: "But the courtiers who mocked Guido in Or San Michele were in their own house. House of . . ." (p. 46). The reference to Guido derives from the *Decameron*, 6th Day, 9th Story, in which Guido Cavalcanti answers the witty insults of a group of his rather rough friends. He goes walking in the Orto San Michele to San Giovanni, where there were many great marble tombs. His friends ride up and see him brooding moodily (like Stephen). They say, "Let us go plague him." Spurring their horses they charge down upon him shouting, "Guido, thou refusest to be of our company; but, harkye, whenas thou shalt have found that God is not, what wilt thou have accomplished?" Guido, seeing himself forced to answer, says promptly, "Gentlemen, you may say what you will to me in your own house," and leaps over one of the tombs and skims away, no doubt smiling a scholar's smile as he leaps along. His friends are puzzled by his inconsequential answer, until one of the brighter ones comes up with the solution: "He hath courteously and in a few words given us the sharpest rebuke in the world; for that, an you consider aright, these tombs are *the Houses of the dead*, seeing that they are laid and abide therein, and these, saith he, are our house, meaning thus to show us that we and other foolish and unlettered men are, compared with him and other men of learning, worse than dead folk; wherefore, being here, we are in our house."[1] This story would appeal to Stephen for two reasons: Guido is accused of free-thinking, which would strike home at Stephen; and it would be a victory for scholarship over anti-intellectualism, which is a sufficiently rare occurrence to make it prized when it does happen. The suppressed word in Stephen's train of thought is, of course, "death." He suppresses another taboo word later on, when he says (not thinks this time), "I will arise and go to my . . ." (p. 506). The hidden word is, of course, "father"; the source is the story of the Prodigal Son, which also furnished a quotation about "filling my belly with husks of swine," and which fits into the anti-paternal complex of the book. Bloom also suppresses a word, though not so completely as Stephen. Bloom repeats a proverb that "a pin cuts lo—" and will not say the last part of the word, which is "love." Bloom mistrusts the word *love* because he knows only too well that love of the sort that is not "the opposite of hate," his hasty definition in the Cyclops chapter, is being made at his expense by his wife and persons known and disliked. (Poor Bloom! Everyone is so tactless about his marital misfortunes. McCoy chooses the worst way in the world to ask about the backing of Molly's proposed tour; he asks, "Who's getting it up?" and Bloom shows that he catches the *double-entendre* by his uncomfortable and hasty outline of the financial structure of the tour. Also the loafers in Barney Kiernan's saloon can find nothing but unfaithful wives to talk about in his presence, which finally irritates him sufficiently to answer the fool of a Citizen's anti-Semitic bawlings.) We would miss several rich and meaningful touches to the subtle and complex texture of the novel if we lose the thread of the thought every so often simply because we lack a part of a quotation. Ariadne's clue of thread is dangerously weak in spots; it is no disgrace to grope and feel about us on our way back on the path to the clearing of the Beast.

Study of inhibitions on subvocalizings leads to another, more complex subject: the articulations of the interior monologue. It has long been recognized that *Ulysses* does not consist solely of random thoughts jotted down, although the novelist Dorothy Richardson seems to have made that mistake when she took her conception of *Ulysses* as a model for her own novels. Actually there is constant evidence of subconscious workings under the oral façade (or really the *sub-oral façade*). Everyone knows of the Penrose touch; Bloom tries to remember the name of a young man whom he once knew, and fails; he goes on to think of other things and people, and a few pages later suddenly remembers that the man was named Penrose, showing that his mind was working all the time "in inarticulate counterpoint" to his stream of subvocal comment, on the task that he set himself, to remember a name of a character who might be important in the story (as a surrogate for Stephen?). This episode has not really been used as the basis of a consistent theory of Joyce's construction of a stream of consciousness, but other examples could be instanced to show the contrapuntal and "reciprocal" nature of the thought processes of Bloom and of Stephen. For example, an incident on p. 102, in the Hades Episode, is much less innocent and much more meaningful, both for the revelation of the character of Bloom and for the general theory of subvocalisms as used by Joyce, than it seems. Bloom remembers a lively description of the Glasnevin chaplain by Si Dedalus, who said that "he had a belly on him like a poisoned pup." This word *poisoned* should ring bells for any Joycean; Bloom's father poisoned himself with aconite. Bloom *could* not approve of Si Dedalus' joke without seeming to the reader callous and indifferent to the fate of his "poisoned Pop." The fact is, of course, that he is not, and that he really resents Simon's joke. We can tell that he does by the phraseology of Bloom's next thought: "Most amusing expressions that man finds." The word *amusing* gives the whole show away. A man in Bloom's social position in the year 1904 would never say that a thing was *amusing* if he really enjoyed it; the word had acquired by then the aura of condescension that still clings to it. (It probably received its death-blow when Queen Victoria was *not* amused, in the first person plural.) No, Bloom is "faking" a reaction; he feels that he *ought* to approve the joke. It is (objectively) humorous, and Bloom is "Anglo-Saxon" enough to have a horror of the accusation of the lack of a sense of humor that some commentators have found a distinguishing characteristic of the English-speaking peoples. Of course, the cold sound of "that man finds" helps along the impression of a "bump" in the interior monologue. This "bump," caused by the conflict between a conscious desire to appreciate a joke and an unconscious resentment of one of the elements of the joke, can only thin out the texture of the interior monologue at the point at which it occurs; if the resentment had been strong enough he would not have felt the obligation to react to its humor; if he had resented it less his reaction (subvocally) would probably be more in the whole-hearted vein of "Wow! Beef to the heels!" that occurs later, although it probably never would involve gales of laughter. (Bloom, like Ulysses, does not have an overpowering sense of humor. If you recall, Odysseus never smiles except when he is planning an exceptionally dirty trick; it is as much a part of him as his thick neck, which, by the way, is a Bloom characteristic also; he wears a size 17 collar (p. 695).)

This resentment possibly paves the way for Bloom's willingness to disregard Simon's legal claim to Stephen as his son later on in the book; the resentment festering inside of Bloom could emerge as a general feeling that Stephen was too fine to be saddled with such an insensitive father. Bloom appreciates sensitivity toward the feelings of others; he is very grateful to Martin Cunningham for his intercession in the unfortunate discussion of suicides that begins in the funeral carriage. Now, assuming that this is a valid and useful insight, and is symptomatic of a general theory of psychology in *Ulysses,* how is this category to be inserted into a study of *Ulysses?* Should there be a preface containing various headings and subheadings on various stubborn topics that will not reduce themselves to alphabetical cataloguing under the key words? Or do you think that the reader will look up such an innocent-appearing phrase as explained above under the key word *amusing?* Readers' comments would be appreciated.

I have been studying *Ulysses* for seven years now, and since I first bought my copy I have been finding useful information on difficult points in almost every book, magazine, throwaway, piece of music and scholarly article that I have come across. Some of the discoveries have bordered on the risky. For example, in Handel's *Acis and Galatea,* libretto by John Gay, the uncouth giant Polyphemus (*absit nomen*) sings of his love for the delicate Galatea in a famous, beautiful and completely ludicrous bass-baritone aria, "O Ruddier Than the Cherry." In the introductory recitative to this aria, which Joyce most probably knew, there occurs the unusual line "Bring me a hundred reeds of decent growth / To make a pipe for my capacious mouth." Now what are we to make of the fact that the word *capacious* occurs prominently in the Cyclops Episode, in a wonderful burlesque description of the burly hero himself, the Cyclops-Citizen, the Polyphemus of the Pubs? Is this coincidence? I would hate to think so. Is it *unconscious* imitation? There is no such thing in Joyce. Is it a symbolic device to indicate the basic unity of all Polyphemoi? This seems most likely, I would say. Yet how is the problem this raises, the question of the construction of *Ulysses,* to be solved? Could all of the complex facets of this problem be crowded into a note under the word *Cyclops,* or should it also be discussed in the Preface?

I have tried to indicate some of the discoveries I have made in the past few years on difficulties and cruxes in *Ulysses;* I have also tried to show some of the difficulties in organizing a book of these insights. I have said little about the great streams of symbols that underlie the book, like

Father, Mother, Death (beastly or spiritual), Authority, and the rest, which certainly are too involved and demand too much attention to be relegated each to its own little paragraph under its own little heading. Besides, who would know to look them up in their alphabetical order? I hope that readers can assist me on this point and on many of the other points involved with the construction of a responsible aid to the reading of *Ulysses*. The more provocative and useful letters would be printed in some future issue of the *JJR*, to be used by me or by someone else engaged on such a project as annotating *Ulysses*.

Notes

1. This discovery was made independently by Marvin Magalaner of CCNY.

9

The Anti-Semitic Limerick Incidents and Joyce's "Bloomsday"

MARVIN MAGALANER

The events which befall Leopold Bloom, in Joyce's *Ulysses*, do not occur in a vacuum. He may represent Everyman and at times he may bear distinguishable characteristics of Christ.[1] But first and foremost, he is a Jewish-born man, living in Dublin on 16 June 1904. His inescapable Jewishness, furthermore, is adduced by Joyce as a principal reason for Bloom's overpowering loneliness on that day. He cannot feel comfortable on the way to Paddy Dignam's funeral, even among his friends, when the conversation turns to the exploits of a Dublin moneylender "Of the tribe of Reuben." Lawyer Menton snubs him at the cemetery. Even his symbolic son, Stephen Dedalus, feels that the touch of Bloom's hand on his own is different from that of other men. "Stephen . . . thought he felt a strange kind of flesh of a different man approach him, sinewless and wobbly and all that." Finally, Bloom is threatened with bodily violence by the anti-Semitic nationalist in Barney Kiernan's pub.[2]

An investigation of the climate of tolerance toward Jews in Ireland during the year in question reveals that Joyce had wisely selected 1904 as the date of the events in his novel. Undoubtedly other, unrelated circumstances also dictated his decision.[3] Yet, if his hero was to be a persecuted Dublin Jew, no better year for summing up attitudes toward Irish Jewry in modern times could have been chosen.

Prior to the twentieth century, there had never been a "Jewish problem" in Ireland, possibly because there had been such an insignificant number of Jews in that country. In 1871, the Jewish population numbered

Marvin Magalaner, "The Anti-Semitic Limerick Incidents and Joyce's 'Bloomsday,'" *PMLA* 68 (December 1953): 1219–1223. Reprinted by permission of the Modern Language Association of America. Copyright 1953.

258 people. Twenty years later, the number had increased to 1,779, owing mainly to the influx of settlers from Russia. By the time of Bloomsday, there were fewer than four thousand Jews in Ireland, enough apparently to antagonize some of the native Irish population into open violence.[4] This vitriolic outburst of anti-Semitism, and its more philosophical aftermath, became big news on the front pages of leading newspapers and magazines in Dublin during the middle months of 1904—that is, close to the very day in June on which Mr. Bloom embarks upon his fabled odyssey.

That Joyce was aware of the topical controversy can hardly be doubted. If he did not see references to it in the *Freeman's Journal*, to whose pages he alludes occasionally in his fiction, he could have found it in one of Dublin's most influential literary periodicals, *The All Ireland Review*. Edited by the venerable Standish O'Grady, whose voluminous writings on Irish myth and history had created a background for the Celtic Renaissance, the review showed an interest in continental literature which must have had Joyce's eager support. In its issue of 2 January 1904 O'Grady had gone so far as to begin publication serially of an article by Ivan Tourgenieff (sic) on "Don Quixote and Hamlet."[5] It is difficult to believe that a young man whose stories of this period bear the marks of this Russian, and of Chekhov, Hauptmann, Maupassant, Ibsen—and whose interest in Hamlet furnishes material for a major motif in *Ulysses*[6]—should not have kept up with the articles in *The All Ireland Review*.

What controversy would Joyce have found in the periodical? On 23 April 1904, under the headline "Stoning a Rabbi—Crusade Against Jews at Limerick," the *Review* printed a short news note recording the fact that "John Rahilly, aged 15, was charged with being one of a number of boys who . . . stoned the Rev. Elias B. Levi . . . and two of his companion Israelites" (v, 200). The judge, who said that he was determined to stop such outbursts, sentenced the boy to one month's imprisonment. Following the news article, liberal-minded O'Grady comments editorially that the affair "reveals a scandalous state of things, which is a disgrace to the whole country." He shows particular courage when he adds:

> It is publicly stated that the persecution originated in a fierce anti-Jew sermon, preached by a Roman Catholic priest in Limerick. Whether this be so or not, it is difficult to believe that the priests and the Bishop of Limerick could not put an end to it if they tried . . .
> These Limerick Jews seem to be a very harmless body, neither

money-lenders nor extortioners; just traders trading in clothes, and selling the same at no more profit than is permitted. . . .

It is certainly high time for the Church of the people to exert its authority over the people, and end this vile persecution.

O'Grady's public reacted to these mild and unexceptionable words occasionally with restraint and reason, but more often with loud-mouthed vituperation. For every letter which came to the *Review* upholding the editor's plea, many bitter denunciations of O'Grady and the Jews were found in the mail. A correspondent who signed himself "M. Y." said on 30 April: "I think Jew-baiting is not based on religious motives either here or elsewhere. Still persecution is persecution and I am glad you have sounded a note of justice" (v, 211). Such reasonableness met the head-on attack of "S. A." on 7 May: "I was grieved . . . to see the line you took about the Jews. They are killing the place [Ireland] with extortion. . . . Indeed, I think it is a great pity that the Irish are prevented from driving all the Jews out, who will do them as grievous harm as they have done everywhere else" (v, 224). These remarks are reminiscent of the words of Mr. Deasy, the anti-Semitic headmaster in the Nestor episode of *Ulysses*. "Ireland," he says (p. 37), "has the honour of being the only country which never persecuted the jews. Do you know that? No. And do you know why?" His laughing reply to his own question is simply, "Because she never let them in." Joyce knows the standard responses in the catechism of anti-Semitism.

More significant than the epigrammatic utterances which are given above are the fuller, slanted accounts of attitudes toward the Jews, which appeared in the *Review* and were answered by the editor. "A Black Northman" makes no bones about his stand:

Since Father Creagh, C.SS.R., delivered his anathema against the Parasites, there has been much talking, much writing, much holding up of hypocritical holy hands. We Irish find it hard enough work to maintain a merest living in a country that should be our own by every right of descent . . . Yet, because one man in Ireland is of heart high enough to say a word in defence of his own—his beggarly own—he is condemned on all sides as a bigot and a fanatic. Ireland's body is a body diseased; there is a strange sickness upon her that saps herself while it feeds the Parasites. If she is to survive as a nation she must rouse herself and shake off the Parasites, who, if they could, would bleed her blue veins white. I happen to know Father Creagh . . . than

whom . . . there is no braver soul breathing in Ireland today. A heart
of flame burns within him—of love for the oppressed—and . . . of
holy hatred for the oppressors. (7 May, p. 224)

O'Grady's answer to this tirade is couched in terms which recall the wise
father rebuking the unruly child for raising his voice. He takes the position that if one believes the rabbi's statement that the Limerick Jews are
neither moneylenders nor extortioners, there can be no grounds for persecution. "You evidently don't believe the Rabbi; believe, on the contrary,
that the Limerick Jews cannot differ much from Jews everywhere else
. . ." The modern reader may smile at this evidence of latent anti-Jewish
sentiment even in the remarks of one who is making a plea in their be-
half. O'Grady goes on to admit that he does not know for certain the facts
of the Limerick situation. He proceeds to widen the issue. Assuming for
the sake of argument that "Northman" is correct in his estimate of Jewish damage to the economic life of Limerick, he raises the "great general
question . . . Have you yourself, nay has any man in Ireland, thought out
the right answers to the questions: 'What is usury?' 'What is extortion?'"

The editor advances to an indictment of Gentile businessmen. "The Jews
have not taught us these vile tricks and dishonest shortcuts to wealth; we
had them and practised them all long before he came, and are at them still,
and would be at them were we to expel the whole race of Jews en masse
to-morrow." If there were no Jews in Ireland, "our own Irish Christian usu-
rers . . . would be at just the same bad work, only without competitors."
O'Grady has only praise for the "more calculative heads" of the Jews; for
the fact that they "don't drink," and for the way they "concentrate upon
the game with an intensity of purpose of which we are incapable." He concludes sarcastically, "If it is as you say [in the north], your starved condition
up there ought to be a good protection against the Jews" (7 May, p. 224).

About one month before Bloomsday, a correspondent signing herself
simply "A Jewess" came forward with the Jewish view of the controversy.
Like Bloom himself, she can speak mildly yet firmly against the tenuous and fuzzy attacks of the anti-Semitic letter writers: "I won't comment
on the assertion that 'the Jews are killing Limerick'; that thirty-five families can destroy a town of a good many thousand inhabitants is, perhaps, rather a compliment than an insult." She demands to know on what
grounds the Black Northman condemns Jews as parasites. Spain, the
reader is reminded, drove out all Jews. "Will you, or any of your anti-

Semitic correspondents, hold up the Spain of today as an example of prosperity and progress . . . or compare her to the Spain of the Moors, when the great Jewish Doctors . . . flourished" (14 May, p. 232).

It is enlightening, and perhaps significant, to compare Mr. Bloom's remarks on the same subject, made in the Eumaeus episode of *Ulysses*: "Jews, he softly imparted in an aside in Stephen's ear, are accused of ruining. Not a vestige of truth in it, I can safely say. History—would you be surprised to learn?—proves up to the hilt Spain decayed when the Inquisition hounded the jews out and England prospered when Cromwell, an uncommonly able ruffian . . . imported them" (p. 628). "A Jewess," however, shows herself to be more aggressive than Bloom is: "Let 'Black Northman' *prove* that any Jew in Limerick resorted to illegal or immoral means . . . and *then* let him explain by what right any individuals or any Government . . . should persecute . . . thirty-five families because even a dozen persons of the same faith have sinned."

In replying to these forthright remarks, the honest but transparent O'Grady exhibits many typical reactions of Gentiles to Jews—reactions found in *Ulysses* and elsewhere. He pledges that he will try to be fair to both sides in his magazine but confesses to "certain sub-acid reflections . . . of a time when, young and foolish, and 'in a hole,' I visited a pair of gentlemen of your great race and left their little office with £25 in my pocket indeed, but also after having left behind me with them my promise to pay £30 in three months. That was a grand interest! Near 100 per cent per an.!" The inevitable result is easy to predict! "I paid it all right . . . but had I not, those gentlemen would have established over me for life a lien upon all my industries" (14 May, pp. 232–233).

O'Grady then resorts to the platitude, certainly sincere in this instance, of separating a whole people into the categories of bad Jews and good, my-best-friend types of Jews. Speaking of broadminded Semites, he says: "You are a good example yourself, I know; but I wish you would marry us more and not be so proud and aloof; but I suppose that would interfere with the heritage. Do you still hold that you are to give us the Messiah, in whom all the families of the earth are to be blessed? I mean the question very seriously."

Slowly, during the month of June 1904, the controversy disappeared from the public press. The persecution in Limerick, as an active movement, died away for two reasons. First, the boycott against Jewish tradesmen was successful enough so that only half a dozen Jewish families remained in that city. Furthermore, the Jewish population found a staunch supporter in Parnell's partner, the founder of the Land League, Michael Davitt. His letter to the *Freeman's Journal*, protesting "as an Irishman, and as a Catholic, against this spirit of barbarous malignity being introduced into Ireland, under the form of a material regard for the welfare of our workers," brought a cessation of overt acts against the Jews. But Davitt went further: "The Jews have never done any injury to Ireland. Like our own race, they have endured a persecution, the records of which will forever remain a reproach to the 'Christian' nations of Europe. Ireland has no share in this black record. Our country has this proud distinction . . . of never having resorted to this un-Christian and barbarous treatment of an unfortunate people."[7]

Several weeks after this public airing of the racial discrimination issue, Joyce left Ireland for good, to make his home on the continent. He carried with him, as a reading of *Ulysses* indicates, a clear mental and emotional picture of the Dublin he left behind him. From that time forward, he was able in his writings to draw upon fragments of that picture—the physical environment, the people, the speech, the local shops, the smells—as he needed them. Having selected as his central character a Jew, he wished, I think, to establish a frame of reference against which the reader might place the attitudes of Jew and non-Jew toward each other in the Ireland of that period. His meeting Nora Barnacle on 16 June 1904 had made that day especially memorable to him. But the Limerick affair and the ensuing discussion of it in the Dublin press may very likely have given him the background of tension which he was seeking.

Notes

1. S. Foster Damon, "The Odyssey in Dublin," in *James Joyce: Two Decades of Criticism* (New York, 1948), pp. 203–242.

2. James Joyce, *Ulysses* (New York, 1934), pp. 92 ff., 114, 644, and 339.

3. One of these unrelated circumstances, pointed out to me by Professor Joseph Prescott, is alluded to by Maria Jolas in her remark that Joyce and Nora Barnacle "first met on . . . June 16th 1904." (*British Broadcasting Company's James Joyce Memorial Broadcasts by His Family and Friends*, Part I, p. 27.)

4. Bernard Schillman, *A Short History of the Jews in Ireland* (Dublin, 1945), p. 128.

5. Translated by T. W. Rolleston, *All Ireland Rev.*, v (2 Jan. 1904), 5–6.

6. See the Scylla and Charybdis episode.

7. Schillman, *Short History of the Jews*, p. 137.

I V

Foundations of
Finnegans Wake

Finnegans Wake stands as the academic equivalent of the Bible. It sits on the bookshelf of every literature professor and graduate student in the country, and yet for many it changes its location only when its owners move or when one of the coffee table legs gives way and a stack of otherwise unused tomes serves as a replacement. Nonetheless, a significant number of individuals do take pleasure in reading *Finnegans Wake*, and an impressive number of contemporary critics—commentators like Geert Lernout, Daniel Ferrer, Roland McHugh, Vincent Deane, and Margot Norris—have facilitated the process with diverse approaches for comprehending a number of different areas in the text.[1]

At the same time, many students of *Finnegans Wake* do not realize that recent yeoman efforts at interpretation rest on the achievements of stunning preliminary work done up to half a century ago, though the interpretive heritage of Joyce's final work has a much earlier genesis. Wherever one chooses to mark the beginning of scholarly work on *Finnegans Wake*, the origins of the critical commonplaces that arose from pioneering studies and that now facilitate sophisticated contemporary responses may have been obscured by more recent readings. Nonetheless, as is the case with Joyce's other works, returning to early, formative assessments to see precisely how various critics arrived at these insights offers a deeper understanding of the fundamental assumptions informing much contemporary criticism. Even more than in the case of the early commentaries on *Ulysses*, a significant amount of contemporaneous criticism of *Finnegans Wake* appeared during its composition process, and the origins of and motivations for much of it complicate efforts to understand subsequent interpretations.

As Joyce grew in experience as a writer, he also developed a less confrontational approach in dealing with his readers.[2] This is not to say that he compromised his artistic vision in any way. Rather, a duality obtained, for he came to understand the need to persuade both ordinary readers and critics of the value of his new approach in form and content even before the completion of his full text. The previous section notes some of the comparable tactics that he employed in garnering support for *Ulysses*. In the promotion of *Finnegans Wake* Joyce elaborated on lessons learned from some of the harsh responses that certain readers made to his earlier works, in an effort to forestall a similar reception of a far more demanding work.

As early as 1924 fragments of *Work in Progress* (as the project would be known until *Finnegans Wake* was published in 1939) began to appear in little magazines like the *transatlantic review* and in monographs from small publishers like Corvinus Press.[3] This practice of a gradual and sustained introduction to the radical rhetorical form that characterized Joyce's final work would continue until 1938. Almost all of *Finnegans Wake* appeared serially over the course of its composition, and readers interested in Joyce's writing had the opportunity to see and discuss the bulk of the material by the time the completed version appeared.[4] While the process prepared readers for the radical experience that the full-length account would produce, a number of longtime supporters—Ezra Pound and Stanislaus Joyce among them—read these fragments with increasing concern, and expressed deep disappointment in the new direction Joyce's writing was taking.[5]

Joyce anticipated such resistance, and, relatively early on, he began to organize responses to the harsher public criticisms. The most notable effort, a 1929 collection of pieces written primarily by friends and admirers, displayed a range of responses from erudition to playfulness.[6] The twelve essays and two letters that make up *Our Exagmination Round His Factification for Incamination of Work in Progress* cover diverse topics, from the literary tradition with which Joyce associated himself to the narrative's unique style, and despite the diversity of tone all were composed with the intention of dispelling the impressions of inaccessibility and incomprehensibility that had grown up from early criticisms of the work.

Like the examinations that both Gilbert and Budgen made of *Ulysses*, much of the material appearing in *Our Exagminations* went beyond simple textual criticism. From varied points of view and with varied tones, its essays aimed as much at persuasion and validation as at explication. In consequence, some of the contributions now seem more useful as artifacts of literary history than as hermeneutic documents. Nonetheless, the collection established an important point that would offer legitimacy to the efforts of a great many subsequent writers: *Work in Progress* (and its metamorphosis as *Finnegans Wake*) could sustain the same kind of critical scrutiny, whatever biases the essayists might have, as more conventional works.

Critics without a personal attachment to Joyce generally waited until the work appeared in full to respond, though a number had doubtless followed its evolution through its episodic publication. Within two years of the publication of *Finnegans Wake*, Edmund Wilson wrote an important analysis that had an impact greater and more lasting, and some would argue less salubrious, than all these previous efforts upon the way readers came to understand Joyce's writing.[7] The essay is a revised version of Wilson's *Wake* reviews of June 28 and July 12, 1939, in the *New Republic*, and it marked an important stage in the development of *Wake* criticism.

Wilson's commentary gave an American audience a simple but revelatory approach to Joyce's work. With a profound sensitivity to the text, Wilson offered analyses along conventional lines that suggested a narrative accessibility heretofore unseen by others. Without claiming to present a definitive view, he attempted to identify the distinctive features of Earwicker's character, and to explain the language, myth, and psychology of the work.

The first book-length examination of the novel appeared in 1944. Joseph Campbell and Henry Morton Robinson in *A Skeleton Key to "Finnegans Wake"* combined summary and analysis.[8] Offering paraphrasing, synopses, and some commentary, the study presented an accessible overview upon which many readers still rely. As perhaps a testament to its durability, only a handful of *Finnegans Wake* scholars have attempted a similar approach.[9]

By offering an effective point of entry into a broad understanding of *Finnegans Wake*, mixing synopsis with explication to lay down a general narrative overview, the Campbell and Robinson book enabled a range of more focused studies. Reference guides quickly became one of the most popular subsets of *Finnegans Wake* criticism. In this area of scholarship, Adaline Glasheen stands as the undisputed pioneer. Her first, second, and third censuses of *Finnegans Wake* combined canny identification of characters, despite the apparent obscurity of many of the allusions, with an increasingly complex commentary on the work as a whole.[10] Although some of the associations she made and some of the criticism she offered in her introductions remain open to question, the interpretive freedom that her glosses of characters provide readers makes her contribution to *Wake* criticism difficult to overestimate. Whatever critique one may make of these volumes, they sparked a long line of valuable reference books.[11]

As valuable as these early works were, however, there remained in them by and large an emphasis on generalization, on summary assessments that gave good overviews but in doing so ran the risk of missing subtleties in the text. It was not until David Hayman's 1958 PMLA essay "From *Finnegans Wake*: A Sentence in Progress" appeared that critics began to see how a careful analysis of the compositional evolution of the creative process could greatly clarify the interpretive possibilities imbedded in Joyce's prose.[12] In a brilliant interpretation that combined biographical evidence with draft material, Hayman showed how to bring conventional critical language to bear upon the most unconventional of prose narratives. His meticulous examination of the sinuous development of just one of Joyce's sentences set the paradigm for the elaborate skills that one needs to bring to any reading of *Finnegans Wake* and laid the groundwork for the genetic criticism that he would champion four decades later.[13] Of equal importance, his study demonstrated that, despite the size and complexity of *Finnegans Wake*, one could write useful article-length criticism on various components of the narrative. Critics may now take for granted many aspects of this style of interpretation, but that is because Hayman was among the first to so eloquently lay down the guidelines for pursuing it.

The second piece in this section, Clive Hart's essay "Notes on the Text of *Finnegans Wake*," both built on existing criticism and opened new areas of inquiry. It complemented Hayman's explication with a reasoned illustration of the numerous typographical errors that inhabit the first printing of *Finnegans Wake*, and it drew attention to the relativity of so much *Finnegans Wake* criticism by underscoring the unreliability of portions of the text itself.[14] Highlighting this condition had both a specific and a wide-ranging effect upon *Wake* criticism.

Hart's interest in the textual features of Joyce's work offered an immediate sense of the complex underpinning of the narrative and also prepared readers for the studies of other pioneers in the field: A. Walton Litz, already encountered in the *Ulysses* section, Thomas Connolly, a critic intimately familiar with the Joyce material in the Buffalo archives, and David Hayman, taking a different approach to the material at the British Museum that Walton Litz had analyzed and giving broader attention to the creative process that Litz had identified in the first essay of the *Ulysses* section.[15] Because so much emphasis, then and now, has been placed on interpreting *Finnegans Wake* at the most fundamental levels, the careful attention to the process of composition shown by these men offered important guides for later readers.

Hart would subsequently expand upon this research to produce a book-length examination of the framework that supported Joyce's narrative, *Structure and Motif in "Finnegans Wake."*[16] However, the fundamental, painstaking study that he undertook to ascertain the integrity of the volume not only reconfigured the way critics and readers thought about *Finnegans Wake,* it also illustrated the tenuous authority of any printed document and challenged any easy generalizations critics and readers might make about the text and what constitutes it. Though many scholars have gone well beyond his framework in engaging *Finnegans Wake,* few would have accomplished anything without the scaffolding that Hart provided.

As was the case with the evolution of *Ulysses* criticism, initial work on reference guides and textual integrity laid the foundation for more diverse interpretive explorations of *Finnegans Wake.* Hart offered the earliest example of how the achievements of the 1950s and early 1960s could help domesticate Joyce's final work. In quick succession other critics followed, each adopting a very specific perspective yet each relying upon traditional modes of reading.[17] Viewed as a group, they show the evolution of interpretations of *Finnegans Wake* into studies with more focused topics and making more detailed examinations of selected elements within the text.

Even with the impressive scholarly abilities brought to bear in early *Finnegans Wake* criticism, however, a sense of awkwardness remained as readers attempted to apply orthodox hermeneutics to a highly unorthodox narrative. Robert Boyle's essay "*Finnegans Wake*, Page 185: An Explication," though ostensibly as conventional as those studies just cited, in fact signaled a new commitment to exuberance, even extravagance, in efforts to understand Joyce's work.[18] Boyle's approach might seem at first glance only to expand Hayman's exegetical scope slightly, focusing on a paragraph rather than a sentence. In fact, Boyle's playful yet ingenious reading shows how the application of basic exegetical tools by a skillful critic can produce profound insights.

Boyle came to the text of Joyce's last work uniquely suited to engage it. His Jesuit training not only gave him the background to translate the Latin passage on page 185, it made him familiar with the rich philosophical heritage with which Joyce plays in the paragraph, presenting with Rabelaisian exuberance a caustic satire on the mechanics of writing. With these tools, Boyle's explication exemplified the achievement that comes from a judicious balance of scholarship and close reading and a heightened sense of multiplicity when applied to *Finnegans Wake*, an approach now familiar to us all, though often more honored in the breach than in the observance.

The approach highlighted by Boyle's essay also underscored the interrelatedness of Joyce's work. It acknowledged the narrative's insistent demand that readers move back and forth between passages in *Finnegans Wake*. More significantly, though, it privileged the evocations of other writings in the canon to gain insight on one from its representations within and by another.

Equally important to cultivating this polytextual sensitivity, Boyle reminded readers of the need for engaging Joyce's Catholic/catholic heritage if they hoped to reach a full appreciation of his writings. As the essay made clear, a sense of the intellectual and spiritual environment from which Joyce emerged remains crucial to a full comprehension of his work, as is an awareness of Joyce's marvelous openness to diversity. Readers need to show some facility for the paradoxical intellectual leaps and spiritual connections that inform the narrative.

A full-length example of Boyle's unique ability to engage *Finnegans Wake* did not appear for more than a decade after this essay was published,[19] yet his ongoing involvement with *Wake* criticism had an undeniable effect on other scholars in the field. Roland McHugh, in a riff off the resource guide that he would publish four years later, showed how much one can derive from the doodles that punctuate the text.[20] Patrick

McCarthy, who as a graduate student had worked with Robert Boyle, played off the connections of humor and wit running through the narrative.[21] And John Bishop, in a dense and demanding analysis, used the Egyptian *Book of the Dead* as a template for understanding Joyce's lithe narrative.[22]

From the early 1980s a range of complex and diverse response to *Finnegans Wake* has appeared.[23] The common thread, however, remains the debt all owe to the pioneering scholars like those whose essays appear here. The confidence and energy one finds in contemporary criticism of *Finnegans Wake* stands as the most profound tribute that could be offered to the formative studies upon which they rest.

Notes

1. Roland McHugh, *The "Finnegans Wake" Experience* (Berkeley and Los Angeles: University of California Press, 1981); Margot Norris, *The Decentered Universe of "Finnegans Wake": A Structuralist Analysis*, rev. ed. (Baltimore: Johns Hopkins University Press, 1974); Vincent Deane, Daniel Ferrer, and Geert Lernout, eds., *The "Finnegans Wake" Notebooks at Buffalo: Notebook VI.B.16* (Turnhout, Belgium: Brepols, 2003).

2. The younger Joyce could be unremittingly critical and bitingly satiric, as evidenced by "The Day of the Rabblement," a 1901 essay expressing disgust with the Irish Literary Theatre for succumbing to the demands of Irish nationalism and provincial attitudes, and by "Gas from a Burner," an invective-laden poem written in 1912 bitterly satirizing the publisher George Roberts of Maunsel & Co. for reneging on his contract to publish *Dubliners*. Later responses were far more nuanced.

3. For a detailed account of these publications, see Fargnoli and Gillespie's *Critical Companion to James Joyce*, rev. ed. (New York: Facts on File, 2006), 386–388.

4. For a good survey of contemporary responses to the segments of *Finnegans Wake* that appeared prior to the book's publication, see A. Nicholas Fargnoli's *James Joyce: A Documentary Volume* (Detroit: Gale Group, 2001), 295–316. For reactions of those close to Joyce, like his brother Stannie, see Richard Ellmann's biography *James Joyce*, rev. ed. (New York: Oxford University Press, 1982), 577–579.

5. Ellmann, 577–579, 584–585.

6. Samuel Beckett et al., *Our Exagmination Round His Factification for Incamination of Work in Progress* (Paris: Shakespeare and Company, 1929).

7. Edmund Wilson, "The Dream of H. C. Earwicker," in *The Wound and the Bow* (Boston: Houghton Mifflin, 1941), 198–222.

8. Joseph Campbell and Henry Morton Robinson, *A Skeleton Key to "Finnegans Wake"* (New York: Harcourt, Brace, 1944).

9. Cf. Anthony Burgess, *A Shorter "Finnegans Wake"* (London: Faber and Faber, 1966); William York Tindall, *A Reader's Guide to "Finnegans Wake"* (New York: Farrar, Straus and Giroux, 1969).

10. Adaline Glasheen, *A Census of "Finnegans Wake"* (London: Faber and Faber, 1956); *A Second Census of "Finnegans Wake"* (Evanston, Ill.: Northwestern University Press, 1963); *A Third Census of "Finnegans Wake": An Index of the Characters and Their Roles* (Berkeley and Los Angeles: University of California Press, 1977).

11. These include James S. Atherton, *The Books at the Wake: A Study of Literary Allusions in James Joyce's "Finnegans Wake"* (New York: Viking, 1960); Clive Hart, *A Concordance to "Finnegans Wake"* (Minneapolis: University of Minnesota Press, 1963); Helmut Bonheim, *A Lexicon of the German in "Finnegans Wake"* (Berkeley and Los Angeles: University of California Press, 1967); Brendan O Hehir, *A Gaelic Lexicon for "Finnegans Wake"* (Berkeley and Los Angeles: University of California Press, 1967); Brendan O Hehir and John M. Dillon, *A Classical Lexicon for "Finnegans Wake"* (Berkeley and Los Angeles: University of California Press, 1977); Louis O. Mink, *"Finnegans Wake" Gazetteer* (Bloomington: Indiana University Press, 1978); Roland McHugh, *Annotations to "Finnegans Wake"* (Baltimore: Johns Hopkins University Press, 1980); Vincent John Cheng, *Shakespeare and Joyce: A Study of "Finnegans Wake"* (University Park: Pennsylvania State University Press, 1984).

12. David Hayman, "From *Finnegans Wake*: A Sentence in Progress," *PMLA* 73, no. 1 (March 1958): 136–154.

13. Hayman followed this with *The "Wake" in Transit* (Ithaca, N.Y.: Cornell University Press, 1990). Another critic doing important though always controversial work is Danis Rose. See his *The Textual Diaries of James Joyce* (Dublin: Lilliput Press, 1995). One finds a good summary of the directions inspired by Hayman in *How Joyce wrote "Finnegans Wake": A Chapter-by-Chapter Genetic Guide*, ed. Luca Crispi and Sam Slote (Madison: University of Wisconsin Press, 2007).

14. Clive Hart, "Notes on the Text of *Finnegans Wake*," *Journal of English and Germanic Philology* 59 (1960): 229–239.

15. A. Walton Litz, *The Art of James Joyce: Method and Design in "Ulysses" and "Finnegans Wake"* (New York: Oxford University Press, 1961); Thomas E. Connolly, ed., *Scribbledehobble: The Ur-Workbook for "Finnegans Wake"* (Evanston, Ill.: Northwestern University Press, 1961); David Hayman, ed., *A First-Draft Version of "Finnegans Wake"* (Austin: University of Texas Press, 1963).

16. Clive Hart, *Structure and Motif in "Finnegans Wake"* (London: Faber and Faber, 1962).

17. Helmut Bonheim, *Joyce's Benefictions* (Berkeley and Los Angeles: University of California Press, 1964); Dounia Bunis Christiani, *Scandinavian Elements of "Finnegans Wake"* (Evanston, Ill.: Northwestern University Press, 1965); Bernard Benstock, *Joyce-Again's Wake: An Analysis of "Finnegans Wake"* (Seattle: University of Washington Press, 1965); Anthony Burgess, *Here Comes Everybody* (London: Faber and Faber, 1965), also published as *Re Joyce* (New York: Norton, 1965); Jack P. Dalton and Clive Hart, eds., *Twelve and a Tilly: Essays on the Occasion of the 25th Anniversary of "Finnegans Wake"* (London: Faber and Faber, 1964); Margaret C. Solomon, *Eternal Geomater: The Sexual Universe of "Finnegans Wake"* (Carbondale: Southern Illinois University Press, 1969).

18. Robert Boyle, "*Finnegans Wake*, Page 185: An Explication," *James Joyce Quarterly* 4 (1966): 3–16.

19. Robert Boyle, *James Joyce's Pauline Vision: A Catholic Exposition* (Carbondale: Southern Illinois University Press, 1978).

20. Roland McHugh, *The Sigla of "Finnegans Wake"* (London: Edward Arnold, 1976).

21. Patrick A. McCarthy, *The Riddles of "Finnegans Wake"* (Rutherford, N.J.: Fairleigh Dickinson University Press, 1980).

22. John Bishop, *Joyce's Book of the Dark: "Finnegans Wake"* (Madison: University of Wisconsin Press, 1986).

23. Barbara DiBernard, *Alchemy and "Finnegans Wake"* (Albany: State University of New York Press, 1980); Danis Rose and John O'Hanlon, *Understanding "Finnegans Wake": A Guide to the Narrative of James Joyce's Masterpiece* (New York: Garland, 1982); Kimberly J. Devlin, *Wandering and Return in "Finnegans Wake"* (Princeton: Princeton University Press, 1990); Sheldon Brivic, *Joyce's Waking Women: An Introduction to "Finnegans Wake"* (Madison: University of Wisconsin Press, 1995); Patrick McGee, *Joyce beyond Marx: History and Desire in "Ulysses" and "Finnegans Wake"* (Gainesville: University Press of Florida, 2001).

10

From *Finnegans Wake*

A Sentence in Progress

DAVID HAYMAN

Although it has often been described as a work of destruction, James Joyce's *Finnegans Wake* was designed to be a triumphant reconstruction. It was in reference to this characteristic of his last book that Joyce is reported to have remarked during a visit to Stonehenge, "I am fourteen years trying to get here."[1] The task of reproducing with words the aesthetic unity of the past was an arduous one. For seventeen years Joyce, having at his disposal all the means of knowing and all the methods of expressing, labored to resolve the "proteaform" mass of modern learning in a "faustian fustian" of words. Such a process, the mixing and blending, the ordering and composing, the choosing and discarding, was necessarily a lengthy one entailing numberless revisions which bear "hermetic" testimony to the nature of the creative act while recording the artistic mind in a state of flux. It is self-evident that Joyce's manuscripts for *Finnegans Wake* are of immense importance to the scholar and that the French critic Louis Gillet, intimate though he was with Joyce's creative process, expressed a very limited view when he stated: "On ne comprendra vraiment la pensée de Joyce que le jour où nous l'aurons dans son premier état, avant toutes les retouches dont il l'a compliquée. . . ."[2] As material for the study of Joyce's intentions, as a "key" to the *Wake*, the primitive (first-draft) manuscripts to which Gillet refers are of surprisingly little value; for they generally expose little more than the armature of the work, the fundamental action which the reader might otherwise discern for himself after a brief syntactical search. On the other hand, as an aid to exegesis, the *complete* manuscripts are invaluable. They provide a basis for study of Joyce's method, his

David Hayman, "From *Finnegans Wake*: A Sentence in Progress," *PMLA* 73 (March 1958): 136–154. Reprinted by permission of the Modern Language Association of America. Copyright 1958.

progressive elaboration upon a theme. They furnish material for a close examination of the mental process behind this style and of the organization which enabled Joyce to control the chaos from which he drew his inspiration. To this end, I believe a word-by-word study which questions each aspect of a single sentence in progress would be of greater value than a more generalized discussion of a longer passage. If feasible, a series of such exegetic analyses might aid in more thoroughly illuminating the total stylistic of the book.

It is for this purpose and with the intention of casting the first stone that I have chosen to examine here a sentence of moderate length and complexity which Joyce, beginning in 1924, elaborated over a period of fourteen years. A study of the thirteen-odd stages of its development should give us a reasonable number of insights into the artistic method and into the meaning of Book III, the section of *Finnegans Wake* to which this sentence belongs.[3]

As the plan of *Finnegans Wake* was not completed until 1926,[4] and as there was to be "no beginning or end," Joyce composed his chapters without regard to their final order.[5] Consequently, though the first versions of some of the chapters in Book I of *Finnegans Wake* were among the earliest passages to be written, the first section to be completely planned and executed was Book III. This last is comprised of four chapters, in three of which Shaun, the dream-son of the archetypal father-hero, HCE, appears successively under the names Shaun, Jaun, and Yawn. On 24 May 1924, after he had sketched out III.i and ii, Joyce wrote Miss Weaver that the Shaun chapters describe a postman's journey backward through the night's events, that they are "written in the form of a *via crucis* of 14 stations but in reality [they are] only [the description of] a barrel rolling down the river Liffey" (Add MS. 47489).

The analogies mentioned in this letter only begin to indicate the nature of the complex set of controls Joyce imposed upon himself and of the framework within which these chapters were constructed. Aside from instituting for Shaun a set of character traits appropriate to a hero of Vico's democratic or decadent age, Joyce established *at least* five parody levels of which the movement is both forward and backward. Thus, while Shaun-the-post travels backward, Christ follows in their proper order the fourteen stations of the cross;[6] Buddha under the Bo tree withstands the trials of the night, passes watch by watch through the four steps of knowledge. Coincidentally, Joyce implies that the sun has disappeared and that Jaun, the false sun or shadow-son, is re-enacting the sunset in four positions:

the appearance of the false sun, its static moment near the horizon, its slipping below the horizon, and its disappearance. As to the chronology of these themes, Shaun travels from deepest night to evening, Buddha sits from sunset till sunrise, Jesus suffers from morning to evening, and the false sun shines from the moment of the sun's disappearance till nightfall. Meanwhile, the barrel analogy, a systematic re-enactment of four pages from Mallarmé's poem *Un coup de dés*, links all the others:[7] "Shaun a," or III.i, shows us the empty barrel floating at an angle in the river; in "Shaun b" the barrel, which has begun to take water through its bunghole, is standing up straight with the aid of a weir or a post; "Shaun c" finds the water-logged barrel floating on its side, slowly sinking into the maternal liquid, while in "Shaun d" the barrel has been submerged and we are faced with a view of the sea of life. This barrel, slowly being infused with the dark female fluid, parallels Jesus' torment as he becomes progressively more imbued with the Holy Ghost. It also parallels the experience of the Buddha losing himself in the effort to gain nirvana. As Shaun, it journeys back through the stages of the nocturnal cycle to the Fall with which the book opens. Finally, as the sun, the barrel is slowly engulfed by night. (This movement may also be applied to the stages of the Vichian cycle.)

When applied to the individual chapter, this rich superstructure becomes even more elaborate as Joyce particularizes each analogy, finds further (narrower) identities for his protagonists. Chapter III.ii's Jaun is superficially a somewhat Laforguian hero—blasé and splenetic, a happy-go-lucky priest, a Don Juanish Tristan figure ("Sir Tristram, violer d'amores," p. 3/4), a boyish Tom Sawyer ("topsawyer," p. 3/7), a Saint Patrick ("thuartpeatrick," p. 3/10) come to deliver Ireland to the day. Essentially he stands as the white hope of mankind, the product of centuries of overcivilization, the thin shadow of his forefathers' vitality. As the white hope, he naturally assumes the traits of a savior and of a sacrificial god. Also, as the white hope he is destined to carry the coals of a dying civilization, both figuratively and literally. Thus, on one level he repeats the meaningless dictums, preaches the institutionalized rules of behavior which have long since fallen into disuse and which he himself fails to honor. But on another level he revitalizes the Word, interprets God to man. As the postman, having reached the peak of his possibilities, he distributes the act-become-word which was the sin and the glory of his fallen predecessor. As the priest of cults, he re-enacts the tragedies of Osiris and the Savior. Thus, for one hopeful moment, as the empty husk which formerly surrounded the life-giving fluid Guinness, he promises to stay with us, leaning against the garnered wealth of civilization, the light of the vanished sun. This is the point at which Jaun or the false sun, which swells on the horizon, has reached the static point in his decline, the same that will be repeated in reverse by his backward reflection and morning self, the sunrise. As the Buddha beneath the Bo tree, Jaun is being tempted by the daughters of Mara Pusana, lord of passions, who sing to him of the joys of love. He is literally tormented by devils as he loses himself in contemplation. Finally, as Christ, Jaun is carrying his cross and possibly going through steps four through nine of the *via crucis*.

Examining Chapter III.ii's most generalized plane of action, we find that Jaun, halted in his journey down the Liffey, is propped up against a weir upon which are seated twenty-nine schoolgirls.[8] As soon as he sees that the last of these girls is his sister Issy, he sermonizes her on virtue and the Ten Commandments. He then expatiates on his mission, on his return, on the joyous prospect of seeing Issy again, and on the reforms he would like to put into effect in Dublin. At this point Joyce inserted the earliest version of the paragraph of which our sentence was to become a crucial element:[9]

> I'd ask no kinder fate than to stay where I am this moment catching trophis of sturgeon by the armful and what I'd *make by poaching I'd put into the poteen & before you knew where I was I'd be rolling over in tons of cash but I'd be anxious about the terrible cold in the air that* WD [would] PERISH THE DANES.[10]

Jaun's statement is a two-part explanation of his reasons for staying where he is (i.e., his pleasant occupations during this stay and the wealth which he expects to amass) and his reasons for leaving (i.e., his fears and compulsions concerning the future). Our hero is lazy and a wastrel; he would get rich quickly by "poaching" or capitalizing on the wealth of others, but he would drink and eat up his profits putting all of his wealth in the "poteen" or whisky. The success that he desires is also in keeping with his shadow personality. Like the crass materialist of a decadent age, the antithesis of the hero of the fairy tales or of a more active epoch Jaun would like to be "rolling over in cash" for the benefit of Issy. Even though we find in this evocation of gold ("cash") a prediction of the glory of the sunrise, we are assured that, *au fond,* our hero remains a barrel in the river, capable perhaps of floating in water dyed by the setting sun, but nevertheless a victim of the Fates. To mask this weakness and to motivate his disappearance Jaun expresses fear of the cold air which would destroy him. By means of a reference to "Dane," he evokes his physical aspect as a false sun, bringing out his concern over the transitory nature of the post upon which he is leaning, that is, the Viking wanderer, HCE drunk, or the light of the vanished Helios. In the chapter of the lessons, II.ii, which foreshadows the reappearance of HCE (absent since the beginning of the book), the speaker refers to "Mr. Dane" as "the pillar of the perished and the rock o'ralereality" (p. 289/3).[11]

The pattern established by Joyce for this original or primary paragraph is the one which he later imposed upon each succeeding draft of our sentence. Jaun's humdrum conception of the ideal existence is pitted against the rude facts of fate and a lack of courage; his static dream is opposed to a kinetic reality:[12]

> I'd ask no kinder fate than to stay where I am at this present moment *by local option* in the birds' lodging the pheasants among till well on into the night [sic] I COULD SIT ON MY SIDE TILL THE BARK OF THE DAY. . . . [13]

Fundamentally, our sentence as it first appears—"I could sit on my side till the bark of the day"—functions as a simple reiterative statement, further limiting time, place, and condition, further developing the theme that opens the paragraph. It is inserted as a self-contained unit whose addition has little or no immediate effect on the structure of the surrounding clauses, which are elaborated by its intellectual content. (Most of Joyce's changes are of this order. Rather than revise an entire sentence, he customarily used his primary idea as a base upon which to construct a more complex thought-expression unit.) The whole of this new germ element hangs upon the interpretation given two vague words, "side" and "bark." Even at this early stage Joyce forces his reader to utilize the ungrammatical meanings suggested by his distortions of the language. Thus, "I could sit on my side" is at best an *ambiguous* statement of physical position. Jaun seems to be saying that he is now sitting, but he also indicates a reclining position, that of the floating barrel propped up against "a log." The force of this same nautical analogy reflects upon the rest of the clause. "Bark of the day" may refer to the solar boat of Ra to which Jaun is attached as the reflected glory of the departed sun. Again, the "bark" recalls the barking baboons (i.e., HCE or "Babau," p. 466/1) that were believed by the

Egyptians to herald the sun's matinal appearance. In all of his symbolic identities, Jaun, the last surviving remnant of the disappearing male factor, would like to live through the night to greet the new day, the spring, or the new dawn of civilization.

Already, we detect some of the possibilities to be developed in the second draft. The sentence like the paragraph is a dual entity which opposes a desired stasis to an impending change. To elaborate the pattern thus established, the author must now brush in the implications of the time gap, the conflict, the cataclysm, and the glory to come. He must detail the setting more carefully, describing the actions of his hero as he awaits the dawn. He must suggest not only the actual sunrise but also the emotions it arouses in the heart of the character, its significance in the book, and its relation to the book's symbolical basis.

But the process is painfully gradual. In Draft 6,[14] or the heavily revised first typescript of this chapter, with corrections dating from 1924–26, we may approximate three distinct evolutionary stages resulting from three separate revisions:[15]

> I could sit on ~~my~~ *one* side till the bark of the day *for to watch how* ~~the~~
> *my* [sic] *my nocturnal goose would lay her golden egg for* [sic] *behind me in the shy orient.*[16]

Joyce's first change, "one" for "my," seems to add a note of detachment to Jaun's position—he wishes to see himself as a disinterested spectator. The "side" has become more manifestly one side of the barrel, the setting sun, the barque, or "one side" of a log or a tree. When we consider the nature of the other additions, "one" enriches the meaning of "till." Jaun would like to "sit *beside* the bark of the sun till the night prepares to give birth to the new day." The Egyptian sunboat is now associated with the goose that will lay her golden egg in the east as Jaun watches from his vantage point. The replacement of the word "the" by "my" strengthens the hero's sun aspect. Perhaps he too has been hatched out of a goose egg. His desire to watch the sunrise "behind" him (his progress as the sun's shadow is from east to west) highlights the already present, dual aspect. In spite of his reluctance to move, and like the hero of the fairy tales and myths, he will have to suffer hardships in order to bring back the goose egg upon which our happiness depends. On this level at least, he remains a reluctant hero who has no control over his own movements.

If we accept the bark-log association, Jaun is leaning against the day-post-HCE. In the beginning of III.ii his means of support is described as a "butterblond . . . exsearfaceman" (p. 429/19–20) in reference to the light and the heat of the sunfather from whom the son derives his existence. Another analogical level makes of the log a fertility symbol and of Jaun the corn or harvest god. This is clearly implied by the reception he receives from the twenty-nine pupils of St. Bride's night school. As the chapter opens, these girls have gathered about the "yellowstone landmark." Jaun arrives, perfumed with "wild thyme and parsley," doffing a "hat with a re-inforced crown," and wearing his hair in "golliwog curls"; and they dance up to kiss the "post"[17] (Jaun or the log) in a simulated harvest dance.[18] Again, the log is the Bodhi tree of enlightenment whose protection Buddha employed to help him withstand the terrors of the "four watches of the night." There is an evident but valid contradiction between Jaun's wish to stay, a craven desire contrary to the dictates of his mission, and the Buddha's resistance to movement, his steadfast observance of a vow.

The major addition to the draft is an account of the "goose's" laying of the dawn egg. By means of this adverbial phrase Joyce motivates his hero's action and elaborates upon the theme of the "bark of the day." We may infer from the context that the author was quite aware of the goose's wide religious significance as a soul bird. According to the Hindoos, Brahma, the breath of life, "progenitor of the Universe," was hatched from a golden egg laid by the Supreme Spirit. For the Egyptians, whose sun was said to have been laid by "the primeval goose," Osiris was the son of Seb, an anthropomorphized goose.[19] By extension, Jaun's bird will lay the egg from which the new Christian world (the millennium) will emerge after the culmination of Jesus' sacrifice. Buddha's Brahma will eventually provide him with the divine knowledge to which he aspires. Osiris' Seb will make possible the god's physical renewal. While, on the material level, Jaun's goose will provide him with wealth and sustenance, his breakfast.

The second stage of the draft reads as follows:

> I could sit on one side till the bark of the day *when the rugaby moon had rolled west through her scrummages* for to watch how carefully my nocturnal goose*mother* would lay her *new* golden *shee*egg for [sic] ~~behind me~~ *down under* in the shy orient.[20]

Here Joyce introduces a third aspect, the dualistic interpretation of the moon's nightly journey. To describe his moon, the author evolved a rich series of play images well suited to Jaun's adolescent and childish or Tom Sawyer–like identity. But the pleasure element innate in sports was clouded for Joyce by prior associations.[21] "Rockaby" and "Rugby" are both descriptive of the moon which rolls across the sky, but "Rugby" completely negates the dreamy quality of the other word and evokes the turmoil of a game field. The moon is destroying the worn-out remnants of civilization, preparing for the new day, but it is also reinforcing Jaun's lazy mood, lulling him to sleep. Again, although the cloud image implicit in "scrummages," baby talk for small clouds, is primarily a restful one, the duality is confirmed by the brutally kinetic football scrimmage.

As we might expect, the lunar image yields a rich harvest of associations. For the early Christian and the ancient Hindoo the crescent moon, symbolized here by a cradle, meant the land of heaven (*Lost Language*, I, 44). Likewise, the crescent with the circle (i.e., the ambiguous shape of our moon as a Rugby-ball cradle) signified the kingdom of heaven or the ultimate perfection of the millennium (I, 56). Joyce pictures a paradise surrounded by cloudlike angels. Still faithful to Egyptian, Hindoo, and Christian symbology, he depicts the moon as preparing the way for the hero's return. As such, "she" is a "destroyer of foes" (I, 107–108), a powerful light image in a darkened world.

Joyce does everything he can to help the reader fill in *Finnegans Wake*'s symbolic patterns. Thus, the goose that laid the golden egg has become a nocturnal symbol for pleasant dreams and light fantasies. This marriage of images continues and amplifies the above-mentioned theme of "Rockabye Baby" while injecting a further set of conflicts. By the portentous placement of the word "mother," Joyce makes it clear that "goose mother" is more than a reference to that good old lady Mother Goose or even to the creator goose; it is also a pun on nightmare or "smother."[22] Likewise, in reference to "Rockabye Baby," we remember that the cradle will fall, and we find therein an echo of the primal fall from innocence, that of Adam. This is of course confirmed by the fact that Jaun is an aspect of that first man, HCE, and that he shares and relives the tragedy of the *father's* guilt as he leans against the post of *his* memory.

Again in the Rugby-Fall context, as Joyce's friend Samuel Beckett has pointed out to me, mother goose's "she-égg" is, according to Freud, a symbol of defecation (see French argotic sense). The little boy's world of Shaun, like the subconscious world of HCE, sees defecation as a catastrophic act worthy of the closest attention. As the night, Shaun's goose mother lays the new sun; for the sun must, like the Phoenix, be born afresh each day. The goose's giving birth to the light parallels the creation of darkness by HCE defecating in Phoenix Park. Appropriately, both acts lead to the destruction or fall of their perpetrators.

In this valuable egg, laid for Jaun "down under" or in Australia, we find a new aspect of the get-rich-quick motifs present in the early versions of the paragraph. Both "down under" and "for to" remind us of the language of the adventurous emigrants whose motives the speaker shares. It would seem that he wishes to move only after his fortune has been *carefully* provided for.

The true nature of the egg's location becomes clear when we associate Joyce's sentence with Harold Bayley's discussion under the chapter heading "Down Under" of the prehistoric *"Dane* holes" which dot the English and Irish countrysides. (See Joyce's "perish the Dane.") These holes, Bayley states, had nothing to do with the Danes, whose appearance they antedate. Instead, they represent perhaps the dwelling places of some ancient troglodites, that is, "the Children of Don or Danu," the Danaan. In *Finnegans Wake*, the blood of Finn, the Dublin giant, whom Joyce patterned after the English Penrith giant, is "Danu U'Dunnell's" ale (p. 7/12).[23] Of more direct interest is the fact that the primitives "believed that the Life of the World, in the form of the Young Sun, was born yearly anew on 25th December, always in a cave: thus caves were invariably sacred to the Dawn or God of Light, and only secondarily to the engulfing powers of Darkness . . ." (*Archaic England*, p. 765). The Danaan's caves and the barrow of the Penrith giant are therefore similar in nature to the Phoenix' pyre: the home of the issuing soul or sun or race, and the labyrinthine testing ground of the dismembered hero. If we may presume that Joyce had these interpretations in mind, Jaun links himself not only with the sun but also with the prehistoric cradle of life, the birthplace of all ancestors. In a world where actual time and place do not exist, our protean hero visualizes himself as being in two places at once. As the false sun he is either sitting down, waiting for the daybreak or, the moon having completed her journey, he has already bridged the night and is sitting "on one side" of the sun bark, below the horizon or in a dene cave, watching his "goosemother" lay the new day. Hence, the action is, now more than ever, dualistic: the hero is at once neglecting and fulfilling his function.

With the "when" clause—"when the moon had rolled West through her scrummages"—Joyce introduced into a basic evening-morning, death-resurrection context a solid time element. He hoped thereby to complete the motivation of Jaun's behavior, suggesting the texture of the nocturnal gap: the ordeal of the sacrificial hero, his dying into evening, and the dismemberment which must precede the recovery, that is, the nature of the hero's accomplishment. But this new element, as we have seen, only halfway fulfills its purpose. The sentence is still primarily concerned with the morning and evening worlds, the poles of its action. The new clause vacillates between these two major elements but possesses no ground of its own. Joyce was later to recognize that, in what amounts to a ritualistic or semi-incantatory situation, emotional distance must intervene between *theophany* and the ritual death.

Nevertheless, the author has established a basis for further development, a solid armature which will adhere to and generate a meaningful structure for the future. The sentence, as it first stood, was itself an elaboration on an already-existing theme. As such an elaboration should, it helped supply color and mood. Our sentence now stands in relation to its future elements, as the paragraph once stood in relation to it.

> I could sit on one side till the bark of the day *laughing at the sheep's lightning* ~~while~~ *till I'd followed with my nephewscope* ~~when~~ the rugaby moon *cumuliously* ~~had~~ rolle~~d~~*ing himself* west through ~~her~~ *the* scrummages for to watch how carefully my nocturnal goosemother would lay her new golden sheegg for [sic] down under in the shy orient.[24]

The two major addenda in this revision both contribute to the sense of chronological continuity required by the dramatic context. The first, "*laughing at the sheep's lightning*," gives Jaun at least two occupations as he awaits the dawn. He will continue to enjoy the fireworks that accompany the sunset, that is, the lighting of the sunboat or ship. He will count sheep. But in spite of his flippant manner, uneasy rests our hero's head; for the sheep in question are jumping over the insomniac's proverbial fence and the sheet lightning, though in itself harmless, is frequently a presage of trouble and may well be a result of the moon's battle with the clouds. A further aspersion is cast on Jaun's courage by an earlier association. In the "Circe" chapter of *Ulysses*, Zoe, the harlot, sees courage in Stephen Dedalus' palm. This he denies while his friend Lynch quips, "Sheet lightning courage" (p. 547). We may also see in the lightning a symbol both of the fall of Satan and of the nocturnal predominance of Jaun's brother Shem. As Jaun knows, his satanic twin is the possessor of the "proud lightning of the intellect" (*Ulysses*, p. 51).

"... ~~while~~ *till I'd followed with my nephewscope*" evidences already some consistency in Joyce's preference for the vague "till," though the versatility of this chameleon word only becomes apparent when it is examined in the light of the three "till's" employed in the final version of the sentence. In the present context, "while," with its simple evocation of continuity, lacks the dual or "timeless" inference of a word which suggests continuous action but with an added note of finality. Other aspects of this clause, such as the kinship suggested by "nephew," are far less clear. Perhaps, if we consider, as some myths do, the moon to be the brother of the female night or the male sun, the child born of the conjunction of the day with the night is the moon's nephew. When we recall that the sentence is illumined by the setting sun, we are tempted to consider the satellite in a ritual context. The bloodshed caused by its struggle with the clouds identifies it with the sacramental bread immersed in wine, symbolic of Jaun's destiny as a Christ figure. Christ-Jaun, the illegitimate son of the Holy Ghost, might then be the nephew (nephew being the son of a priest) of God, the savior whose return will be signaled by the "bark of the day." (See Joyce's application of this theme in *Ulysses*: "My mother's a jew, my father's a bird" [p. 20].)

In keeping with the above, the allusion to "cope" introduces an element of the ecclesiastical garb, and the "nephew's cope" becomes the badge of office of a celebrant following the host in a procession. Since the cope was originally worn as a protection against inclement weather, Jaun will be protected both by his cloak and by his religious function from the ravages of the coming storm-catastrophe. In all events the "nephew-scope," as part of the hero's accouterment, gives its possessor special rights and privileges and a clearer view of the proceedings which will lead to the great event. A type of telescope or "nephoscope," it might also reinforce the static element in the sentence by permitting Jaun to *witness* from afar while giving him special insight into the nature of the new era.

Appropriately inserted into the lunar phrase, "cumuliously" describes the nature of the moon's action as it rolls toward the seated or floating figure of our hero. The "rugaby moon" is fighting its way through cumulous clouds (suggestive of a coming storm), gaining in size like a snowball rolled through the snow. Its approach is like that of a conquering hero, a Julius Caesar—that is, Iullii, or a god or god surrogate, a pathfinder. Clearly, such a deity can only be male, but in affirming this, Joyce weakened the nocturnal predominance of the female so evident in the last draft. No longer does a *female* moon roll across the sky to watch the female goose prepare the new day which will be female or a "she egg" until it breaks out of its all-containing unit, the subjective shell of night.[25] By introducing an imposing male force, Joyce has created a new polarity for his sentence.

In relation to the secondary levels, "himself," "sheep's," and "lightning" all possess magical qualities. Taking these elements one at a time, we find first that the moon is male in several important religions. It is outstandingly so in the Egyptian where the god Thoth, "bearing on his narrow ibis head the cusped moon,"[26] is the scribe who invented letters, the judge of the dead, the possessor of dark knowledge (Hermes Trismegistus was his medieval cognomen).[27] According to myth, Thoth was installed as vicegerent taking the sun's place at night.[28] In *Finnegans Wake* he is reincarnated in Shem-the-pen, HCE's dark son, who is responsible for "lettruce invrention" (p. 424/20). Shem, like Thoth, is a *wandervogl* (p. 419/14); he too possesses infinite knowledge of the dark powers. As the moon, he shares with Jaun-the-shadow-sun the reflected light of the vanished Helios. Jaun calls him "Dave the Dancekerl," the "mightiest penumbrella I ever flourished on behond the shadow of a post!" (p. 462/21–22). He is, then, the modern equivalent of the nocturnal eye of Horus. (In II.iii, which recounts the conquest of the sun, HCE is variously named "ahorace" (p. 325), "horces" (p. 322), "Horuse" (p. 328).) Jaun, as Osiris, sees in him both a continuator and an enemy, both a wanderer, whose journey must be followed by the new day, and a Cain (or diabolic Typhon-Set) who wittingly destroys his brother by goring him with a phallic tusk.

The newly introduced Christian liturgical motif ("cope") and the Buddhist parallel may both be interpreted in a similar way. Thus the moon represents the all too substantial Mara, god of sensual lust, who appears as an ambiguous enemy of the spiritual light throughout *Finnegans Wake*. (On p. 122 we witness the comic battle between God and O'Mara, while on p. 460 "Mrs. A'Mara makes up" with "Mrs. O'Morum." See also p. 407, "Mara O'Mario.") The evil principle is here pictured as leading his marshaled host across the night sky in an effort to intimidate the sedentary Buddha. Meanwhile, as the principle of spiritual light, enemy of sensuous clouds or temptations, the moon is the Vedic "destroyer of foes" or Buddha's active spirit striving for total illumination (*Lost Language*, I, 108). For the Christian, also, Shem's moon, the bright possessor of dark truth, personifies two mutually contradictory existences. He is Dave, the paraclete, Shaun's own shadow, who will continue the existence of the god and pursue the god's ends till the dawn. Paradoxically, he is also Lucifer, the lightning of the intellect, the once bright god become an enemy and relegated to the night. Consequently, Shaun, who is often identified with Michael, is shepherd of God as opposed to Shem's Nick, the devil horrifying the innocent sheep after the defeat of the hero.

(A positive interpretation of Lucifer's role is also possible. Lucifer is the moral garbage collector who makes Christ's work possible. Bayley explains brother killing as the murder of love by learning. After cataloguing the pairs of opposites he states that "probably LUCIFER, the fallen angel, was originally the twin brother of his opponent MICHAEL . . . subsequently one revolted against the other . . ." [*Lost Language*, II, 28]. In mystic lore, love and learning are the two sons of wisdom [see ALP] [ibid., I, 272].)

Jaun's function as the youthful Christ places him in a primitive Christian context as the "Good Shepherd," an Abel figure awaiting Cain-the-tiller's blow. (See the repeated use of "till" in our sentence.) Like the Good Shepherd, Jaun wishes to remain with his flock. Like Him also, his excuse for leaving is a *wholly* plausible one: he must prepare the coming era of salvation—he must fulfill the hero's duty. In such a setting the moon is the physical reflection of the deed, the proof of the existence of the godhead. Like the sheet lightning, his action is full of portent but heatless: *fearful* for the wicked or impure, but *sublime* for the pure.

(A citation taken from *A Portrait of the Artist* illustrates the fact that Joyce has woven his own terror into the fabric of this sentence. "I fear many things," says the demonic Stephen Dedalus, "dogs, horses, firearms, the sea, thunderstorms, machinery, the country roads at night" [p. 287]. Earlier, in reference to his aesthetic, Stephen said, "Terror is the feeling which arrests the mind in the presence of whatsoever is grave and constant in human sufferings and unites it with the secret cause" [p. 239]. Seeing himself as the mirror of the human "constants," the artist has bestowed fresh life upon his youthful theory.)

All things considered, the hero's moment of inaction has been altered but slightly by Jaun's statement of function. Even the sentence's rich possibilities, the elements that I have discussed in connection with this draft, have yet to be affirmed symbolically by later developments. In its stark economy the passage still lacks the sensual aspects which would make it more portentous, more human.

This being so, it is interesting to note that the modifications visible in the next draft possess only the humblest of virtues. At this point, Joyce, evidently thinking of his sentence as a fully developed entity, began to apply its superficial gloss:

> laughing *lazy* at the sheep's
> my *old* nephewscope
> rolling himself west*asleep*
> golden sheegg for *me*.[29]

Adding another static nuance to Jaun's position, "lazy" suggests a semi-prone attitude ("layzy"), that of the insomniac. In choosing this word, as in selecting the next addition, "old," Joyce was influenced by the tonal quality of his context. Through his reference to the age of the "nephews-cope," the author hoped to evoke, first, the stability of Jaun as an institution capable of acquiring and conserving possessions and, second, the hero's place in the future era, which will provide him with a new cope. The next element, "asleep," gives added emphasis to the nursery-rhyme quality of the phrase without detracting from its more ominous aspects. The sleeping moon rocking through the little clouds is closely linked to the triumphant Rugby-ball moon beating its way to the west, slipping "west-asleep" through the clouds toward his resting place.[30] Meanwhile, Shaun's relationship to the new sun is further defined by "for me." The new egg is his in at least four ways: he will be hatched from it; he will be rejuvenated by it; he will be saved by it; he will be enriched by it.

The polishing process continues in Drafts 4 and 5, which may be treated as a unit, the material in the fifth draft providing us with final developments of two puns begun in the fourth:

> till I'd followed ~~with~~ *through* my ~~old~~ *upfielded* nephewscope the rugaby moon cumuliously *goa*rolling himself westasleep ~~through amuckst~~ the ~~scrummages skyscrums~~ CLOUDSCRUMS—[31]
> cumuliously *god*rolling himself westasleep amuckst the cloud-scrums[32]

The corrections and revisions in these two drafts all tend to point up the already existing sport-bloodshed motifs while complicating the pun structure of the sentence. After exchanging the *poor* words "with" and "old" for the rich ones "through" and "upfielded," Joyce found it necessary to replace a second "through" in order to avoid a weak repetition. These insertions also affect the interpretation of "cope" elaborated in my discussion of the preceding draft. In the religious context, "followed through" must be interpreted as "followed through the grace of" or "by means of." The "field" in "upfielded" is then the decorated part of the priestly vestment.

"Followed through" expresses more clearly the action of observing with the aid of a telescope. Simultaneously, it calls to mind Jaun's position as he gazes up from the bottom of a floating barrel, subject to the vicissitudes of the life liquid, which it no longer contains but which will brook no denial. HCE's shadow form links the eternal Yin-Yang pair. His Guinness barrel once contained the stout "made from Liffey river water." Whereas the fluid stout is the blood of Jaun's father, the river of life is his mother. This wooden husk, this shell, is what remains of a man after his demise: his reputation, his life's work, his "bark." Clinging to lifeless modes and empty credos, Jaun's decadent spirit is symbolized by the hollowness of his barrel. The river of life, true to her function, will eventually wash such light material out to sea, where, once again full of vital liquid, it will regain its former validity as a male force. Colored by this promise of rejuvenescence, both "followed through" and "upfielded" suggest aspiration and achievement, active participation; both share in the combative aura of sports. There is innate in these expressions a vivacity which evokes hoards of images whose turbulence conflicts sharply with the startling quiescence of their context and of the age. The achieved effect is describable only in terms of an action-still photograph whose petrified movement threatens to break its bounds.

The prefix "goa," which might well have been a slip of the pen, adds little more than a slight Western tang to the sentence. In its final form, however, "god-rolling" reinforces the above-mentioned aspects of the moon as god surrogate. The familiar dualistic note is struck by the combination of the awesome aspect of the raging god with the clownish aspect of the moon who goes "drolling."

"Amuckst," the word Joyce chose as a replacement for "through," throws the suggestive balance of the cloud passage towards blatancy. Its colorful sensual connotations outweigh the simple social meanings, "among" or "amidst," by their inference of grime ("muck"), bloodshed ("amuck"), and by the suggested picture of evening clouds dyed with the blood of the setting sun, an orgiastic scene. This situation is aggravated by the suggestive element of "moon madness" (i.e., to run amuck), which adds to the dangers of the night. To balance these nuances, the author crossed out "scrummages" with its brutal denotation, substituting for it the more childish and hence more indirect "sky-scrums." Shortly thereafter, Joyce must have found this pun on clouds as the crumbs scattered in the sky singularly non-evocative. As a unit it has no substantial meaning; when broken down, its elements ("sky's crums" or "sky scrums") fail to jell in the reader's mind. Indeed, even the inference of "scrummages" is somewhat smothered by the abbreviation. Chosen for clarity's sake (Joyce has too often been accused of not wishing to communicate), the two final variants emphasize the nursery-rhyme effect while directing the reader's attention toward "crumbs" and "scrums" or the dramatic depiction of the havoc wrought by the moon as he progressively scatters his cumulous enemy. The final variant "cloudscrums" ensures the static emotional balance of the pun cluster, "westasleep," "amuckst," "cloudscrums."

The second of the above-treated drafts dates from April 1928. During the four years that had elapsed since 1924, nine revisions had been written. Joyce was already working from *transition* page proofs. At that stage the sentence placed Shaun in conjunction with the larger natural phenomena: the solar and lunar cycles, the cloud formations, and the lightning. His drama, like that of Max Müller's solar heroes of mythology, was basically an astral one. Draft 12 marks the beginning of a trend toward greater integration, the introduction of the themes and patterns already established for the paragraph and for the book.

> I could sit on one side till the bark of the day *for hoopoe's hours,* laughing lazy at the sheep's lightning and crekking jugs at the grenoulls, ~~and~~ *leaving tea for the trout* AND BELEEKS BELLEEKS FOR THE WARY, till I'd followed through my upfielded nephewscope the rugaby moon cumuliously godrolling himself westasleep amuckst the cloudscrums for to watch how carefully my nocturnal goosemother would lay her golden sheegg for me down under in the shy orient.[33]

Due perhaps to the brevity of the 1924–26 sentence, as well as to a lack of detachment, Joyce had heretofore neglected to incorporate the background motifs, the rich bird, fish, and animal references which had long been present in the surrounding sentences. Functionally, these references replace conventional description, contributing to the passage a rich Garden of Eden backdrop which helps situate the action on several planes while providing no positive clues for the identification of locale or epoch. Furthermore, they contribute to the evocation of certain specific attitudes and analogies. For example, the three types of creatures abounding in Jaun's garden are suggestive of three locations: the heavens or "birds' lodging" (p. 449/17–18), the earth or "upon this earthlight" (p. 449/7), and the water world implicit in the phrase "flashing down the swansway, leaps ahead of the swift MacEels . . ." (p. 450/5–6). For each of these we find a symbolic manifestation of the hero: earth / the landbound postman, water / the barrel, air / the false sun—echoes all of the mystic trinities. Again we may equate these elements with three realities being portrayed simultaneously: the temporal (i.e., Shaun-the-post, Tristan, Tom Sawyer), the priestly (i.e., liturgy and ritual), and the godly (i.e., Osiris, Christ, Buddha). More generally, by suggesting a Garden of Eden and making of our hero a childlike Adam, successor to his father in a recreated world, this "pastoral" setting amplifies the paradox already visible in earlier drafts. We may assume that Jaun is not a true Adam; as a child of decadence, he is preparing himself intellectually for the new era, "going primitive." In the coming age he will be, or he hopes to be, the reincarnation of the original father, living the life of the romantics' "happy savage." Indeed, perhaps the passage's rich esoteric symbolism was included for a similar reason, the portrayal of man's search for lost truths and occult secrets as characterized by such late mystical beliefs as Theosophy, Rosicrucianism, or Gnosticism.

The pre-Fall atmosphere is also consonant with the sentence's ominous dual aspects: God-the-Avenger is present in the lightning, the bark, and the moon. The scene thus set is Phoenix Park where the wonderful sun bird dies and is reborn, where HCE sins and falls, where the youth prepares to assume the rights of manhood. It is the locale of the sacrificial death of the Nature god, of Buddha's denial of the flesh, that is, the garden of sensual delights or Buddha's second watch. By the sheer weight of this imagery we are brought to feel the nature of the loss sustained by the hero on being banished from or on leaving this world.

Letters as well as words become for Joyce applicable at once as sounds, shapes, and symbols. The nature of the resulting effects, available only after close study, is best illustrated in our sentence by the cluster "for hoopoe's hours." Prolonging the cyclical aspect both audibly and visibly, "hoop" and "oe's" are both circle words; the sound "hours," like the clock face which it brings to mind, may be conceived of as being *round*. The existence of a hidden pun on the French word *oripeau* ("'or hoopoe's"), that is, something that has a false brilliance, is substantiated by the more accessible "for who pose." Jaun-the-setting-sun would like to sit still till his hour returns; he would like his refracted glitter to last the night through. In James Frazer's *Golden Bough* we read that the Swabians believe in the hoopoe's power to find the magical spring wort, supposed by them to bloom only on the night of the summer solstice.[34] The renewal element implied here gains force when we recall that this bird, whose nest is notoriously malodorous, is said to have an affinity for excrement (see also "sheegg"). An even stronger affirmation of the return theme is found in the predominant role played here by the shape and meaning of the letter *O*, the circle that will return us to the past while bringing us to the future. Clearly, as a unit containing exactly five of these circles, "fOr hOOpOe's hOurs" may have a special and perhaps a mystical signification. For the Pythagoreans the number "five" typified light, and we are told that five circles were the Mayan and Egyptian symbols for "daylight and splendour."[35] In this connection we note that Joyce was quite conscious of the esoteric association implicit in letters. He appreciated the mystic value of the *E*, regarded as the symbol of light sacred to Apollo by dint perhaps of its five points and its position as "fifth character in the Egyptian, Phoenician, Greek and Latin alphabets . . ." (*Lost Language*, I, 291). Thus on page 454 of *Finnegans Wake* Jaun intones, "Shunt us! shunt us! shunt us! . . . Sacred ease there!" "Alpha and omega" are evoked in reverse order when, in her ritual address to the dying god, the priestess Issy speaks of "oval owes and artless awes" (p. 458/36). Again, in the majestic opening of ALP's chapter, the *O* synthesizes woman's unity in function:

O

tell me all about
Anna Livia! I want to hear all. (p. 196)

Although I do not believe that Joyce ever went to the extremes of a Rimbaud or a René Ghil in establishing color or tonal values for the letters of the alphabet, I am convinced that he was acutely aware of the effects that can be achieved by means of the careful manipulation of significant sounds and shapes. Perhaps we may discount as early experimentation the letter experiences described in *A Portrait of the Artist as a Young Man* and in *Ulysses*, but we are forced to affirm that the "Professor's" analysis in I.v of the letters used in ALP's "Mamafesto" is more than a satirical "legpull."[36] When he speaks of a "bullsfooted bee" (p. 120/7), of "those throne open doubleyous . . . seated with such floprightdown determination and reminding uus ineluctably of nature at her naturalest" (p. 120/28–33), or of "that strange exotic serpentine, since so properly banished from our scripture" (p. 121/20-21), or again of the "trim trite truth letter" (p. 120/3–4), the author is no more nonsensical than when in that very same passage he mentions the sentence "to be nuzzled over a full trillion times for ever and a night till his noddle sink or swim by that ideal reader suffering from an ideal insomnia" (p. 120/12–14). ALP's letter is after all just another aspect of Joyce's gest book, and Joyce was never so serious as when he jested.

" . . . *leaving tea for the trout*" continues the alliterative mode, the jingle tone so well fitted to the gentle dullness of a Jaun. In order to kill time during the night, the postman is picnicking alongside the river. Tea, the first of the elements that he will leave behind him, is the fortune-teller's medium of knowing the future. But these leavings are more than presages, they signify the past; like the excavated detritus of dead cities, they illuminate stages of civilization. Jaun wishes to continue the developmental process begun by his father, leaving a further stratum of history. In the hope of gaining a measure of immortality, he is doing his bit to maintain the stream of life. Furthermore, the T or Tau as the mark of Thoth, the "truth letter," is equivalent to the word of God, symbolized also by the pages or "leaves" of the Bible or by the cross of Christ. "Tea" is then another variant for ALP's letter of life: the *word* as transcribed by Shem-the-pen, the garbled message brought to light by the culture-hero, Jaun, who has received it from the dark powers.

Significantly, in I.v we learn that a mysterious tea stain served as a signature for the letter of ALP (p. 111/20–24),[37] whose symbol is the "trout."[38] In III.i, the narrator (Shem?), after completing an account of Shaun's symbolic repast (the postman is feeding on the legacy or flesh of the father), addresses a prayer to ALP in the role of the matriarchal goddess of tea: "Ever of thee, Anne Lynch, he's deeply draiming: Houseanna. Tea is the Highest! For auld lang Ayternitay" (p. 406/27–28). The last word in this citation combines most of the nuances already treated with the associations *a-t-t-a*: the "first and the last, the last and the first" (letters of the Hebrew alphabet or the Greek *a-o*).[39]

By implication, Jaun's tea offering is also a "ritual of aversion" directed towards ALP as the force which has imprisoned the male light.[40] It is characteristic of all such gifts that the giver does not *bestow* but *leaves* or even *throws* his offering to the hated and feared god. Then, like Orpheus, turning his back towards the dread spot (see Jaun, "I'd followed through my upfielded nephewscope"), he quits the shrine. Jaun's "tealeaves," "jugs,"[41] and "bel-leaks" are appropriately base, as are the three forms of the deity, "frogs," "trout," and "the wary."

" . . . *and belleeks for the wary*," with its reference to Belleek ware (the Irish porcelain), completes the tea imagery and provides the archeologist with his shard of modern man. Joyce's alteration of the spelling to "beleek" may have been a simple error, but more likely it was a first effort to imitate the shrieks of the two girls surprised by HCE while they were urinating in Phoenix Park. "Bel eeks" now becomes even more appropriately "belle-eeks" or "belle-leeks." Also implicated in that crime are the "wary" or those who are capable of profiting by the lessons of the past, the three soldiers or warriors ("war-y"), that is, the trinity, or a configuration of treacherous demigods who spied on HCE and published his crime. The fact that these soldiers are also associated with racing "touts" adds further significance to the word "trout." Jaun, whose function in life is to deliver the letter, will use his power to prevent others from falling as his father fell. Here we may read an aspect of Jaun's heroic function: he will deposit the word that will save us or he will take upon himself the onus of the crime, leaving holy shrines, sacred or vestigial fires dedicated to the solar god Baal or Bel.[42] On the other hand, Jaun's decadent character is revealed by the interpretation "I will leave the girls to the soldiers; I will leave revelation to those who are strong."

A third lazy occupation, "*crekking jugs at the grenoulls*," takes us back to the garden where the first man was confronted with amphibious life and where Jaun awaits the sunrise. There is more than a hint of the primordial in the appearance of a frog (*grenouille*). According to the Egyptian creation tale cited above, frogs were on the hill which stood alone above the floodwaters of the earth. (Also on that hill was the goose egg containing the solar goose, which, once hatched, flew across the sky to make earthly life possible.)[43] This early flood myth is vaguely reminiscent of our own Genesis. The flood, like the sunset, was at once a sign of God's wrath and His love. Jaun, sitting beside the crematory pyre of the sun bird, reaffirms his desire to survive the catastrophe with its annihilation of values in order to participate in the slow reconstruction.[44] This is signified by his "tossing jugs," that is, the shards, or "cracking jokes" at the frogs, symbols of new life ("grenoull," "renoull," renewal). The lighthearted tone of this phrase is, however, balanced by the overtones of brutality and by Jaun's own fear. The hero's *genoux* are "knocking" or "crekking" together (Gilbert, p. 70).

A further aspect of the destruction-renewal theme is found in the sounds "jug" and "brékkek." T. S. Eliot uses the Elizabethan "jug jug" of the nightingale in his *Wasteland* to signify sordid love. Again, in "Sweeney Among the Nightingales," he compares his hero to a gory Agamemnon sung over by that bird. In spite of its role as a harbinger of the spring, the nightingale is traditionally associated with the night, lovers, sadness, and loss, all predominantly female associations belonging to the low ebb of male existence. Joyce gave point to all of these interpretations when, to the next draft of another sentence in this paragraph he added the reference, "naughtingerls juckjucking benighth me" which yields the interpretation, "naughty girls-nightingales joking-singing beneath me in the night in their effort to benight me."[45] (Jaun is referring to his physical position as the sunset.)

Jaun's "crekking" recalls the Aristophanian frog sounds figuring in a Joycean description of the beginnings of life after the Fall: "What clashes here of wills gen wonts . . . Brékkek Kékkek Kékkek Kékkek Kóax Kóax Kóax!" (p. 4/2). A few pages later Joyce amplifies this theme by linking it directly to the sunrise and the breakfast egg: "there'll be iggs for the brekkers come to mournhim, sunny side up with care."[46] Like so many others, this passage probably owes its development to a reciprocal interchange. Thus, the author waited four revisions and two years after writing the above before he inserted the postdiluvian nuance in our sentence, completing the association "eggs," "frogs," "morning," "sunrise," "care."

As the major elements in the phrases added by this draft have strong sexual connotations, we may detect a note of hypocrisy even in Jaun's gift giving. The two feminine receptacles, the jug and the cup, are both discarded by the sterile publicist, who leaves them and the tea to the fertile trout and frog and the omnipresent trio. Symbolically, Jaun-Buddha is renouncing the meager pleasures of the flesh, but as the shadow or mime hero, the follower of ritual, Jaun can only invoke the shadows of deeds. As the vestige, he is refusing a right he does not possess, the right to create. Though he glories in and associates himself with the heroic past, his is but a tentative existence. His picnic litter is indeed a mere approximation of the barrowful of rubbish left his heirs by that fallen Titan, the true Hero (p. 26).

In adding the pretty details, "cracking jokes with the frogs," "leaving my picnic litter," Joyce took care to maintain the original balance of mood.

The next three *transition* proof sheets (two dated 5 June and one 13 June 1928) perfect the balance between earthly and cosmic realities. (Two of these drafts are complementary parts of a single revision of the corrected proofs. The third, however, is composed mainly of corrections for a poorly set final *transition* proof sheet.)

> the bark of the [sic] ~~day~~ *Saint Grouse's*
> I could sit on one side till the bark of the day for hoopoe's hours, laughing lazy at the sheep's lightning, *hearing the mails across the nightrives (peepet! peepet!) and whippoorwilly in the woody (moor park! moor park!), as peacefed as a philopotamus,* and crekking jugs at the grenoulls, leaving tea for the trout . . . [47]
> I could sit on ~~one~~ *safe* side till the bark of the day *Saint Grousers* for hoopoe's hours . . . and whippoor willy in the woody . . . my up-fielded ~~neph~~viewscope . . . [48]

If the elements added by Draft 12 are, superficially at least, life aspects to be rejected by Jaun, the better part of those of this draft are passively accepted through his hearing. They are the prophetical noises, equivalents of the primitive "bark of the sun." Appropriately, Joyce began by eliminating the direct sun reference in favor of contradictory elements concealed in "Saint Grouse's." Besides its more evident bird signification, "grouse" means "complain." The holy one who *rouses* us with his bark, *complaining* of our misdeeds, is the angel of the reckoning or the Christ or the hound of heaven. The variant "grousers" gives point to this hound nuance by adding a hunting element through which Joyce represents at once the hunted and the hunter. In *Finnegans Wake*, John Peel, the fabulous sportsman, is a sunrise symbol while Humpty Dumpty is a symbol of the sunset or fall. Peel, with his barking hounds and his "halloo," was capable of waking the dead. But these barking hounds are perhaps counterparts of the devils and angels who will ferret out sinners on the day of judgment or who will lead the rejoicing righteous to the pearly gates. Joyce must have had this in mind when, later in 1928, he included in his fable, "The Ondt and the Gracehoper," the expression "grousious me."[49] He who damns us can also save. He who awakens us raises us and bestows upon us the joy of living.

While making Jaun's neutral position all the more clear by adding a further note of repose, the new version of "I could sit on one side"—"I could sit on safe side"—also contributes to the dualism of the sentence:

Jaun's "on safe" is also "unsafe." Joyce, who considered the *S* a serpentine letter, was addicted to the use of the triple form as in Sanctus Sanctus Sanctus: "Sandhyas! Sandhyas! Sandhyas!" (p. 593/1), "She, she, she!" (p. 570/24), and so on. Both good and bad serpents, the Satan of the garden and the king serpent of the protecting Bodhi tree are invoked by this alliterative group as is the doomed Sidon, "sit-on," the powerful *democratic* citadel of the prosperous Phoenicians.[50]

By changing "nephew" to "neview" Joyce indicated that Jaun's vision is limited by the nature of his being. Incorrigibly sterile, he lacks both foresight and insight. Just as his "follow through" is a useless act as compared with the trail blazing of the hero, his "neviewscope" is but one of many examples of how Jaun practices the fine art of self-deception. Paradoxically, but on a mystic level, the "neviewscope," by denying the visual, forces the hero to discover more excellent truths while following the mystic leader.

First of the direct auditory evocations, "hearing the mails across the nightrives," recalls Jaun's function as postman while introducing the brother battle of the "males" or that of knights in armor ("mail"), the quarrel between the two banks of the river of life. This last aspect is well developed by Joyce in the "Anna Livia Plurabelle" chapter (I.viii): "Reeve Gootch was right and Reeve Drocked was wrong."[51] The nocturnal reversal of roles evident in the sex of the sun is also expressed here by the fact that the left bank or Shem was right and the right or Shaun was wrong. Jaun's euphoric mood would not necessarily be disturbed by these sounds; he would continue to be a bystander. However, the ominous overtones and the call to duty are not calculated to put his mind at ease, especially since the mails are no doubt transmitting news of the catastrophe, marshaling forces for the recovery. The battle allusion is considerably enriched by two references; the first, from Plutarch, may well have been in the back of Joyce's mind at this point: "It is an observation, also, that extraordinary rains pretty generally fall after great battles, whether it be that some divine power thus washes and cleanses the polluted earth with showers from above . . ."[52] After that fabulous brother battle fought by the Mookse (Shaun) and the Gripes (Shem), that is, the fox and the grapes, across the banks of the Liffey, we read of a similar rain:

Ah dew! Ah dew! It was so dusk that the tears of night began to fall, first by ones and twos, then by threes and fours, at last by five sixes of sevens, for the tired ones were wecking, as we weep now with them. *O! O! O! Par la pluie!* (p. 158).[53]

In "*(peepet! peepet!) and whippoorwilly in the woody (moor park! moor park!)*" the bird sounds made by the "mails" are full of portent. Both of the parenthetical expressions, which belong to the tonal backdrop of this passage, are reminiscent of Dean Swift's amours with his Stella and Vanessa.[54] The same elements reinforce the semi-incestuous infantilism of HCE's crime. "Peepet," a variant of Stella's pet name for Swift, is linked to "peacefed" and "belle leeks" by its urination associations, while by its defecation nuance *pet* (French) recalls the "sheegg," clearly linking HCE's crime with his creative act. Onto this cluster of Fall and Crime symbols is grafted a new element, the romance of Tristan and Isolde or young love as opposed to old. Though this is primarily a Shaun-Issy motif and therefore indigenous to this chapter, Tristan as the young HCE and Jaun as the Tristan-shadow are respectively symbolic of the daybreak and the "dayfall," the successor and the precursor of the hero. The "mail" or armor image recalls Tristan's dress, while the woods image and the sounds "we poor will lie in the woody" recall the scene of the famous "Wood of Morois" escapade, an incident reflected also in Jaun's chivalrous behavior towards Issy.

"... *as peacefed as a philopotamus*" reminds us once more of the river in which Jaun is floating and of Jaun's amphibious state. More than ever, the setting with its combined forest-river elements recalls those two Alpha and Omega events, the creation and the flood. As a "river-lover" or "philopotamus," Jaun associates himself with the prototypic crime and with the criminal, HCE, who loves the river Liffey. Furthermore, the slothful, overstuffed, piglike animal is the image of Shaun's unproductive gluttony. Before leaving his picnic litter he will stuff himself full of food. Characteristically ungenerous, he will leave only waste, "tea leaves and leaks." Not all of the "philopotamus'" associations are distasteful, however. The "peaceful" river lover is also an Egyptian river god, an ascetic devotee of the life forces or a mangled Osiris. He clearly symbolizes the nature of and the reason for the hero's sacrifice. Such a "peace" is a hard-earned victory in whose benefits we all share. Consequently, Joyce salutes the departing Jaun with a parenthetic listing of words for peace in many languages: "Frida! Freda! Paza! Paisy!" (pp. 470–471). These words accompany him as he floats down the Liffey, which is doubtless the river of peace and renewal prophesied by Isaiah for the faithful: "For thus saith the Lord, Behold I will extend peace to her like a river . . . then shall ye suck . . ." (LXVI.12).

The sixteenth draft, completed in 1936, is the end product of several minor revisions undertaken over a period of seven years. Consequently, these *transition* pages are generously annotated in a variety of Joycean scripts. (Joyce's handwriting varied with the state of his eyesight.)

> I could sit on safe side till the bark of Saint Grousers for hoopoe's hours, laughing lazy at the sheep's lightning, *hearing the wireless harps of sweet* DEAR *old Aerial* and the mails across the nightrives (peepet! peepet!) . . . [55]

The abortive shift from "dear" to "sweet" is another sign of the workings of Joyce's mind. Neither word adds a great deal to the context, but "sweet" carries, in addition to its pleasant emotional denotation, an overtone of sensation which reinforces the food aspects of the sentence. Joyce sacrificed the rhyme effect (a poor one) "hear"—"dear"—"Aer" for these added nuances.

The author's reference to Aerial's instrument evokes the pleasing tones, the refined music of the Aeolian harp or of the sprightly Ariel as opposed to the "tempest" aspect of Shakespeare's spirit being and the dark implications of the news that the "wireless harps" transmit. Perhaps Jaun's harps carry the thunder presaged by the lightning. There is some indication that we have to deal with those wind instruments commonly known as "bull roarers," by means of which primitive races throughout the world imitate the divine wind calling for heroic sacrifice—the death into rebirth of the initiation ritual.[56] For the supercivilized Buddha these noises are Mara's threats which the hero must ignore (transcend); but they are also the half sounds of his detached world or the true peace. For the ordinary hero they are a challenge which he must at all costs answer, but which he strives vainly to ignore. They assure us that Jaun's static desires will be thwarted by his kinetic function; for, like the rabbit in *Alice in Wonderland*, the postman is a victim of his own time complex; he is imperiously called upon to fulfill a duty. These intuited terrors, darker for their invisible nature, will be richly elaborated in succeeding drafts. The time interval has been filled. Now the drama must be underlined:

I could sit on safe side till the bark of Saint ~~Grousers~~ *Grouseus* for hoopoe's hours, laughing lazy at the sheep's lightning, ~~hearing~~ *and turn widamost ear Dreamily to the drummling of snipers,* hearing the wireless harps of sweet old Aerial and the mails across the night-rives . . . [57]

Though it weakened the hunting nuance and perhaps obliged Joyce to add a new phrase, "Grouseus" or "grace-us," by deepening the last-judgment aspect, which now permeates the first part of the sentence, gives new force to the image of the frightened "sheep's lightning." Here is the holy personage who will give the signal for the separation of the sheep from the goats; here is the two-sided, love-and-hate-bestowing Father, a god or his god surrogate for whose existence Jaun finds affirmation in the noises of the night.

While indicating the nature of one of these sounds, the insertion "and turn a widamost ear dreamily to the drummling of snipers" does yeoman's service, linking several of the ideational strands. Through it Joyce introduces a new bird name which compensates for the lack of animal elements in the "Aerial" phrase. Then, using "widamost ear," he links the visual elements with the auditory: one "opens wide his eyes" although one may "keep his ears open." There is also something visual in the possible interpretations—"moist tear" for "wide-a-most ear" and "witness" for "widamost." The total context would confirm our belief that Shaun is only feigning to be relaxed and disinterested (see also "neviewscope"). The "drummling of snipers" compensates for the lost hunting nuance in "grousers" and, by its war implications, reinforces both the soldier aspect of "mails" and the element of the soldier spies in "trout" and "wary." "Drummling" refers to the drumming sound made by the snipe's wings, and to the noise made by the hunters' or soldiers' (i.e., snipers') guns. Perhaps it is also a reference to a "drummlin" or an oval hill which would correspond to the feet or barrow of the giant Finn-HCE. This would be the ideal location for the war or hunt, the place where the devils have chased their victims. (By adding a reference to *Hell* to his next draft, Joyce gave weight to this interpretation.) Once dead, the hero becomes part of the landscape. His mound becomes the abode of the hidden forces which correspond to the world's evil, the ancestral demons.

With the inclusion of Joyce's addition to the second galley proofs of

Finnegans Wake, our passage lacked but one syllable ("leaves") of the published sentence. Consequently, for the sake of brevity and clarity, I shall indicate below the variants from the two drafts within the formal unity of the printed version.

> I could sit on safe side till the bark of Saint Grouseus for hoopoe's hours, *till heoll's* ~~horerisings~~ *hoerrisings,* laughing lazy at the sheep's lightning and turn a widamost ear *dr*eamily to the drummling of snipers, hearing the wireless harps of sweet old Aerial and the mails across the nightrives (peepet! peepet!) and whippoorwilly in the woody (moor park! moor park!) as peacefed as a philopotamus, and crekking jugs at the grenoulls, leaving tea*leaves* for the trout and belleeks for the wary till I'd followed through my upfielded neviewscope the rugaby moon cumuliously godrolling himself westasleep amuckst the cloudscrums for to watch how carefully my nocturnal goosemother would lay her new golden sheegg for me down under in the shy orient.[58]

Characteristically, Joyce's last changes lean heavily upon poetic devices. Both the rythmic and the visual patterns are visibly improved by the addition of the echoing "leaves," while the double *l* in "till" finds its reflection in "heoll's" and "hoerrisings." Of more consequence is the fact that the *o* and *e* in "hoop*oe*'s" gain in symbolic portent when combined with those in "heoll's hoerrisings" to form the first of an alternating departure-return series, *oe, eo, oe.* Throughout his sentence Joyce opposes *e*'s and especially double *e*'s to *o*'s and double *o*'s but only here does he associate them in this manner, employing them as rising and falling vitalities, new manifestations of the eternal conflict between darkness and light. Man's unity in diversity is then symbolized by a digraph. His state depends upon the precedence of one or the other letter. In "heoll" for example, *o* or the disk of light preceded by *e* or delphic dark wisdom is a symbol of the fall or light eclipsed by intellect. But this too is equivocal because *eo* is Greek for *dawn* or *daylight.* (Though we may suppose that these clusters are not the only ones devised by Joyce for this pattern, I will content myself with these few tentative observations designed to illustrate the thoroughgoing nature of Joyce's organization, his manner of underlining desired effects. It may be noted in passing that these letter aspects belong to Joyce's later innovations, that they are consistently and deliberately emphasized by the author, that their function is pre-eminently reiterative.) These same paradoxical interpretations may be applied to the *word* "heoll" which the Celts use to signify the Sun (*heol*), but whose most accessible meaning is "Hell-Sheol" or a combination of two conceptions of the afterworld.[59]

Briefly then, Jaun is stating his desire to remain beside the sun's or Hell's horizon until the dawn when all arise or until Christ, the hound, will come to harrow, that is, "till," Hell. More poignant is the adolescent hero's acknowledgment of his duty to await Aeolus' (Eol's) arising or the sound of the bullroarers which will summon him to the test. Here, as though to demonstrate the debased state of the heroic currency, Joyce links the awesome voice of God to the clamor of newspaper and radio, that is, "Aerial" and the "mails." Perhaps the noise of that wind is vaguely present in "for hoopoe's hours, till heoll's hoerrisings," while the note of "horror" carried over from "*horer*isings" is intended to imply Jaun's mood. Such effects predominate in this last insertion, a penultimate piece of virtuosity. I believe that an identical love of effects motivated the late addition of "leaves" by which Joyce dotted a final *i*, applying a light touch of birdness ("teal"), a fortune-teller nuance, and a final alliterative twitch. For indeed he had long since completed this subdivision of his mighty structure, leaving little or nothing to chance or to the reader's innocent whim.

To sum up, in the case before us now, the story of a sentence's evolution is the tale of the gradual mobilization by the artist of all the tools available to him. Built, literally constructed, within a tactile framework of the established mysteries, myths, and symbols, the finished piece revolves like a carved bead about the central axis or universally accepted situation. While maintaining a static-kinetic balance through thirteen successive changes, while placing all movement in the future, while making it all tentative and equivocal, Joyce nevertheless suggests an infinite variety of actions and provides for a delicate variation in mood. Working under self-imposed restrictions, he produces skillfully manipulated paradoxes from which arise the synthetic experience of the reader. Here, the crucified Christ and the abstracted Buddha mix their respective roles and remain intact;[60] terror is akin to peace; the sublime meets and occasionally submits to the inroads of the ridiculous; yet the finished product makes lively sense to men of our generation.

By approaching several levels of this sentence simultaneously, I have attempted to show how Joyce reconciled a variety of seemingly contradictory accounts of the hero's approach to the brink of the abyss, how he

chose or formed words and even arranged letters to fit his evolving pattern. I have tried to indicate how Joyce managed to integrate a great mass
of esoteric knowledge into an experiential mold. In retrospect, the three
aspects of James Joyce's style best highlighted by this study are: the degree to which this knowledge is organized and controlled, the essentially
poetic nature of the means, and finally the end which these means were
intended to serve.

Joyce's new language demanded an even more rigid control than did
the stylistic quirks and symbolism of *Ulysses*. Even if we neglect the series
of parallels imposed by the author upon his chapter, section, and book,
our sentence remains an example of the extremes to which planning can
go. When he composed the first draft of his sentence, Joyce established a
frame of reference vague enough to support elaboration. At that point the
aspects fundamental to the action were present, but instead of splitting
this unit in order to make of it his armature, Joyce preferred to safeguard
its primitive integrity while elaborating by repetition the two final elements, "till" (or the duration) and "the bark of the day" (or the objective).
Thus, two drafts later, three basically ambivalent thought units enjoyed
equal emphasis: Jaun's rest, the moon's journey (i.e., the nature of duration), and the Sun's rebirth (i.e., the protagonist's motivation). In 1928,
when Joyce became aware of the need for further coordination, he recognized also the all-inclusive nature of his primary element. Thereafter,
he concentrated on the elaboration of Jaun's nocturnal activities, which
he modulated by means of strong interior references to the other two
aspects. As the expanding sentence demanded new organizing principles,
Joyce systematically developed such devices as the sensory climate of the
sedentary decadent. An analysis of the completed sentence reveals that
Jaun's sense of touch is evoked in the passages concerned with physical
aspects of his lazy nocturnal activities; his ears are treated to a variety of
sounds; his taste buds are titillated by the prospect of his picnic, of being "peacefed," of eating the "sheegg"; his eyes are pleased by the gentle
prospects of the heavens and of the hunt; and his nostrils are filled by the
odor of corruption which pleases his age—the stench of the hoopoe's nest,
of "sheegg," and of the crime, his overcultivated and abandoned heritage.
Meanwhile, Joyce tied Jaun to the soil of the book, elaborated and skillfully joined together the major motifs. Imperceptibly, he superimposed
upon the original triple division a four-part series of balanced opposites,
a résumé of *Finnegans Wake*'s book structure. Even though the last of

these parts to be developed stands first in the order of the sentence, there is every indication that Joyce had in mind a minutely organized progression of ideas. Thus, the complex rise-fall, heaven-hell evocations, whose generalized impersonality recalls the larger revolutions of the cycle, blend smoothly into overtones of the heroic crime, the creative-destructive act of the Father. This last is followed by the black-white, good-evil structure of the brother battle with its lunar aspects. Finally, in Part IV of the sentence as in Part IV of the book, Joyce briefly elaborates the maternal echo of the Father's act as the female sows the seed of her own dissolution.

The elaboration of the paragraph follows roughly the same pattern as does the development of the sentence. Coordination works two ways: echoes of the last-judgment motif are added to the sentence before ours in the course of the heavy revision of Draft 6, "breezes . . . do be devils to flirt." The fox-hunting motif with its John Peel elements is supported first by the addition, "I'll nose a blue fonx" (Draft 14), and later by "the fox! has broken at the coward sight . . ." (Draft 18). Sooner or later all the themes and background elements are held in common by the sentence and the paragraph. If, as I mentioned above, the germ of our sentence follows the essential movement of the germ paragraph, the completed sentence is ideationally an echo of the paragraph as it now stands.

The movement of the preceding sentence parallels that of our own, consisting first of a statement of Jaun's desire to stay put, "leaning on my cubits," which is followed by a description of how he plans to pass the first five or six hours of the night (until "twoohoo the hour") gathering in the natural riches ("pinching stopandgo jewels" and "catching dimtop brilliants"). It concludes, as does the paragraph, on an ambiguous note of terror and peril: he fears the owl's cry "twoohoo" and the breezes that "do be devils to play flirt." The sentence we have been studying prolongs Jaun's projected stay till daybreak at which time the predicted sunrise will bring material or spiritual success or the "golden sheegg." Joyce begins our sentence on the same suppressed note of terror which punctuated the preceding one, but here he reverses the emotional progression, ending on a series of pleasant associations, that is, the sunrise as glory. Jaun's fears are sufficiently sublimated by this to permit him to expatiate in the second part of the paragraph on his future success.

Joyce's interest in narration is so secondary that, once the narrative content of a passage or of a chapter has been mapped out, he deliberately covers up the marks of his artistic act, turning his attention to the thickening of effects, and to the rarefication of nuances by means of subtle transitionary devices, shifts of interior mood and psychology. Here perhaps we have a major key to the essential novelty of Joyce's sentence.

In the conventional novel the sentence tends to be a linear construction. The reader lets his eyes follow its development and draws from it material capable of preparing him for what is to come. In our sentence, however, Joyce is dealing with a poetic moment of doubt, a pause, which can hardly be isolated from all other such moments in man's history. Jaun's hesitation can be considered only in conjunction with the mass of experience that went into the epiphany of its revelation: the total being, a semi-mystical combination of Braman-Atman, the self-nonself of man. Joyce's sentence, therefore, as I have tried to demonstrate, does not in any real sense advance the action or the argument of the paragraph. His "action" is essentially static, an embroidery about a theme or an instant. His book is broken up into sentences very much like the one we have examined. These, in the last analysis, resemble nothing more than views of a cross section of some organism seen under varying lighting conditions and from a variety of different angles. The sentence, therefore, tends to atomize *the* meaning in favor of the *many possible* meanings rendering an *impression* to which all *ideas* are secondary. In spite of its total union with its context, the minor organism has a life of its own. The reader approaches it well supplied with images and impressions gathered from his experience with other parts of the book, but he is obliged to isolate this element, to subject it to a searching scrutiny before he can safely replace it in its context.

Toward the end of the last century, Mallarmé, who was himself writing an "omnibus" work for humanity, *Un coup de dés*, sanctified poetic obscurity: "La contemplation des objets, l'image s'envolant des rêveries suscitées par eux, sont le chant . . . [The poet must not deny] aux esprits cette joie délicieuse de croire qu'ils créent."[61] Indeed, the most obvious result of a technique such as Joyce's is to oblige the reader to retrace the steps of the artist's creative process in order to garner not only the intellectual but also the emotional wealth, the *song*. Joyce's sentence is a construction built about a central armature and composed of parallel entities linked together by association and applicable on several levels simultaneously. These "entities" we have already examined closely. They are the thought subdivisions of the sentence, the phrases that Joyce attached to his armature from which they draw deeper life. Like musical overtones, they are designed to blend into the whole once they have been understood or assimilated, but like our sentence, they assert their individual rights until they have been at least emotionally comprehended. Each of these units, as we have seen, tends to reinforce some elements in its fellows; therefore the total meaning is gradually revealed, if not as fact plainly stated, at least as the play of light so aptly described in another of Mallarmé's statements: "[words] . . . s'allument de reflets réciproques comme une virtuelle traînée de feux sur des pierreries . . ." (*Œuvres*, p. 366). To link these elements and to achieve the effects desired, Joyce used all the technical devices at his disposal from letter significations through alliteration, rhyme, and onomatopoeia. In an effort to explore all the surfaces of his subject he invented words, changed syntax, used puns; in an effort to keep the sentence intact he availed himself of these devious means to reiterate basic themes. Thus, through "heol," "tea," "sheegg," "belleek," "hoopoe" scintillates the "light" that one desires, that of the living Father, which is symptomatic of eternal good, enlightenment or wisdom.

The "ideal reader" of such a structure will discover first the imposed rhythm (Joyce's germ sentence is a metered statement of Shaun's attitude), then the armature, which is readily available as the grammatical core of the sentence. This armature, being sufficiently elastic to permit several interpretations, leads the reader past the background effects, which aid in establishing the climate, and along each of the parallel subdivisions. As he follows these strands of associations, he will notice antennae of possible meanings which are subject to justification by associations latent in other subdivisions. He will relate these meanings to different levels of the narrative until, finally, he begins to achieve insight into the total thematic effect. Step by step he will recreate the poem.

In its nature, this cognition differs radically from the logical apprehension of technical and didactic language. Even after reaching the point of "complete comprehension," even after understanding thoroughly in all its particulars the variegated structure, the reader carries away an impression rather than an image or a concept, an experiential reference which may be highly personal. Joyce has ensured this effect by establishing interior conflict or tension within even the smallest units of his sentence, by employing vague words in eternally expansible contexts. The sensibility has absorbed a multitude of complex images, mostly self-contradictory, which, by their interaction, defy "comprehension." Logic tells us that the human mind, like the human eye, perceives only a limited number of images simultaneously. To achieve a synthesis, it must neglect the particular and the contradictions inherent in any juxtaposition of particulars. A synthesis then is far from being the true view towards which Joyce aimed when constructing his sentence. That the reader of *Finnegans Wake* never arrives at such a static overview is a tribute to rather than a criticism of Joyce's method. Knowledge of the existence of further reaches is as important as perception of intellectual content. Thus the *content* of our sentence—glossed superficially by my analysis—could be elaborated ad infinitum, its consequences being boundless.

If we set aside *Finnegans Wake*'s formal aspects, we may conclude that the book, like our sentence, differs from other poems only in its scope, which Joyce widens to provide a greater area for contact. The interior world was for James Joyce what the exterior world was for the impressionists, "an ensemble of colored vibrations which vary constantly." Using images familiar to each of us, Joyce permits all the possibilities of a given situation to interact. The reader is exposed to a new way of feeling, of perceiving. He encounters levels not only of meaning but also of sensation, attacking simultaneously or individually the various strata of consciousness. The perceptive reader need hardly perform exegeses or catalogue sensations. His personal receptors will receive and retail the positive emotional weight of the phrase. He need only read and reread at intervals to receive a kaleidoscopic or prismatic series of views, all incomplete but all provocative, the same that any man might see when in the process of self-examination:

Now, to be on anew and basking again in the panaroma of all flores of speech, if a human being duly fatigued by his dayety in the sooty ... were at this auctual futule preteriting unstant, in the states of suspensive exanimation, accorded ... with an earsighted view of old hopeinhaven with all the ... ways to which in the ... course of his tory will have been having recourses, the reverberration of knotcracking awes, the reconjungation of nodebinding ayes, the redissolusingness of mindmouldered ease and the thereby hang of the Hoel of it, could such a none, whiles even led comesilencers to comeliewithhers and till intempestuous Nox should catch the gallicry and spot lucan's dawn, byhold at ones what is main and why tis twain, how one once meet melts in tother wants poignings, the sap rising, the foles falling, the nimb now nihilant round the girlyhead so becoming, the wrestless in the womb, all the rivals to allsea, shakeagain, O disaster! shakealose, Ah how starring! but Heng's got a bit of Horsa's nose and Jeff's got the signs of Ham round his mouth . . . then *what* would that fargazer seem to seemself to seem seeming of, dimm it all?

Answer: A collideorscape! (*FW*, p. 143)

If the truth of one man's vision can be measured in terms of the coincidental insights of others, we may ascertain how close Joyce's theory if not his practice has come to reality by reading the following revealing citation from Franz Kafka's diaries:

I stare rigidly ahead lest my eyes lose the imaginary peepholes of the imaginary kaleidoscope into which I am looking. I mix noble and selfish intentions in confusion; the color of the noble ones is washed away, in recompense passing off onto the merely selfish ones . . . as I stand here in my misery, already the huge wagon of my schemes comes driving up behind me, I feel underfoot the first small step up, naked girls, like those on the carnival floats of happier countries, lead me backward up the steps . . . Rosebushes stand at my side, incense burns, laurel wreaths are let down, flowers are strewn before and over me; two trumpeters, as if hewn out of stone, blow fanfares, throngs of little people come running up, in ranks behind leaders . . . the heavens strain to open to disclose a vision to me, but then stop . . . Was this the ultimate given to mankind?[62]

This then is the account that Joyce made of his artistic intention. The study of his sentence has shown some of the salient aspects of the poetic method through which he hoped to reach his ends. Only the individual reader can give us news of his success.

Notes

1. Statement by Mrs. Kathleen Griffin on the BBC Third Program, Pt. II, "The Artist in Maturity," 17 Feb. 1950.

2. *Stèle pour James Joyce* (Marseille, 1941), pp. 127–128. A remarkably complete collection of the *Finnegans Wake* MSS is now in the possession of the British Museum where it was deposited by Miss Harriet Weaver. In the course of this article, these manuscripts, BM Add MSS 47471–89, will be referred to by their catalogue numbers. For a brief account of the nature of the collection see John J. Slocum and Herbert Cahoon, *A Bibliography of James Joyce, 1882–1941* (New Haven, 1953), pp. 145–148.

3. "I could sit on safe side till the bark of Saint Grouseus for hoopoe's hours, till heoll's hoerrisings, laughing lazy at the sheep's lightning and turn a widamost ear dreamily to the drummling of snipers, hearing the wireless harps of sweet old Aerial and the mails across the nightrives (peepet! peepet!) and whippoor willy in the woody (moor park! moor park!) as peacefed as a philopotamus, and crekking jugs at the grenoulls, leaving tealeaves for the trout and belleeks for the wary till I'd followed through my upfielded neviewscope the rugaby moon cumuliously godrolling himself westasleep amuckst the cloudscrums for to watch how carefully my nocturnal goosemother would lay her new golden sheegg for me down under in the shy orient" (New York, 1947), p. 449. For the sake of brevity I shall designate sections of *Finnegans Wake* by means of Roman capitals (Joyce's: I, II, III, IV); chapters falling within sections will be indicated by lower-case letters (I.i, II.ii, etc.); page and line numbers will be separated by a diagonal line.

4. In a letter dated 21 May 1926, Joyce tells Miss Harriet Weaver that he finally has the book "fairly well planned out in [his] head." The final plan was fixed only after the inclusion of I.i in Dec. 1926, more than 3 years after he had begun writing (Add MS. 47489).

5. Ibid., letter to Miss Weaver, 8 Nov. 1926.

6. In *Dublin's Joyce* (Bloomington,1956), p. 362, Hugh Kenner convincingly develops *Finnegans Wake's* liturgical analogies in sequential order. According to his analysis, the 14 stages of the cross are confined to Ch. III.ii. Although Kenner's arguments supporting this last contention sound very convincing, Joyce indicated clearly in his letter of 24 May 1924 (above) that he thought of the Shaun chapters as a solid unit. As it happens, the 2 other analogical levels mentioned by Joyce clearly hold for all 4 chapters. Indeed, the first 2 chapters were composed and, for 3 consecutive drafts, revised as a unit. Furthermore, Kenner's liturgical progression would be somewhat reinforced by the inclusion of III.i and III.iv in his calculations. For purposes of this study, therefore, I shall assume that Joyce applied the *via crucis* to both the chapter and the section simultaneously, making Jaun a priest in the smaller unit and a Christ in the other. In all events, it should be stated that no single level of analogy can provide the "key" to *Finnegans Wake*, which depends for its meaning on total effects.

7. For further details see my study, *Joyce et Mallarmé*, II (Paris, 1956), 80–84.

8. These too are representative symbols of many of the aspects of *Finnegans Wake*: the multiplicity of a democratic age which destroys the tendency to exert a unified effort; the nature of broken light which has lost its whiteness, being dispersed by a prism; the disappearing process of the hero, whose virtue lies in his essentially macrocosmic nature.

9. Joyce first conceived this passage in 1924 while revising the 3rd draft of Ch. III.ii. In the course of this early revision he interpolated a multitude of additions, but as this is an attempt to isolate the fundamental elements upon which the paragraph is constructed, most secondary and tertiary revisions are omitted from the citation of what appears to be Joyce's first continuous sentence. Italics and small capitals indicate respectively the 1st- and 2nd-degree additions which I have felt obligated to include.

10. BM Add MS. 47482b, p. 30.

11. Joyce was revising III.ii and II.ii practically simultaneously.

12. I have deliberately glossed over the greater part of the implications of this paragraph in an effort to simplify the presentation of the skeletal elements. In like manner I

shall generally avoid indulgence in too meticulous a reconstruction of the many phases of Jaun's existence as they are effected by Joyce's *retouches*. The analogical aspects which will be alluded to throughout the exegesis should suffice to establish the extent to which Joyce integrated his material.

13. Draft 4, 1924 (BM Add MS. 47482b, pp. 53b–54).

14. In Draft 5, which Joyce completed before Oct. 1924, our sentence remains unchanged.

15. According to his letters Joyce reworked *Shaun abc* in 1925 and again in 1926 (BM Add MS. 47489).

16. Draft 6 (BM Add MS. 47483, p. 117). This version is only an approximation of the 2nd stage of the sentence's chronological development.

17. Page 430/6, 29, 17–18, 23, 20.

18. Harold Bayley describes the Greek festival of the laurel bearer where the principal actor wears his hair loose under a golden wreath as he leads a band of maidens. The author cites in this connection a Guernsey harvest dance known as "A mon beau Laurier." "In this ceremony the dancers join hands, whirl round, curtsy, and kiss a central object, in later days either a man or a woman, but, in the opinion of Miss Carey, 'perhaps originally either a sacred stone or a primeval altar'" (*Archaic England*, London, 1919, p. 541). Much of the data used in this article to explicate Joyce's mythological analogies is to be found in Bayley's 2 books on symbology, *The Lost Language of Symbolism* and *Archaic England*. These books contain such a surprising number of clues to the esoteric meanings of this sentence and, in general, to the analogies in *Finnegans Wake* that I am strongly tempted to place them among Joyce's source books.

19. Bayley, *The Lost Language of Symbolism*, I (London, 1951; first pub. 1912), 93–94—hereafter referred to as *Lost Language*. Like Joyce, Bayley equates these with the tale of the goose that laid the golden egg.

20. Draft 6 (BM Add MS. 47483, p. 117).

21. In *A Portrait of the Artist as a Young Man* Joyce describes Stephen's impressions of a rugby game: "He was caught in the whirl of a scrimmage and, fearful of the flashing eyes and muddy boots, bent down to look through the legs. The fellows were struggling and groaning and their legs were rubbing and kicking and stamping" (New York, 1916), p. 4. This same image reappears in *Ulysses* where a more mature Stephen watches a game from Mr. Deasy's window: "Again: a goal. I am among them, among their battling bodies in a medley, the joust of life." Joyce continues with an evocation of the "uproar of battles, the frozen deathspew of the slain . . ." (New York, 1946), p. 33.

22. "A fiend or incubus formerly supposed to oppress people during sleep" (*Webster's New Collegiate Dictionary*).

23. In another context Bayley mentions the existence of an "Adam's Grave" or "Giant's Grave near Edenhall by Penrith . . ." (*Archaic England*, p. 746). For further information on the derivation of Joyce's Giant see Joseph Prescott, "Concerning the Genesis of *Finnegans Wake*," *PMLA*, LXIX (Dec. 1954), 1300–02, and Walton Litz, "The Genesis of *Finnegans Wake*," *N&Q* (Oct. 1953), pp. 445–447.

24. Draft 6 (BM Add MS. 47483, p. 117).

25. ALP is elsewhere called "Mrs. Moonan" (p. 157/15).

26. *A Portrait of the Artist*, p. 264.

27. See also William Y. Tindall's article, "James Joyce and the Hermetic Tradition," *JHI*, XI (Jan. 1954), 23–39.

28. Max Müller, *Egyptian*, in *The Mythology of All Races*, XII (Boston, 1918), 34.

29. Draft 7, clean copy of 1st typescript (BM Add MS. 47483, pp. 144–145).

30. Stuart Gilbert, *Our Exagmination Round his Factification for Incamination of Work in Progress* (Paris, 1929), p. 70, sees in "westasleep" a reference to the song "The West's Asleep."

31. Draft 8 (BM Add MS. 47483, p. 173).

32. Draft 11, April 1928—1st *transition Mag.* proof sheets (BM Add MS. 47483, p. 188).

33. Draft 12, 16 May 1928—2nd *transition* proof sheets, many changes (BM Add MS. 47483, p. 198). Third-level additions are indicated by boldface.

34. London, 1914–17, XI, 70, n. 2.

35. *Lost Language*, I, 267. Bayley also states that the "*khu* or intelligent portion of the Egyptian soul was figured as a crested bird [or Phoenix], perhaps the crested bird known nowadays as a *hoopoo* or *pupu*; Khu was the God of Light, and in ordinary use the word *khu* meant *glorious* or *shining*" (II, p. 117).

36. See *Portrait of the Artist*, pp. 193, 274, 187, 255, 262, etc.; for *Ulysses* see Tindall, *James Joyce: His Way of Interpreting the Modern World* (New York, 1950), p. 10.

37. We are told that the "*signa tau* or *signature*" is the "mark of enlightenment mentioned in Ezekiel as being branded on the foreheads of the elect" (*Lost Language*, I, 293).

38. Joyce establishes this association in one of his notebooks (Univ. of Buffalo collection of Joyce MSS).

39. "The expression 'last' is generally misunderstood in this connection, the truer implication being the end of the last days and the dawn of the new era or beginning" (*Lost Language*, I, 73).

40. See Jane Harrison, *Prolegomena* (New York, 1955), pp. 8–9.

41. Traditionally *thrown* to Hecate "at the meeting of three ways" (ibid., p. 38).

42. See Belleek as a Baalbec or shrine to Baal, the sun (*Lost Language*, I, 150). The "belleeks," like the "tea," have both light and dark significations.

43. Adolph Erdman, *La religion des Egyptiens*, trans. Henri Wild (Paris, 1937), p. 86.

44. On one level Jaun associates himself with birds. Thus he *is* the hoopoe; he exchanges nightingale calls with the frogs; he lodges with the "pheasant." Indeed he *is* the "phaynix"; "Shoot up on that, bright Bennu bird!" (473/17).

45. Draft 14 (BM Add MS. 47483, p. 217).

46. Added July 1926 (BM Add MS. 47472, p. 15), *FW*, p. 12/14–15.

47. Draft 13, 5 June 1928—3rd *transition* proof sheets, many revisions (BM Add MS. 47483, pp. 209, 217).

48. Draft 14, 13 June 1928—4th *transition* proof sheets, obviously reset, numerous omissions (BM Add MS. 47483, p. 225).

49. Draft 1 (BM Add MS. 47483, p. 83), *FW*, p. 415.

50. J. Campbell, *The Hero with a Thousand Faces* (New York, 1956), pp. 31–33.

51. Galley proofs for *Anna Livia Plurabelle* (New York, 1928) (BM Add MS. 47474, p. 259). See *FW*, p. 197, for a final version.

52. *Plutarch's Lives*, Modern Lib. ed. (New York), p. 507.

53. The major portion of this was already present in fair copy dated 27 Aug. 1928 (BM Add MS. 47473, p. 231).

54. Cf. J. Campbell and Henry M. Robinson, *A Skeleton Key to Finnegans Wake* (New York, 1944).

55. Draft 16, completed 1936 (BM Add MS. 47486a, p. 88)—*transition* pages annotated in the margins in ink at different periods, the annotator's handwriting varying from addition to addition.

56. *Lost Language*, I, 87–88; Campbell, *The Hero with a Thousand Faces*, pp. 138–139.

57. Draft 17, *transition* pages and typed correction sheets (BM Add MS. 47486b, pp. 325, 391). Joyce, in an effort to make his changes clear to the printers of *Finnegans Wake*, listed on separate sheets all the revisions included in Draft 16; but a final rereading seems to have led to further corrections both on the separate sheets and on the *transition* page proofs.

58. BM Add MS. 47487, p. 170b; all but *leaves* which is to be found in *FW*, p. 449.

59. *Lost Language*, I, 329. In applying this word Joyce is juxtaposing 2 fires, that of life and that of death.

60. Joyce has succeeded in making the ritual contemporaneous with the act and both contemporaneous with the reader's perception of them. "Only in its twofold unity of then and now does a myth fulfill its true essence. The cult is its present form, the re-enactment of an archetypal event, situated in the past but in essence eternal" (W. F. Otto, "The Meaning of the Eleusinian Mysteries" in *The Mysteries*, New York, 1955, p. 29).

61. *Œuvres complètes* (Paris, 1945), p. 869.

62. *Diaries, 1914–23* (New York, 1949), pp. 40–41.

11

Notes on the Text of *Finnegans Wake*

CLIVE HART

In the July, 1956, issue of this journal [*Journal of English and Germanic Philology*], Fred Higginson noted twenty-nine passages from *Work in Progress* which were omitted from the final text of *Finnegans Wake*.[1] His list of emendations is based on a collation of *Finnegans Wake* with the early printed versions but does not take into account any of the manuscript material in the British Museum (Add. MSS 47471–47489). These MSS give valuable information regarding the history of the omitted passages and reveal that six of the omissions quoted by Higginson (those at 90.28, 138.30, 145.19, 188.01, 485.10, 497.05) were in fact deleted by Joyce at various stages during the preparation of the final text. In the light of the information available for the remaining twenty-three passages I have, in the following notes, amplified some of Higginson's comments, to which I refer in each case by the relevant page and line number. In addition, I have supplemented his list with eight more passages from the early printed texts which seem to have been unintentionally omitted from *Finnegans Wake*, together with two unpublished alterations to I, vi, and some interesting MS additions to a copy of the *transatlantic review* version of II, iv. Where practicable, Higginson's form of presentation has been retained. A few corrections of minor textual errors in his article are enclosed in parentheses. The two changes in I, vi were made on the same proof, and at the same time, as the other omissions from the chapter which appear in *transition 6* and it is not clear why they alone were never printed. It is possible that Joyce deleted them at the last minute, but there is no evidence to support this and I have included them here for the sake of completeness

Clive Hart, "Notes on the Text of *Finnegans Wake*," *Journal of English and Germanic Philology* 59 (1960): 229–239. The *Journal of English and Germanic Philology*, copyright 1960 by the Board of Trustees of the University of Illinois. Used with permission of the author and the University of Illinois Press.

(138.24, 138.25). A letter from Paul Léon to Harriet Weaver, dated 19-7-38 (Add. MS 47481, f.61) indicates that the additions to II, iv were made in about mid-1938, while Joyce was simultaneously working on Book IV. The revised copy of *transatlantic review* was sent to Miss Weaver with the letter and it seems likely that Joyce later forgot about it in the rush to have *Finnegans Wake* ready for his fifty-seventh birthday.

8.36   (For "in" read "on.")

44.24   (For "Sh sh sh! Sh sh sh! Sh! Sh! Sh!" read "*Sh sh sh! Sh sh sh! Sh! Sh! Sh!*")

87.04   (For "door-bringing" read "doorbringing.")

88.20   On the copy of *transition* 4 from which the proofs for I, iv were set up Joyce changed the word "belly" to "bauck" (Add. MS 47475 f.126).

138.24   "whom[, the toady,] is"—MS addition to a late proof of *transition* 6. This addition was never printed. (Add. MS 47473, f.243.)

138.25   for "liberal" read "lubberal"—MS change on the late proof. Never printed. (Add. MS 47473, f.243.)

141.14   This phrase was an addition to the late proof mentioned above (Add. MS 47473, f.246). The word "dinell" in *transition* 6 is a misprint for the MS "divell" and is corrected in ink in the copy from which the proofs for I, vi were set up (Add. MS 47475, f.54). This passage, and those listed by Higginson and myself at 141.32, 142.23, 142.24, 159.26, 159.28, 160.22, 162.35, 163.23, 163.25, 165.13, were never printed in *Finnegans Wake* because the proofs for I, vi were prepared from a copy of the "First Edition" of *transition* 6 which does not contain them. Together with "The Mookse and the Gripes" they were added as a Stop Press to the "Second Edition." The printer of *Finnegans Wake* was to set "The Mookse and the Gripes" from the amplified text which appeared in *Tales Told of Shem and Shaun* (Paris, 1929). This is apparently the reason for Joyce's use of the First Edition of *transition* 6 which conveniently omitted the unwanted earlier version of the fable. He seems to have forgotten about the other last-minute changes and additions that had been made some ten years before.

141.32   These changes were originally made on the late proof mentioned above. The word "Whittingdon" in *transition* 6 is a misprint for the MS "Whittington." (Add. MS 47473, f.247.)

142.23   for "daimons" read "fateful changending constancies"—The change was first made on the late proof (Add. MS 47473, f.247) and is printed in *transition* 6 (September, 1927), p. 93.

142.24 for "feekeepers" read "feedkeepers" and for "their" read "our free"—Changes first made on the late proof (Add. MS 47473, f.247) and printed in *transition* 6 (September, 1927), p. 93.

142.24 (For "*For/sennat*" read "*For-/sennat*.") This passage is clearly added in Joyce's hand to the late proof (Add. MS 47473, f.247) and since it makes excellent sense at this point there is no reason to suppose that it does not belong here.

159.26 (For "Schmeid" read "Schmied" and for "Motto!" read "Motto:.") This passage was originally added to the late proof (Add. MS 47473, f.250). In *transition* 6 the comma after "Samsen" is misprinted as a stop.

159.28 for "gem" read "germ"—Change made on the late proof (Add. MS 47473, f.250) and printed in *transition* 6 (September, 1927), p.106.

160.22 There is no MS version of this insertion in the British Museum. It was apparently one of the very last changes to be made.

163.06 (For "*sein*" read "*fein*.")

163.23 "sinequam [nunc] to"—Omission supplied from *transition* 6 (September, 1927), p. 106c. The addition was originally made on the late proof (Add. MS 47473, f.252). It is misprinted "nune" in *transition*.

282.28 This passage, which has quite a complicated history, should read as follows: "arecreating em om [/and ingreasing om and moultipiecing om rightleft by/] lumerous." The first fair copy has "arecreating em in lumerous" (Add. MS 47478, f.4). The first proof of *transition* 11 prints this as "arecresting om in lumerous" (Add. MS 47478, f.14). The second proofs also have "arecresting om in lumerous" but on one copy there is a MS revision—the word "in" is deleted and the phrase "and ingreasing om and moultipiecing om rightleft by" is substituted (Add. MS 47478, f.26). The page proof of *transition* 11 has corrupted the insertion by printing "rightleft by" at the beginning instead of at the end: "arecresting om rightleft by and ingreasing om and moultipiecing om lumerous" (Add. MS 47478, f.37). The whole of the interpolation is omitted from the proof for *The Muddest Thick* (Add. MS 47478, f.44) but the misprint "arecresting" is rectified: "arecreating om lumerous." Finally, *The Muddest Thick* (*Tales Told of Shem and Shaun*, Paris, 1929) changes this to "arecreating em om lumerous" (Add. MS 47478, f.68) and this version persists thereafter.

293   under the geometrical figure add: "Fig. I.—*Bass*."—Omission supplied from *transition* 11 (February, 1928), p. 14. (Cf. "in Fig., the forest," *Finnegans Wake*, 294.3).

294.20   for "lydia's, with" read "lydia's. Doweth knoweth him, with"—Omission supplied from *transition* 11 (February, 1928), p. 15. Omitted from the proofs for *The Muddest Thick* (Add. MS 47478, f.57), and thereafter.

297.23   (If the first of these omissions is to be restored, "stream's" will have

297.27   to be modified to its earlier form: "stream." For "three-ingles" read "threeingles.") An undated letter from Joyce to Elliot Paul (Add. MS 47478, f.25) seems to indicate that these passages were first interpolated by Paul at Joyce's direction. The letter reads, in part, as follows:

Dear Mr Paul: If compatible with existing text and still possible make the following changes please: . . .

wedgemidden of the stream lying low on his rawside And (something follows here which I forget but if compatible add) diesmal he was laying him long on his laughside

Joyce seems to have forgotten that the phrases had already been included in substantially the same form a page or so further on (see 301.26–29) and their later deletion from page 297 probably corrects an unwanted repetition.

386.12   "Johnny. [From the urizen of speeches.] Ah"—MS addition to *transatlantic review* I (April, 1924), made in mid-1938. Never printed. (Add. MS 47481, f.63.) The allusions to Blake's Zoas in this passage and in those listed below at 388.10, 390.34, 392.14 seem to overstress an already obvious identification and it may be that Joyce finally decided to omit the insertions for this reason.

388.10   "Marcus. [Tharmaz Syphon Mark.] And"—MS addition to *transatlantic review* I (April, 1924), made in mid-1938. Never printed. (Add. MS 47481, f.64.)

389.01   "brethren, [construing and glosing and] droning"—MS addition to *transatlantic review* I (April, 1924), made in mid-1938. Never printed. (Add. MS 47481, f.64.)

390.34 "Lucas. [For the luvah the lauds Lucas.] And"—MS addition to *transatlantic review* I (April, 1924), made in mid-1938. Never printed. (Add. MS 47481, f.65.)

391.35 "truth, [crosshatching or no,] unfriends"—MS addition to *transatlantic review* I (April, 1924), made in mid-1938. Never printed. (Add. MS 47481, f.65.)

392.14 for "Matt Emeritus?" read "Matt, the grand old Urthonian?"—MS addition to *transatlantic review* I (April, 1924), made in mid-1938. Never printed. (Add. MS 47481, f.65.)

545.26 This passage appears to have been unintentionally omitted in the considerable confusion which arose when the typescript for *Haveth Childers Everywhere* was prepared by a variety of hands.

One of the most striking and disturbing facts to emerge from even a cursory examination of the British Museum MSS is that the text of *Finnegans Wake* is corrupt almost throughout. A very large number of alterations and additions to proofs and typescripts never reached the printing stage, due largely to the extreme untidiness of the material the printers and typists had to work from. A few other passages have been corrupted during the processes of amplification of the early printed versions for the final text. In all, there are several hundred such corruptions. Except for those in II, iv, listed above, they are on the whole unimportant when considered individually, and most of them involve only one or two words each, but *Finnegans Wake* would undoubtedly be the richer for their restoration.[2] With one or two exceptions I have not attempted, in preparing the following list, to emend corrupted passages if the meaning of the text, though impoverished, remains clear, but have restricted myself to a few of the more obvious cases where corruptions tend to confuse the sense or involve punctuation inconsistent with the conventions adopted by Joyce elsewhere in the book. It should be pointed out that the printers who set the type for the First Editions reproduced their copy with extraordinary accuracy and that almost all the misprints ante-date their work.[3]

Any alterations to the text of *Finnegans Wake* other than those listed in the *Corrections of Misprints* must always be suspect, but it seems reasonable to assume that most of the points I have noted below are in fact errors overlooked by Joyce when he was preparing his list during the anxious months at St Gérand-du-Puys.[4] It must, of course, be remembered that the MSS in the British Museum are far from complete and that the missing material may bear authorization for some of these typographical peculiarities.

FURTHER CONJECTURAL EMENDATIONS

9.02   for "Sunshat" read "Sun'shat"—The apostrophe appears in the corrected galleys for I, i (Add. MS 47476 A, ff.4, 137; Add. MS 47476 B, f.280). Its subsequent omission seems to be a printer's error.

10.08–09   for "bluddle/filth" read "bluddle-/filth"—The separation into two words first occurs in the proofs for I, i (Add. MS 47476 A, ff.5, 138; Add. MS 47476 B, f.281). The omission of the hyphen seems to be a printer's error.

37.36   for "wi'fennel" read "wi' fennel"—The words first occur in notes for addition to the copy of *transition* 2 (May, 1927) from which the proofs for I, ii were set up. Here they are clearly separated (Add. MS 47475, ff.17, 192), but are joined in the proofs, apparently by printer's error (Add. MS 47476 A, ff.22, 158; Add. MS 47476 B, f.307).

42.01   for "further—intentions—apply—tomorrow" read "further-intentions-apply-tomorrow"—It is a characteristic of Joyce's handwriting that wide spaces are left on each side of a hyphen. Typists working from his fair copies often reproduced this spacing with the result that hyphens became indistinguishable from dashes. The printer was led astray by this in several cases (see below). The hyphens in this word were first replaced by dashes in the proofs for *transition* 2 (Add. MS 47472, f.324).

42.12   For "araun." read "araun!"—The phrase "seinn fion, seinn fion's araun!" is a late addition to the proofs for I, ii. The exclamation mark occurs in the notes for insertion in all three proofs in the British Museum (Add. MS 47476 A, ff.26, 160; Add. MS 47476 B, f.309). Its later omission is almost certainly unintentional.

42.17   for "fellow—me—lieder" read "fellow-me-lieder"—The phrase first occurs as a MS note for insertion in the proofs of I, ii, where it reads "fellow—me—lieders" (Add. MS 47476 B, f.434). In the later typed notes the "s" has been dropped but the spacing of the hyphens remains (Add. MS 47476 A, f.161; Add MS 47476 B, f.310).

46.07   for "And'tis" read "And 'tis"—The words are separated in the second typescript (Add. MS 47472, f.224) but are joined in the proofs for *transition* 2 (Add. MS 47472, f.327), apparently by printer's error.

47.05   for "Messrs." read "Messrs"—Joyce disliked the use of the stop after Mr, Mrs, Messrs, Dr, St, etc. In the *Corrections of Misprints* he deleted all such stops except in this and four other cases (see below) which apparently escaped his notice.

50.23   for "Nawlanmore and Brawne.)" read "Nawlanmore and Brawne?)"—The interrogation mark occurs in the MS addition to the first proof for I, iii, where the passage first appears (Add. MS 47476 A, f.33). It is corrupted to the stop in the typed notes for the other proofs (Add. MS 47476 A, f.169; Add. MS 47476 B, f.318).

56.11   for "power of his sword.)" read "power of his sword!)"—The passage first occurs in a MS addition to the proofs for I, iii. The exclamation mark is lacking in every case, but this would seem to be an oversight (Add. MS 47476 A, ff.35, 173; Add. MS 47476 B, ff.322, 435, 441).

56.35   for "orfishfellows'" read "or fishfellows'"—The passage in which these words occur first appeared as a late addition to two of the proofs for I, iii (Add. MS 47476 A, f.173; Add. MS 47476 B, f.322). In both of these notes the words are separated.

62.25   for "Errorland. (perorhaps!)" read "Errorland (perorhaps!)."— The stop was first shifted in the proofs for *transition* 3 (Add. MS 47472, f.340). It would be more consistent with the rest of the chapter to retain the stop after "Errorland" and read "(Perorhaps!)" for "(perorhaps!)" but there is no authorization for this in the MSS.

67.26   for "name.)" read "name)."—The stop is in the correct position in the second typescript (Add. MS 47472, f.246) but not in *transition* 3 (June, 1927), p. 45.

69.06   for "Peannlueamoore There" read "Peannlueamoore. There"—
The phrase "Where Gyant Blyant fronts Peannlueamoore" is
added on all three proofs for I, iii, after the word "wall." (Add.
MS 47476 A, ff.43, 182; Add. MS 47476 B, f.331). The stop after
"Peannlueamoore" is lacking in every case and the printer does
not supply it. The omission is probably an error but cf. 365.12:
"dollymaukins Though."

87.15   for "twenty-four" read "twentyfour"—The word is printed
solid in *transition* 4 (July, 1927), p. 54. The hyphen arose when
the word was broken at the end of a line in the proofs for I, iv
(Add. MS 47476 A, ff.53, 194; Add. MS 47476 B, f.343).

98.31   for "Cassidy—Craddock" read "Cassidy-Craddock"—As above
(42.01). Late addition to the proofs for I, iv (Add. MS 47476 A,
ff.59, 200; Add. MS 47476 B, f.349).

104.24   for "Geese; Gettle" read "Geese, Gettle"—The semi-colon first
occurs in a typed note for insertion in the proofs for I, v (Add.
MS 47476 B, f.353) and appears to be a typist's error.

120.30   for "loo—too—blue—face—ache" read "loo-too-blue-face-
ache"—As above (42.01). The dashes first replaced the hyphens
in the *Criterion* version of I, v (*Criterion* III, 12, July, 1925, p.
506).

122.14   for "wi'yer" read "wi' yer"—The words are separated in all versions up to and including *transition* 5 (August, 1927), p. 28.
They are joined in the proofs for I, v, apparently by printer's
error (Add. MS 47476 A, ff.73, 216; Add. MS 47476 B, f.365).

124.07–12 This typographical carnival has suffered more corruption than
any other single passage in *Finnegans Wake*. In each successive version some detail of the text has disappeared. The passage first appeared in some notes for addition to the second
typescript of I, v. The following emendations are based on the
typescript of these notes (Add. MS 47473, f.56):

line 8   for "they" read "the͡y"
line 9   for "ad" read "ád"
          for "provoked" read "provòked"
          for "ay" read "by" (? The change to "ay" was
          probably intentional)
          for "of" read "òf"

for "Brofèsor" read "Brofèŝor—The word was originally "Profèsor" but the "P" was changed to "B" in the revision of *Criterion* for *transition* 5 (Add. MS 47473, f.100).

lines 9–10   for "Brèak—fast—table" read "Brèak-fast-table"—As above (42.01).

line 10   for "*piquéd*" read "*piquéd*"

line 11   for "notion" read "nòtïön"

for "of" read "òf"

for "time" read "t̄ime"

for "ùpon" read "ùpòn"

for "plane" read "plāñe"

for "sù"fàç'e'" read "sù"fáç'e'"

for "pùnct" read "pùnc̄t"

for "oles" read "'oles"

line 12   for "sic" read "*sic*"

for "iSpace" read "iSpåce"

137.07–08   for "Canterel—Cockran" read "Canterel-Cockran"—As above (42.01). Addition to the proofs for I, vi (Add. MS 47476 A, ff.80, 223; Add. MS 47476 B, ff.372, 454, 463, 465).

140.23   for "how'tis" read "how 'tis"—The words are separated in the second typescript (Add. MS 47473, f.157) and were first joined in the galleys for *transition* 6 (Add. MS 47473, f.199).

140.28   for "mills'money" read "mills' money"—The words appear unseparated in *transition* 6 (September, 1927), p. 91, apparently due to a printer's error. The galleys for *transition* 6 have "mills money," with the apostrophe added by Joyce as a MS correction (Add. MS 47473, f.200).

141.33   for "name Tik" read "name. Tik"—In the *Corrections of Misprints* Joyce called for stops at the analogous positions 142.02, 142.05, 142.07. The omission of a correction here is probably an oversight.

152.02   for "true'tis" read "true 'tis"—The words were first joined by the printer of *transition* 6 (September, 1927), p. 100, but they are clearly separated in the typescript (Add. MS 47473, f.208).

179.28   for "Dr." read "Dr"—As above (47.05).

183.25–26   for "schoolgirl's" read "schoolgirls'"; for "wives" read "wives'";

for "vice abbess's" read "vice abbesses'"—All the nouns in the list from "schoolgirl's" (183.25) to "godmothers'" (183.28) should clearly be plural possessives. The first fair copy of the passage has "schoolgirls'," "wives'," and "one abbess's" (Add. MS 47474, f.11). In the first typescript (Add. MS 47474, f.31) "vice" replaces "one," but the apostrophe in "abbess's" is not shifted; it is in this typescript that the apostrophe has been dropped from "wives'." The second typescript corrupts "schoolgirls'" to "schoolgirl's" and thereafter the words remain unchanged.

184.03–04 for "upheavals distortions" read "upheavals, distortions"—The comma is lacking from the galleys for *transition* 7 (Add. MS 47474, f.96) and subsequently, but appears in all earlier versions.

220.03 for "St." read "St"—As above (47.05).

221.01 for "St." read "St"—As above (47.05).

222.09 for "l'm" read "I'm"—In the type used for the version of II, i printed in *transition* 22 (February, 1933), "1" is difficult to distinguish from "I." The corruption, which first appears in *The Mime of Mick Nick and the Maggies* (The Hague, 1934), may have arisen because of this.

267.02–03 for "Multimim/etica" read "Multimim-/etica"—The First Edition has "multimim-." The *Corrections of Misprints* changes this to "Multimim," but the omission of the hyphen is probably an error.

285.25–26 for "bully/clavers" read "bully-/clavers"—The First Edition has "bully-" but the *Corrections of Misprints* has "bully" in the emendation for ll. 23–25. The omission of the hyphen is probably an error.

287.27 for "*demun*" read "*demum*"—The word appears as "*demum*" in every version up to and including *transition* 11 (February, 1928), p. 9. From *The Muddest Thick* proofs onwards (Add. MS 47478, f.48) it becomes "*demun*." The overtone of "demon" may have pleased Joyce, but there is no authorization for the change in the MSS.

311.18 for "thee. O Connibell," read "thee, O Connibell,"—The comma, which is obviously necessary for the sense, was first replaced by the stop in the typescript (Add. MS 47479, f.25).

320.31 for "drain" read "drain!"—The exclamation mark appears in all versions up to and including *transition* 26 (February, 1937), p. 44, but is omitted from the proofs for II, iii (Add. MS 47479, ff.157, 174).

329.05   for "Briganteen—General" read "Briganteen-General"—As above (42.01). The dash first appears in *transition* 26 (February, 1937), p. 51.

370.34   for "ahull onem Fyre" read "ahull onem! Fyre"—The exclamation mark appears in the galleys for II, iii. Its subsequent omission is presumably a printer's error.

397.15–16   for "quad/rupeds" read "quad-/rupeds"—The word appears as "quadrupeds" in all the early versions, including the proofs for II, iv (Add. MS 47481, f.168). The later omission of the hyphen is presumably a printer's error.

404.11   for "now'twas" read "now 'twas"—The words are separated in all versions up to and including the second typescript (Add. MS 47483, f.54) but are joined in the second proofs for *transition* 12 (Add. MS 47483, f.104). The change may be authorized on the opening pages of the first proofs (which are missing) but this does not seem likely.

406.17   for "while'twas" read "while 'twas"—The words are separated in all versions up to and including the second typescript (Add. MS 47483, f.56) but are joined in the second proofs for *transition* 12 (Add. MS 47483, f.103). Same comment as for the preceding item.

420.27   for "Mr." read "Mr"—As above (47.05).

499.20   for "wi'that" read "wi' that"—The words are clearly separated in the typescript (Add. MS 47484 A, f.198) but are joined in the proofs for *transition* 15 (Add. MS 47484 B, f.372).

557.19–20   for "amazingly frank" read "amazingly, frank"—(?) The comma appears in the fair copy (Add. MS 47485, f.3) but not in *transition* 18 (November, 1929), p. 213.

562.20–21   for "They are and they seem" read "They are? And they seem"—The interrogation mark and the capital appear in the fair copy (Add. MS 47485, f.9), but not in *transition* 18 (November, 1929), p. 216.

587.30   for "MacCawthelock? Who" read "MacCawthelock?—Who"—The dash appears in the fair copy (Add. MS 47485, f.25) but not in *transition* 18 (November, 1929), p. 234. (Cf. *Finnegans Wake* 587.05, 587.19, 587.24, 587.36, 588.13.)

614.01   for "bonding. Mopsus" read "bonding, Mopsus"—The comma appears in all versions up to and including the proof for Part IV (Add. MS 47488, f.214). The sense seems to indicate clearly enough that the stop in the final text is an error.

Even if the conjectural changes and additions listed above are ignored, users of the latest editions of *Finnegans Wake*, both English (1950 and later printings) and American (eighth printing, 1958, and Compass paperbound, 1959) must take into account the fact that their texts contain an appreciable number of new errors introduced since the publication of the First Editions. Most of these have arisen during the process of incorporation into the text of the *Corrections of Misprints*.

In the following lists of errata, changes and omissions have been supplied from the First Editions (London, New York, 1939) and the *Corrections of Misprints in "Finnegans Wake"* (London, New York, 1945).

ENGLISH:

8.27	for "'MacDyke'" read "MacDyke"
8.27	for "'O'Hurry" read "O'Hurry"
14.07	indent paragraph beginning "566 A.D."
22.07	for "'a forethought'" read "a forethought"
32.32	for "of problem" read "of the problem"
132.36	before "hecklebury" insert comma
158.05	before "I see" place dash and indent
161.36	after "outnullused" insert stop
219.17	for "cellelleneteutoslavzend-latinsoundscript" read "cellelleneteutoslavzendlatinsoundscript"
261 fn. 4	note in *Corrections of Misprints* should read "for 'the burglar's' read 'her burglar's'" (last word of note already deleted)
271 fourth note, left	after "sake" insert comma, and for "*chawley.*" read "*chawley!*"
274 third note, left	for "*olive hunkered*" read "*olivehunkered*"

282.27	"and" badly printed
290.26	for "for'twas" read "for 'twas"
299 second note, left	italicise colon
305 note, right	above "CUNCTITI-" add "COME SI/COMPITA" and align "COME SI" with line 3 of the text. Delete the second "IOIOMISS" (opposite l. 20 of the text). The *Corrections of Misprints* does not authorize the deletion of "COME SI/COMPITA." The second "IOIOMISS" is the last line of the old setting of the note in larger type (see below).
305 fn. 3	for "M" read "Mac"
310.09	for "(that)" read ", (that)"
322.01	indent
399.12	delete note in *Corrections of Misprints* (already incorporated)
406.01	for "or" read "of"
425.08	"trouble" badly printed
566.26	for "porkego." read "porkego!"
618.31	no indent (caused by deletion of initial letter of line)
626.34	for "isht" read "wisht"

In all the English printings from 1946 onwards the right- and left-hand marginal notes in II, ii are set in rather smaller type than was used in the First Edition. In some cases the reset notes have been very badly positioned on the page so that they no longer align with the relevant part of the main text. The following changes should be made:

RIGHT-HAND NOTES

In every case place the first word of the note opposite the first line of the paragraph in the text to which it refers.

LEFT-HAND NOTES

262 note 2: place first word of note opposite line 15 of text
267 note 3: place first word of note opposite line 27 of text
269 note 2: place first word of note opposite line 24 of text
277 note 2: place first word of note opposite space between lines 6 and 7 of text

277 note 3: place first word of note opposite space between lines 9 and 10
      of text
277 note 4: place first word of note opposite line 13 of text
277 note 5: place first word of note opposite line 15 of text
278 note 5: place first word of note opposite line 22 of text
307 note 1: spread type so as to occupy the whole column
308 note 2: align each item in the note with the corresponding word in
      the text.

AMERICAN:

42.07	for "firestuffostered" read "firestufffostered"
98.25	delete "of"
127.26	for first "or" read "of," and for second "or" read "on"
136.36	for "mountaen" read "moontaen"
272 fn. 1	for "ma'am? says" read "ma'am?, says"
305 fn. 3	for "M" read "Mac"
342.04	for "*howbeit*;" read "*howbeit*,"
365.12	after "dollymaukins" delete stop
390.17	for "Deaddleconch" read "Deaddleconche"
406.01	for "or" read "of"
438.28–29	for "therein-/under" read "therin-/under"
566.28	for "Then," read "Then."

This edition also incorporates the unauthorized conjectural emendations which I have listed above for 183.25 and 267.02.

Notes

1. *Finnegans Wake* is published in England by Faber & Faber Limited, London, and in the United States by The Viking Press, New York. I am grateful to the administrators of the James Joyce Estate for permission to quote from the MSS, and to Mr. M. J. C. Hodgart, of Pembroke College, Cambridge, for many valuable suggestions.

2. I hope to publish shortly a full set of textual variants for *Finnegans Wake*.

3. R. MacLehose and Company Limited, The University Press, Glasgow.

4. See Patricia Hutchins, *James Joyce's World* (London, 1957), p. 206.

12

Finnegans Wake, Page 185

An Explication

ROBERT BOYLE, S.J.

The artistic mirror of James Joyce, when he held it up to nature, reflected with the intensity of a Freudian age the hidden, festering corners of the human spirit. Like Chaucer's mirror and Shakespeare's and others of our greatest artists, Joyce's reflected sanctity only obliquely. Those critics who see Bloom as the embodiment of charity should, in my judgment, seriously check their critical mirrors. They err, I opine, almost as badly as those valiant few who believe that the stuffy Platonist representing Christ in *Paradise Regained* reflects divinity. Joyce's mirror, as I see it in mine, reflects evil far more profoundly than it directly reflects good, and, to his glory as an artist, he insisted upon expressing that evil in the matter of his art as perfectly as anyone has done it in English.

With extraordinary directness and courage, Joyce set out to turn vulgarity and scatology to his artistic purpose. He uses them in many ways, but the one principal way which will concern us in this paper is to explain and to justify his own artistic practice. He wants also to excoriate the work of artistic Philistines, some of whom used scatological terms in speaking of Joyce's work. But mainly, in *Finnegans Wake*, he wants to justify himself more effectively than Stephen Dedalus was ever able to do, and to do so in a pioneering use of Swiftian scatology turned effectively to an artistic end. His success, or lack of it, may perhaps be more objectively judged after a study of the page with which this paper deals.

Like most of the chapter in which it appears, the Latin passage of page

Robert Boyle, "*Finnegans Wake*, Page 185: An Explication," *James Joyce Quarterly* 4 (Fall 1966): 3–16. Reprinted with permission from *James Joyce Quarterly*. Copyright 1966.

185 of *Finnegans Wake* deals with events in Joyce's artistic career. A literal translation of the Latin should make a helpful beginning to discussion:

> First of all, the artificer, the old father, without any shame and without permission (or, perhaps, pardon), when he had donned a cope and undone the girdles, with rump as bare as on the day of birth (literally: as bare as though it had been born), approaching himself to the viviparous and all-powerful land, weeping and groaning the while, defecated (literally: emptied) into his hand; and secondly, having unburdened himself of the black living thing (or, possibly, of the black air), while he beat out the battlesignal, he placed his own faeces, which he entitled his "purge" (possibly: the sinking of his star), in a once honorable vessel of sadness (or, once procuring honor for sadness), and into the same, under the invocation of the twin brothers, Medardus and Godardus, he pissed happily and melodiously, continuously singing with a loud voice the psalm which begins, "My tongue is the reed of a scribe swiftly writing." Finally, from vile crap mixed with the pleasantness of the divine Orion, after the mixture had been cooked and exposed to the cold, he made for himself imperishable ink.

The names at the top of page 185, "Robber and Mumsell, the pulpic dictators," give us the setting for the Latin passage. George Roberts and Maunsel and Co., the Dublin publishers, frustrated the publication of *Dubliners* over a period of several years, an agonizing procedure for Joyce. Ellmann gives the whole story.[1] The legal advisers who cautioned against publishing a book with names of private concerns and of persons (shades of Notre Dame and *John Goldfarb, Please Come Home!*) are characterized in Latin terms which mean "book" and "anus." "Codex," however, lends itself easily to the punning "tail" or "penis," either of which goes ideally well with the second term and with the Latin passage to follow. "Father Flammeus Falconer" refers to the Dublin printer connected with Maunsel and Co., John Falconer, who, according to Joyce, burned the sheets of the book.

Joyce's first draft of this chapter, reproduced in David Hayman's invaluable *A First-Draft Version of* Finnegans Wake (Austin, 1963), pp. 108–112, contains the following relevant passages:

> boycotted, local publican refuse to supply books, papers, synthetic ink, foolscap, makes his own from dried dung sweetened with

spittle (indelible ink) writes universal history on his own body (parchment) . . . Sings hymn: Lingua mea calamus scribae, veliciter scribentis. . . . Primum flens et gemens in manum suam evquacuavit (shit in his hand, sorry) postea stercus proprium, good appellavit dejectiones meas, exoneratus in poculum tristitiae posuit, eodem lentiter et melliflue minxit psalmum qui incipit *Ligua mea calamus scribae velociter scribentis* magna voce cantitans (did a piss, say he was dejested, asks to be exonerated) demumque ex stercore turpi cum divi Orionis, jucunditate encaustem sibi fecit indelibilem (speaking of O'Ryan, the devil's own ink)

One or two things relevant for my discussion of the finished text and the second draft might be mentioned. "Dried dung sweetened with spittle," since it is to be used to open eyes, to bring light, possibly is based in part on the preparation Christ made to open the eyes of the man born blind in *John* 9/6: "With that, he spat on the ground, and made clay with the spittle . . ." Joyce drops this allusion, choosing instead his urine theme to develop the image of the artist's vocation. Secondly, "veliciter" looks like a portmanteau word combining "velociter" with "feliciter." Joyce knew Latin too well to write down such a mistake, I would judge. For example, in the second draft, Mr. Hayman notes "sic" after Joyce's "appellaviat." I believe, as I discuss later in this article, that Joyce was working for the portmanteau effect in Latin as he does in English. Further, he can be extremely sophisticated in these Latin puns and double meanings. For example, in draft two, page 113 of *First-Draft*, among the answers to the riddle, "When is a man not a man?" one of the answers, not included in the final text, is, " . . . et enim imposuit manus episcopas fecit illum altissimis sacerdotem . . ." Thus a man is not a man when the episcopal hands have made him a priest to (or for) the highest (or the lowest). "Episcopas" is not a conventional form, however; "episcopales" would be the expected word. But neither is it a mere mistake. Joyce knows that "manus" is feminine, and in constructing an adjective of the noun "episcopus" he makes it possible to suggest that the ordaining bishop is an old woman. He dropped the clause, and I suspect he did it because it would distract from his later treatment of the artist as priest. Here the point would be that a priest is not a man. He wants no suggestion later, I suggest, that an artist, who is in an even higher sense a priest, is not a man.

The following answer in the riddle in draft two, "when pigs begin to fly," intrigues me with its proximity to the bishops since I think that Joyce, in his final draft, does tie up bishops and pigs in the word "porporates."

The second draft of the chapter, which Mr. Hayman includes because the first draft is so fragmentary and confused, is more useful for my purposes. On page 118 of *A First-Draft Version*, from which page all further quotations of the second draft are taken,[2] the passage under discussion appears thus:

> Naturally he never needed such an ~~alcove~~ alcohove for his purpose and when George W. Robber, the ~~paper state~~ paper king, boycotted him of all stationery and muttonsuet candles for any purpose he went away and made synthetic ink ~~for~~ and unruled ~~foolscap~~ parchment for ~~it~~ himself ~~with~~ out of his wits' ends. How?

"Muttonsuet" already implied, I suppose, that the writers Roberts would print were sheepish followers of classical traditions. Joyce then, wishing to bring in also the Catholics, the *Pulpit* dictators, who objected to *Dubliners* on moral or religious grounds, substituted "sensitive" for "unruled" as an adjective for "parchment," so that he could add "romeruled" as the perfect adjective for "stationery." "Parchment" he changed, perhaps because, since it turns out to be his own skin, the word made too close a tieup with "muttonsuet." And "sensitive" both fits with his idea of the suffering and responsive artist and matches better with "synthetic."

The most significant addition, however, is the statement that Shem "winged away on a wildgoup's chase across the kathartic ocean . . ." So Joyce as Icarus winged away to France, to become the exiled Irishman, or wild goose. His going across the "kathartic" ocean calls to mind the bitter ode he wrote during this period of difficulty, "the Holy Office." The title suggests his notion of the artist as priest of the eternal imagination, and the name he gives himself as artist is "Katharsis-Purgative." Aristotle's use of Καθαρσις leads Joyce to the bitter, scatological pun. He thus expresses his determination to deal directly with the human filth to which "that motley crew" hypocritically close their eyes:

> That they may dream their dreamy dreams
> I carry off their filthy streams . . .
> Thus I relieve their timid arses,
> Perform my office of Katharsis.

In his second draft, Joyce wrote:

Let the manner and the matter of it for these our sporting times be veiled cloaked up in the language of ~~blushing~~ blushfed cardinals ~~lest~~ that the Anglican ~~cardinals~~ cardinal, not reading his own ~~words~~ rude speech, may always behold the scarlet brand on the brown of ~~the~~ her of Babylon and yet feel not the pink one of his own damned cheek.

Joyce's reference to the *Sporting Times*, a newspaper which attacked the "filth" of *Ulysses*,[3] bolsters his resolve to explain in Latin his method of obtaining the proper ink and paper for his writing. Latin suggests the Church of Rome, and cardinals are the chief speakers of the tongue there. Cardinal suggests scarlet (bringing in the scarlet woman or the apocalyptic whore of Babylon) which suggests blushing. The shift from Latin into English calls in the Anglican clergy, who are here oddly cardinals, but less pronouncedly so, pink rather than scarlet. These presumably will either not understand the Latin or will read it with the comfortable assurance that its hideous vulgarity owes its existence to the Church of Rome. "Blushing" becomes "blush-fed," which no doubt contributes to the change of the first "cardinals" to the final "porporates," derived from the purple of the cardinals and bishops, and suggestive of the disease attendant to too much food and drink. Perhaps we can also make out "porpoise," with its "fish," symbol of Christ, aligned with "pork," Mr. Casey's notion of "the tub of guts up in Armagh."[4]

The second "cardinal" becomes "ordinal," appropriately distinguished from "cardinal," as in numbers. The fact that one of Roberts' attorneys was English may furnish an added basis for concealing the description from the Anglican clergyman. "Speech" becomes "dunsky tunga," which, besides suggesting heaviness ("dunt") and English weather ("dun sky") and Eastern languages ("Tungus"), foreshadows the psalm to be loudly sung a few lines below, which in English goes, "My tongue etc." "Her of Babylon" ("her" in Dublin accent becomes "whore"), the ordinary Reformation designation for the Roman Catholic Church, has indeed a Codex of Canon Law in Latin. Furthermore, her writers of moral case books, when writing or translating into the vulgar tongues, used to leave in Latin those cases which dealt with violations against sexual morality, partly at least to spare the blushes of the innocent or prudish. Joyce, though, I am inclined to suspect, since on the next-to-last page of this chapter he becomes "unseen blusher in an obscene coalhole," here feels minutely closer to the "blushfed porporates" than to the "Anglican ordinal."

I will now take up the Latin passage phrase by phrase, indicating as well as I can what clearly appears in the text, and adding speculations of my own which seem at this time helpful.[5]

1) "Primum opifex, altus prosator . . ." Joyce here translates literally the terms with which *Portrait* ends, "Old father, old artificer," referring to his Father-in-Arts, invoked in the passage from Ovid which opens *Portrait* and called upon again in the final prayer which concludes it. Stephen, the Icarus figure, intends to grow into another Daedalus, the maker of art, the "opus-facio," and appeals to his "old father," his "pro-sator" or "before-sower," to give him the daily bread of art, experience transmuted into the radiant word. Both of the terms are additions to the second draft, which begins "Primum ad terram etc."

2) "ad terram viviparam et cunctipotentem . . ." Joyce might be referring here to his harried trips back to Ireland to see if he could there get *Dubliners* published and get some money; in that case, the adjectives are surely ironic, in the light of the paralysis and sterility which *Dubliners* so vividly portrays. He could, though, be referring to what he (and the young Stephen) hoped from the France to which he flew, which would fit well enough with the later invocation of the French saints Medard and Gildard. Line 33 of this page, "gallic acid on iron ore," may suggest that Joyce wrote: "ad terram viviparam et cunctipotentem," shifting from a negative to a positive attribution. If he had added the intended object of "sine," we could no doubt better judge whether he means to refer to Ireland or to France or to both. The adjectives fit well with the France described in the last act *of Henry V*; but Ireland is described in *Portrait* as the old sow that devours her young. The pun implied in the first syllable of "cuncti-potentem" further tends to identify Ireland, as bitter young Stephen saw her.

3) "sine ullo pudore nec venia . . ." This phrase rather argues that he is thinking, at least primarily, of his return trips to Ireland, since the young Joyce would have no special shame in taking off for Paris, surely, and the "pardon," if that is the meaning to be taken, would not there be operative at all. On the other hand, he might be saying that he felt no shame at leaving paralyzed, deaf Ireland and that as a rebel he went without permission, ["exking noblish permish," asking nobody permission, p. 187] since "venia" also permits that meaning.

In the second draft, Joyce had written: "nec ullo pudori nec venia." His change to "sine" called for a change of the second "nec" to "vel," but he missed it or chose to let this stand for some reason. He went correctly from dative to ablative in changing to "pudore." He merely corrects the spelling of "venea." In that spelling, he may have been attempting to suggest venery or Venus. In several places, as I shall indicate, Joyce seems to have had in mind puns and double meaning in his handling of the Latin words, but when, as here, there was no operative function for the word in Latin, he dropped the attempt.

4) "suscepto pluviali . . ." To an ancient Roman, the word "pluvialis" conveyed the notion "of or belonging to rain, rainy." In the course of time, the word came to mean "raincoat, outer garment," and in ecclesiastical contexts, "cope" or "chasuble." Thus the word in the present context suggests rain, which, as we shall see, is tied up with St. Medard and with Orion. Further, the word involves the activity of the priest. Stephen saw himself as "the priest of the eternal imagination," and his work as artist as the "transmuting the daily breath of experience into the radiant body of everliving life."[6] The Mookse of the previous chapter, embodying both Henry II and Pope Hadrian, after he had "vacticanated his ears" proceeded to "put on his impermeable," (152) which would correspond to this taking up of the "pluviali." This phrase recalls the opening of *Ulysses*, also, particularly in connection with the next phrase.

5) "atque discinctis perizomatis . . ." The word "perizoma" is most familiar in its use in the Vulgate for the "coverings" which Adam and Eve made for themselves after the fall (*Genesis* 3/7). Hence the suggestion of a cosmic uncovering fits well with Joyce's (at least young Joyce's) idea of his vocation. As artist, he would tear away the false coverings of shame and hypocrisy from his race. And Buck Mulligan, on the first page of *Ulysses*, appears for his mockery of the Mass and the act of transubstantiation in a dressing gown which is an obvious surrogate for a chasuble, and he is "ungirdled." In Buck's case, the suggestion surely involves his own lack of chastity as well as his blasphemy. In the present context, Joyce, I presume, wants to suggest the necessary frankness and clarity of the artist who dares to hold up his mirror to reflect a hypocritical society.

In correct Latin, the word should be "perizomatibus." This phrase and the one preceding it are additions to the second draft.

6) "natibus nudis uti nati fuissent . . ." Joyce changes the ordinary gender of "nates," no doubt for sound or to suggest the verbal connection here

between "rear end" and "born." The imagery here and in the following lines recalls that of "Gas from a Burner":

I'll burn that book, so help me devil.
I'll sing a psalm as I watch it burn
And the ashes I'll keep in a one-handled urn.
I'll penance do with farts and groans
Kneeling upon my marrowbones.
This very next lent I will unbare
My penitent buttocks to the air
And sobbing beside my printing press
My awful sin I will confess.
My Irish foreman from Bannockburn
Shall dip his right hand in the urn
And sign crisscross with reverent thumb
Memento homo upon my bum.[7]

"Memento homo, quia pulvis es, et in pulverem reverteris," the priest says on Ash Wednesday, echoing the curse of God on the human race in *Genesis* 3/19, as he signs the cross in ashes on the foreheads of the faithful. The speaker of "Gas from a Burner" personifies Roberts, blended, as Ellmann points out,[8] with Falconer. The psalm, the urn, the writing material from the urn, the farts and the groans, and the writing upon the skin all appear on the page we are discussing.

In the second draft, Joyce wrote: "natibus nudix uti nudi fuissent." The coined word "nudix" is perhaps an effort to echo "Codex and Podex" above. No doubt Joyce dropped the effort because "nudix" is meaningless in Latin. Why he decided upon the subjunctive here is a mystery. I suspect that he had the rhythm of some other saying, a motto or proverb, in mind. He changes "nudi" to "nati" primarily, I suppose, to bring in a birth image.

7) "sese adpropinquans, flens et gemens. . . ." At the top of the next page, Joyce speaks of Shem's deriving all history "from his own individual person." This, I suppose, is what "sese adpropinquans" may faintly, if considered by itself out of its context, suggest—his taking himself as his subject matter, as he thought he was doing in producing *Portrait*. As in "The Holy Office," he here, "myself unto myself," interprets himself. The weeping and groaning here contrast with the joy with which he micturates later. The answer to the difference, I suggest, might be found in the quotation from

Portrait in Point 4 above, where the painful "daily bread of experience" is joyfully transmuted into what he in *Ulysses* calls "the word that will not pass away."[9] Shem makes his ink from experience, here as in "The Holy Office" imaged as defecation, mixed with artistic insight or skillful exercise of art, imaged as micturition.

8) "in manum suum evacuavit . . ." The word "emptied" may have had for Joyce some implication of the wholeheartedness of his dedication to his artistic vocation.

9) "highly prosy"—mistranslates, in the tonality of an almost illiterate and hasty reader, "altus prosator," taking "altus" in the sense of "high" and "pro-sator" as if it had something to do with "prose."

"crap in his hand"—the effect of the phrase in Point 8.

"sorry!"—suggested by the last part of the phrase in Point 7.

As his first effort to write this Latin passage, Joyce wrote, "Primum gemens in manum evacuavit." He added after that, "(shit in his hand, groaning)." Thus, it appears, he first intended to translate the meaning of the whole passage, but after the complications had come in, he apparently decided to translate only the most important notions.

10) "postea, animale nigro exoneratus . . ." This I find to be the most puzzling phrase in the passage. Shem has been relieved of the burden of something black and living, unless "animale" here means "air." The bilious humor which produced *Dubliners*, according to its critics, might be involved in the "black." Joyce might be referring to the blackness in which the "nightmare of history" takes place, from which daily experience comes, black until made radiant by the artist. This might be tied up with the "black panther" of *Ulysses*, the frightening threat of the brutal and irrational. It could conceivably suggest that thus Shem relieved the frustrations which daily experience laid upon him. By a good stretch, it could be tied with the Black Mass of *Ulysses*, since "animale" does have a liturgical context in which it means a victim whose life is offered to the gods while the flesh is given to others; Joyce could conceive of his own work as a Black Mass through which the dark spirits of men could be brought to the light, dogs might become gods. Mercius does, on page 193, call Justius (and presumably Ireland, whose womb bore him and paps gave him suck, a reference to *Luke* 11/27) "one black mass of jigs and jimjams . . ."

"Animalis" does primarily refer to air and the movements of air, so that the phrase may basically tie up with the "farts" quoted above in Point 6, and mean that painful black gas has been voided with the faeces. The "animale" instead of the expected "animali" is puzzling, and if taken seriously, could yield a meaning like "having been unburdened of a living thing which lives by a black thing." Both this phrase and the one that follows are additions to the second draft.

11) "classicum pulsans . . ." Stephen's battlecry of "non serviam" comes to mind, and Joyce's proud words in "The Holy Office":

> And that high spirit ever wars
> On Mammon's countless servitors.

Joyce's attack on dead classical forms, as in the Aeolus chapter of *Ulysses*, might by way of pun be suggested, especially in the odd participle. Since the "classicum" was sounded on the trumpet, and "pulsans" means a striking or a plucking, some special meaning probably lurks in their connection. The "Nothung," Siegfried's battlecry which Stephen shouts out in the Circe chapter of *Ulysses* while he strikes the light from the world, inducing the Götterdämmerung into Bella's house, may be echoed here.

12) "stercus proprium, quod appellavit dejectiones suas . . ." He called his faeces "things cast down," or "castings down," but I suspect he is thinking of good things coming from above, of the artist as god casting down his light, not desired by those who love darkness, the "pulpic dictators." They would call it ugly and evil. Or perhaps it merely means that his daily experience is ugly and worthless until through the process to be described he makes of it ink for artistic use.

In the second draft, Joyce wrote: "postea stercus proprium quod appellaviat dejectiones meae . . ." "Appellaviat" might have been some effort to introduce the notion of water into the word by stressing the "lav," and to suggest "alluvial." It is not likely, in the light of the first draft, as I indicated above, to have been merely a mistake. The "meae" should correctly be "meas," as Joyce correctly indicates in the first draft, and suggests, if it is not only the echo of some quotation, that Joyce was thinking of himself in writing the passage and not of Shem, or that he identified himself totally with Shem.

13) "in vas olim honorabile tristitiae posuit . . ." This suggests a funeral urn, containing the ashes of the honored dead over whom the survivors weep. In literary terms this might suggest the ode, at least a threnody. The phrase provides a good description of "The Holy Office," if we take "vas" to refer to the literary form and Joyce's content to refer to "stercus." Perhaps, however, Joyce is referring to the *Chamber Music* poems, songs

in a form once popular with sad lovers. This would tie up better with what follows, and could better recall Bloom's musing on Molly's melodious micturitions, as well as the exhortations on pages 21 and 571: "Lissom! lissom! I am doing it," and "Listen, listen! I am doing it."

In the second draft, Joyce wrote: "in poculum vasum olim honoribilem tristitiae posuit." His first notion was, apparently, "poculum tristitiae," "cup of sadness." "Poculum" he changed to "vasum," probably because this word can mean a container in a sexual context—even more so in the form "vas." "Honoribilem" looks like an effort toward a Latin portmanteau word, combining "honorabilem" and "horribilem." If so, the effort is abandoned in the final text.

14) "eodem sub invocatione fratrorum geminorum Medardi et Godardi . . ." The *Roman Martyrology* (The Newman Press, Maryland, 1962) includes the following pair of saints on the eighth day of June:

> At Soissons in France, the birthday of St. Medard, Bishop of Noyon, whose life and precious death were approved by glorious miracles. At Rouen, St. Gildard, Bishop, brother of the same St. Medard. Both brothers were born on the same day, consecrated bishop on the same day, and on the same day were withdrawn from this life, so that together they entered heaven.

Butler's *Lives of the Saints*, Vol. II (P. J. Kenedy & Sons, New York, 1956):

> St. Medard is a favourite with the peasants of northern France, and his *cultus* goes back to his death in the sixth century; it has been enhanced by the legends that have grown up around his name, as well as by his veneration as the patron of the corn harvest and the vintage . . . St. Medard sometimes is depicted with a spread eagle above his head, in allusion to the tradition that once in his childhood an eagle extended its wings over his head to shelter him from the rain. This story may account for his supposed connection with the weather. The peasants say that if it rains on St. Medard's feast the 40 ensuing days will be wet, and that if, on the other hand, the eighth of June is fine, a spell of forty fine days is to be expected, just like our English St. Swithun. Occasionally the saint is represented with St. Gildard, who is erroneously described as his twin brother, and who as such is commemorated with him in the *Roman Martyrology*. St. Medard for some reason was sometimes depicted in the

middle ages laughing inanely with his mouth wide open ("le ris de St. Médard"), and he was invoked to cure the toothache. Whether his association with dental troubles was the consequence or the cause of this representation, it is hard to say.

The connection of the twins, however legendary, Joyce would, in the light of his twin-patterns in *F.W.*, scarcely relinquish. St. Medard's connection with rain brings him into relation with the life-giving micturition,[10] and his position as canonized bishop of the Church of Rome ties him up both with the "porporates" and with the "pluviale." That last connection again involves him, like Orion below, with rain. His inane laughter fits with the tonality of the passage. And his name suggests the name of one of the persons involved in Joyce's life at the time of which the passage treats, Patrick Mead, editor of the *Evening Telegraph*, the model for Crawford in *Ulysses*, a heavy drinker, and friendly to Joyce (cf. Ellmann, pp. 297–298). St. Gildard's name becomes "Godardi," and as a twin to Mead, Gogarty, another heavy drinker and hazily friendly to Joyce, fits well. Thus the symbolic Mead and Gogarty smile upon the symbolic micturition of Shem-Joyce, as the real characters had no doubt often joined him in the literal act. As Joseph Wilson pointed out to me, Joyce had used the connection of micturition with literature in relation to Gogarty in *Ulysses* (197):

> Quickly, warningfully Buck Mulligan bent down:
> —The tramper Synge is looking for you, he said, to murder you. He heard you pissed on his halldoor in Glasthule. He's out in pampooties to murder you.
> —Me! Stephen exclaimed. That was your contribution to literature.

And it is perhaps relevant that in *Ulysses* both Crawford and Mulligan encourage Stephen's writing; both anticipate that he will produce something living from the experiences he is having in Dublin.

In the second draft, Joyce wrote: "eodem lente ac melliflue minxit . . ." That "lentiter" looks like another, and clever, attempt at a portmanteau word, combining "lentus" ("pliant"), "lente" ("slowly"), and "leniter" ("smoothly, gently"). Under the influence of the inanely smiling saints, however, all these meanings disappear, and are replaced by the psalmistic "laete" ("joyously").

15) "laete ac melliflue minxit . . ." In their farewell urination, Stephen and Bloom revealed their opposed attitudes toward reality, Bloom's

phenomenology, Stephen's mysticism (*Ulysses*, 687–688). Here in *F.W.* urine becomes the means for producing ink from the raw material of experience. The water from outside, which Stephen feared and hated so much, is here replaced by the water which the artist himself produces, and which, in his hands, can become a baptismal channel of life.

16) "psalmum qui incipit: Lingua mea calamus scribae velociter scribentis: magna voce cantitans . . ." The psalm is Psalm 44, which begins, in English: "My heart overflows with a goodly theme; as I sing my ode to the king, my tongue is nimble as the pen of a skillful scribe." "Calamus," a reed, is not without some tonality of the pointing ash-plant which Stephen used, and surely close to the lifewand which Shem lifts at the end of this chapter. He lifts that wand, and those who were dumb cry, reiteratively, "quoi." Their cry goes with the wild-goose image. Stephen became a wild-goose in order to bring the dead to life. This goose-speech is the beginning of life. As the "quoi" of French, it would imply surprise and curiosity at the revelation of the artist, at the coming of life. This is the aim of the Icarus-figure of *Portrait*. Stephen mocks his own failure in *Ulysses*:

> Fabulous artificer, the hawklike man. You fled. Whereto? Newhaven-Dieppe, steerage passenger. Paris and back. Lapwing. Icarus. *Pater, ait*. Seabedabbled, fallen, weltering. Lapwing you are, Lapwing he. (208)

The dative "voci" of the second draft is corrected in this final version to the ablative.

17) "did a piss . . ." from "minxit"; "says he was dejected . . ." from "appellavit dejectiones"; "asks to be exonerated . . ." from "exoneratus . . . cantitans"

18) "demum ex stercore turpi cum divi Orionis jucunditate mixto, cocto, frigorique exposito . . ." The most relevant fact about the handsome and powerful giant Orion we find in *The Oxford Classical Dictionary*: " . . . Hyrieus, eponym of Hyriae, asked for offspring from three gods (their names vary) whom he had hospitably received. They made water (ουρησαυ) on a bull's hide and bade him bury it; in time a child was born, which he called Urion, the name afterwards becoming Orion." Life, and even divine life (as the priest in the Christian tradition effects it through the sacraments), here emerges from the mixture of the bull's hide and the gods' urine. Joyce, or Shem, will produce life from the artist's defecation and his urine. In the case of Orion, urine produced a powerful man,

beloved of the gods, who became a constellation, a divinity. Hence, in Stephen's view of the artist's function as priest transmuting ordinary experience into the radiant body of everliving life, Orion serves as an excellent illustration of the artistic process.

Orion, like Medard, is closely connected with rain:

The constellation of Orion set at the commencement of November, at which time storms and rain were frequent: hence by Roman poets is he often called *imbrifer*, *nimbosus*, or *aquosus*.[11]

No doubt the fact that the mixture in the urn is being mixed, cooked, and exposed to cold has far more significance than I now see in it, but at the moment all I can perceive is that the preparation takes time and suffering. The "denique" of the second draft is changed here to "demum," perhaps to echo "demon." As I will note later, Joyce removed the word "devil" from the final parenthesis of this passage as it appeared in the second draft, and he may have tried to retain some touch of the word in this rather distant echo. Perhaps more useful is the suggestion made to me by Michael Connelly, that since "mum" is a sweet strong beer,[12] Joyce might by the change be indicating that the activity being discussed proceeds "from beer."

19) "encaustum sibi fecit indelibile . . ." Joyce here corrects the "indelibilem" of the second draft. "Encaustum" is certainly ink, but not ordinary ink. It is the purple-red ink of the later Roman emperors (secular "porporates"), the color of royalty, and of blood. It comes from a word meaning "burned in." Only caustic writing, one infers, will follow from its use. If it is applied to the skin, as it is in the last line on the page, it will burn in "corrosive sublimation." But it produces, as the following page states, the "word that would not pass away." This ink is formed from the mixture of painful crap, low, earthy, death symbol; and from his pleasant piss, like rain, a life symbol. Literally, it is made from the ugliness of evil humans, the dead, hypocritical, paralyzed, vulgar, lecherous, classical; and from the artist's literary insight and skill, life-giving, honest, candid, moving, original. Thus the priest of the eternal imagination can bring the true eucharist to an otherwise dead world.

20) "faked O'Ryan's, the indelible ink . . ." from "fecit" and "Orionis." Fred Ryan, together with Eglinton an editor of *Dana*, rejected Joyce's earliest attempt to print a version of *Portrait* (cf. *Letters*, 98). His name, like the first one given to Orion in the myth quoted above, suggests urine without,

in Joyce's treatment here, the elevated symbolic tonality noted in Point 19.

In the second draft, Joyce closed the passage with "(made O'Ryan the devil's own ink)." "Made" translates "fecit," and Joyce no doubt wished to suggest a parallel between making water and making ink. The printer's devil would work in well with Fred Ryan's relationship to Joyce. But apparently Joyce decided to stress the first name of Ryan and to echo more pointedly his treatment of "My unchanging Word is sacred. The word is my wife, to expose and expound, to vend and to velnerate, and may the curlews crown our nuptias! Till Breath us depart; Wamen." (*F.W.*, 167).

This page of *Finnegans Wake*, then, sets forth the philosophy of art, the bitter vulgarity, the delight in word-play, the rebellious blasphemy, the determination to total honesty, the doubt of self, the hatred of hypocrisy, the straining idealism of the youthful Joyce.[13] It prepares us for the naming, on the two following pages, of every story in *Dubliners* ("for the deathfete of Saint Ignaceous Poisonivy, of the Fickle Crowd (hopon the sixth day of Hogsober, killim our king, layum low!)"—"Ivy Day in the Committee Room," 6th of October, Hynes poem and "Et tu, Healy," treating of the priests and crowd who laid low Parnell, "our uncrowned king"; "Petty constable Sistersen," "The Sisters"; "foul clay," "Clay"; "in little clots," "A Little Cloud"; "wrongcountered," "An Encounter"; "an eveling," "Eveline"; "boardelhouse," "The Boarding House"; "after the grace," "After the Race" and "Grace"; "the painful sake," "A Painful Case"; "his country-ports," "Counterparts"; "the dead med dirt," "The Dead"; "arrahbejibbers," "Araby"; "two gallonts," "Two Gallants"; "his murder . . . What mother?" "A Mother."),[14] and for the listing of the chapters of *Ulysses* on page 229 ("Ukalepe," "Calypso"; "Loathers' leave," "Lotus Eaters"; "Had Days," "Hades"; "Nemo in Patria," "Aeolus," in reference a) to Ulysses's adopted name in the cave of Polyphemus, "Nobody," here applied to Bloom—b) to the patriotism in the speeches read in the newspaper office—c) to Christ's statement in *Matthew* 13/57, "Non est propheta sine honore, nisi in patria sua et in domo sua"; "The Luncher Out," "Lestrygonians"; "Skilly and Carubdish," "Scylla and Charybdis"; "A Wondering Wreck," "Wandering Rocks"; "From the Mermaids' Tavern," "Sirens"; "Bullyfamous," "Cyclops," i.e., Polyphemus; "Naughtsycalves," "Nausicaa"; "Mother of Misery," "Oxen of the Sun," reference to the misery of Mrs. Purefoy and the name of the hospital near Bloom's house, the Mater Misericordia; "Walpurgas Nackt," "Circe"). It helps us to see the justice in the charge of Justius:

... and now, forsooth, ... you have become of twosome twiminds forenenst gods, hidden and discovered, nay, condemned fool, anarch, egoarch, hiresiarch, you have reared your disunited kingdom on the vacuum of your own most intensely doubtful soul. (188)

And it helps us to sympathize with the self-knowledge of the artist in our world,

... to me unseen blusher in an obscene coalhole, the cubilibum[15] of your secret sigh, dweller in the downandoutermost where voice only of the dead may come ... (194)

Notes

1. Richard Ellmann, *James Joyce* (New York, 1959), passim.

2. I do not attempt to reproduce all of Mr. Hayman's extremely valuable typographical guides to the development of the text, since for my purpose the crossed-out words give the most useful signals of the veerings of Joyce's intention.

3. Stuart Gilbert, ed., *Letters of James Joyce* (New York, 1957), pp. 183 and 201.

4. *The Portable James Joyce* (Viking, New York, 1955), p. 275.

5. I acknowledge here my considerable debt to my colleague, Father Daniel Costello S.J., head of the Classics Department at Regis College. He has gone over the passage with me, noting the oddities of Latin construction, supplying connections from his knowledge of Latin and Greek myths and authors, and suggesting possible allusions and puns.

6. *The Portable James Joyce*, p. 488.

7. *The Portable James Joyce*, p. 662.

8. *James Joyce*, p. 346.

9. James Joyce, *Ulysses* (New York, 1946), p. 385.

10. Not until this paper had been written did I see Adaline Glasheen's *A Second Census of* Finnegans Wake (Northwestern University Press, 1963), where Medard is identified as a "6th century French bishop, patron of rain." Mrs. Glasheen also helpfully identifies another reference to Medard in which, in a passage dealing with micturition, he is specifically associated with St. Swithun: "Never christen medlard apples till a swithin is in sight" (*F.W.*, 433).

11. *A Smaller Classical Dictionary* (London, 1937), p. 359.

12. Cf. Joseph Campbell and Henry Morton Robinson, *A Skeleton Key to* Finnegans Wake (New York, 1960), p. 28. They identify "mum" in relation to "doublin their mumper" on the first page of *F.W.*

13. The page should certainly be added to the significant passages dealing with micturition which Clive Hart discusses in his excellent *Structure and Motif in* Finnegans Wake (London, 1962), pp. 202–208. And the page bolsters W. Y. Tindall's observation that for

Joyce the act of micturition symbolizes an act of creation—see *Chamber Music* (New York, 1954), pp. 74 ff.

14. James Atherton, in *The Books at the Wake* (New York, 1960), pp. 106–109, lists these titles and gives other information valuable for placing in context the Latin passage I have attempted to explicate.

15. Another fascinating Latin-English portmanteau word, formed of "cubile," the ordinary meaning of which is a couch, a bed, a place to rest, and the English slang "bum," meaning buttocks. It suggests that the low work of Joyce, a resting place for the buttocks, might lead to the secret dreams of the longing spirit as inevitably as do the moonbeam-haunted banks where Shakespeare's Bully Bottom (bilibum) dreamt his dream, "past the wit of man to say what dream it was."

Contributors

Robert R. Boyle, S.J. (1915–1998). Boyle, one of the foremost authorities on Joyce and theology, was an American critic and a Jesuit priest. He was an early contributor to the *James Joyce Quarterly* and one of the first to join its advisory board. He was the author of *James Joyce's Pauline Vision: A Catholic Exposition* (1978) and numerous articles on Joyce. He also published *Metaphor in Hopkins* (1961). Boyle taught at Regis College, Kent State University, and Marquette University. He retired from Marquette in 1981 but remained a mentor to many young scholars.

Edmund L. Epstein (1931–). Epstein, a noted linguist as well as a renowned Joycean, was founding editor of the *James Joyce Review*. He also edited *Language and Style: An International Journal*. His publications on Joyce's work include *The Ordeal of Stephen Dedalus: The Conflict of the Generations in James Joyce's "A Portrait of the Artist as a Young Man"* (1971) and *A Guide through "Finnegans Wake"* (2009). After teaching for a number of years at Southern Illinois University, Epstein is now a Professor of English at Queens College and at the Graduate Center of the City University of New York.

S. L. Goldberg (1926–1991). Goldberg was an English scholar and a student of F. R. Leavis who spent his professional career in Australia, first at the University of Melbourne and then at the University of Sydney, where his controversial approach to criticism produced mixed responses. His most significant contribution to Joyce studies remains his book *The Classical Temper: A Study of James Joyce's "Ulysses"* (1961).

Clive Hart (1931–). Hart is an Australian-born Joycean who has spent most of his teaching career in England. He devoted much of his early Joyce research to *Finnegans Wake* before turning his energies to *Ulysses*.

His publications on Joyce's work include *Structure and Motif in "Finnegans Wake"* (1962), *A Concordance to "Finnegans Wake"* (1963), and *James Joyce's "Ulysses"* (1968). With Fritz Senn, Hart is a founding editor of *A Wake Newslitter.*

David Hayman (1927–). With Walton Litz, Hayman stands as one of the earliest scholars of Joyce's prepublication material. Before retiring from the classroom, he taught at the University of Texas, the University of Iowa, and the University of Wisconsin. Among his books on Joyce's writing are *A First-Draft Version of "Finnegans Wake"* (1963), *"Ulysses": The Mechanics of Meaning* (1970), and *The "Wake" in Transit* (1990).

A. Walton Litz (1929–). Litz was a pioneer in the field of manuscript study of Joyce's writings. His chief work in that area is *The Art of James Joyce: Method and Design in "Ulysses" and "Finnegans Wake"* (1961), which influenced several generations of textual scholars and continues to be the definitive work in the area. Litz spent his teaching career at Princeton University, but his influence went well beyond that institution, as his unfailing generosity and support aided the development of scores of young scholars in the United States and beyond.

Marvin Magalaner (1920–2004). Magalaner, who taught at the Graduate Center, City University of New York, did a great deal of work on Joyce's draft materials. He was coauthor of *Joyce: The Man, the Work, the Reputation* (1956), editor of *A James Joyce Miscellany* (1957, 1959, 1962), and author of *Time of Apprenticeship: The Fiction of Young James Joyce* (1959) and several literary guides.

Robert Scholes (1928–). Scholes has taught at the University of Virginia and the University of Iowa and has been a member of the Department of English at Brown University since 1970. He was an early exponent of the new perspectives in critical theory introduced in the 1970s. Among his works on Joyce is *The Cornell Joyce Collection: A Catalogue* (1961).

Thomas F. Staley (1935–). Staley was the founding editor of the *James Joyce Quarterly*, which he edited from 1963 until 1989, and of *Joyce Studies Annual*, which he edited from 1990 until 2004. Staley also published *An Annotated Critical Bibliography of James Joyce* (1989), *Reflections on James*

Joyce: Stuart Gilbert's Paris Journal (1993), and a number of other books about Joyce and modern literature. For many years he taught at the University of Tulsa and served as its provost. He is now director of the Harry Ransom Humanities Research Center at the University of Texas at Austin, where he also holds the Harry Hunt Ransom Chair in Liberal Arts.

James R. Thrane (1928–1979). Thrane became an assistant professor at the University of Wisconsin–Milwaukee in 1960, the year his Joyce essay appeared. He later taught at California State University at San Diego and published articles on Kipling and on Saki, whose foreign correspondence he was editing before his death.

Thomas F. Van Laan (1931–). Before retiring as emeritus professor in 1997, Van Laan spent thirty-five years in the Rutgers University English Department, serving as its chair from 1982 to 1989. Despite his work on Joyce reprinted in this volume, his primary research and teaching focus has been drama, especially Shakespeare and Ibsen. His work on Ibsen, which won him an appointment to the Norwegian Academy of Arts and Sciences, is still in progress.

Florence Walzl (1920–2001). Walzl taught at the University of Wisconsin–Milwaukee for her entire academic career. She was an early member of the advisory board of the *James Joyce Quarterly*. Although she never published a book-length study on the subject, she was widely regarding as one of the leading authorities on *Dubliners*.

Index

Michael Patrick Gillespie, Professor of English at Florida International University, is the author or editor of twenty-two books, including *The Aesthetics of Chaos* and *Oscar Wilde and the Poetics of Ambiguity,* and *James Joyce's Exilic Imagination.*

THE FLORIDA JAMES JOYCE SERIES
Edited by Sebastian D. G. Knowles

Printed in the USA
CPSIA information can be obtained
at www.ICGtesting.com
CBHW030810080624
9698CB00005B/146